The War on Small Business

ALSO BY CAROL ROTH

*The Entrepreneur Equation: Evaluating the Realities, Risks,
and Rewards of Having Your Own Business*

The War on Small Business

HOW THE GOVERNMENT USED THE PANDEMIC TO CRUSH THE BACKBONE OF AMERICA

Carol Roth

BROADSIDE BOOKS

An Imprint of HarperCollins*Publishers*

HarperCollins books may be purchased for educational, business, or sales promotional use. For information, please email the Special Markets Department at SPsales@harpercollins.com.

Broadside Books™ and the Broadside logo are trademarks of HarperCollins Publishers.

FIRST EDITION

Library of Congress Cataloging-in-Publication Data

Names: Roth, Carol (Carol J. S.), author.

Title: The war on small business: how the government used the pandemic to crush the backbone of America / Carol Roth.

Description: First edition. | New York, NY: Broadside Books, an imprint of Harper Collins Publishers, [2021] | Includes index. | Summary: "For years, government bureaucrats have been looking for ways to destroy small businesses. With coronavirus, they finally had their chance."—Provided by publisher.

Identifiers: LCCN 2021014692 | ISBN 9780063081413 (hardcover) | ISBN 9780063081420 (ebook)

Subjects: LCSH: Small business—United States—History—21st century. | Government aid to small business—United States—History—21st century. | COVID-19 Pandemic, 2020—Economic aspects—United States.

Classification: LCC HD2346.U5 R68 2021 | DDC 338.6/420973—dc23

LC record available at https://lccn.loc.gov/2021014692

21 22 23 24 25 LSC 10 9 8 7 6 5 4 3 2 1

This book is dedicated to my father, Bernie, who loved America and was the embodiment of the American Dream.

This book is likewise dedicated to all the small business owners who, despite the odds, continue to fight and persevere.

Contents

Introduction

In 2010, I wrote a book, *The Entrepreneur Equation*, that warned small business owners about the risks of entrepreneurship and owning a business. I made a case for why it is so hard to be a small business owner and entrepreneur—let alone a successful one. I covered how ideas are easier than execution, why you are never really the boss, the competitive landscape, and why everything takes longer and is more expensive and more difficult than you expect it to be and probably should be. I talked about the challenges of managing cash flow, employees, and customers in an ever-changing world.

With all of the challenges that encompass entrepreneurship, never, ever did I think that the most significant risk facing a small business in the United States of America was the risk of the government shutting them down for months on end and preventing businesses from operating.

Small business is the backbone of any economy. More than 99 percent of all businesses in America and worldwide are small businesses. In the United States, they account for around half the economy, but individually, they remain fraught with risk and fragility. The threats that small businesses face daily are varied and numerous, which is why so many small businesses fail and so many more fail to succeed.

Still, millions of small businesses persevere each day in the face of this multitude of threats. Moreover, the United States attracts entrepreneurs from all around the world because (1) some small businesses grow up to be the biggest companies on the planet, and (2) even those that stay smaller can determine and pursue their own definition of success. Small businesses support families, communities, and economic growth. So it is even more staggering to find that the biggest threat not only to their success but also to their existence is the US government.

Of course, government has always been an economic impediment to small businesses. City and state permitting policies in cities such as San Francisco and New York City prevent those without huge budgets from even being able to open a business. (A 2019 article by the San Francisco Apartment Association says you should have $350,000 to $500,000 in liquid capital because of permit delays just to consider opening certain bricks-and-mortar businesses there.) Licensing requirements and other laws further slant the ability to start and maintain a business toward those who already have created wealth. Licenses, permits, and other government-mandated business requirements are a cash cow for government and their cronies at small businesses' expense. And then there is local governments' penchant for giving tax breaks and other incentives to entice big businesses to their cities and states, without providing the same, or in many cases, anything of substance, for smaller operators.[1]

Then came 2020, when governors and mayors alike, particularly in big and blue states and cities, played an all-out nasty, uneven, and rigged game of picking economic winners and losers. To no one's surprise, this did not work out well for many clout-lacking small business owners. State and local governments decided big retailers could continue to operate while shuttering their smaller competition; smaller retailers, many of which offered the same or similar goods and services, found their businesses shut down. Small companies were forced to close and their employees required to stay home, while bigger companies and those that were well connected could remain open and be the beneficiaries deemed, by government mandate, to be "essential."

The War on Small Business is a book about the aftermath of bureaucrats who want to control everything realizing how hard small businesses are to control. It's a book about the battle between central planning and consolidated power versus decentralization.

When the federal government stepped in with its "assistance" via the Coronavirus Aid, Relief, and Economic Security (CARES) Act, it clearly favored the big, wealthy, and well connected. Whereas the Senate tried to pass a more streamlined assistance bill, Speaker Nancy Pelosi and the House of Representatives wouldn't pass a bill unless it was packed with cash for their cronies. While small business owners were forced to duke it out for limited funding under the Paycheck Protection Program (PPP) provision, the broader CARES Act gave away millions to politicians' buddies such as the Kennedy Center (which ended up furloughing its orchestra and other staff after receiving $25 million, no "strings" attached), colleges and universities, including those that had multibillion-dollar endowments (many that were ultimately shamed into giving it back), and other "friends of government."

Even the PPP itself, a provision of the CARES Act aimed at assisting small businesses, was passed late given the circumstances, after many small businesses were already struggling from the government-mandated lockdowns. Moreover, the CARES Act made small businesses further government victims. The poor structuring of the PPP, whether intentional or not, left commercial banks making the decision to give their best customers (aka larger customers) preference, and initially left many of the smallest entities out in the cold. Though many larger funding recipients were shamed into giving back some of those loans and the PPP funding was ultimately expanded, the smallest businesses suffered to a point where we don't yet know the full damage.

Through these stories and others, I will explore two ideas. The first is about capitalism. Many of the critics on the left are correct that a problem exists. They see individuals and companies such as Jeff Bezos and Amazon achieving unparalleled wealth and value, and they sense something in the country is off course. However, critics consistently get these kinds of conflicts wrong. They think that government is the solution when in fact government created the problem. They misread the signs of impending disaster and too often lobby and fight for measures that will make the situation worse. America's "big business" problem is not what those critics think it is. It's not capitalism that gave the country a slew of companies with outsized power and control. In fact, only free market capitalism can fix it. These critics on the left look at America's greatest strength and mistake it for its greatest weakness.

Before advocating for and advising small businesses, I had a career on "Wall Street." As an investment banker, I worked mainly in what is called corporate finance, where I assisted growing companies such as retailers, restaurants, consumer product companies, and tech companies in raising capital in the markets to grow their businesses more quickly. I continue to be a market commentator on major business and news networks to this day.

I'm appalled by what I've been seeing.

From my courtside seat at the financial markets, it has been gut wrenching to watch the markets morph and see cronyism replace capitalism. I've watched the powerful and well connected work with government to enable a wholesale selling out of Main Street to Wall Street.

Though the path was set in the 1980s, it accelerated in the last twelve years and in 2020 was hiding in plain sight.

While small businesses struggled, Wall Street and the White House pressured the Federal Reserve ("the Fed") to take action to prop up the stock market. Though the markets suffered some initial losses, the Fed's actions enabled the markets to rebound quickly, meaning that many bigger companies didn't share in the sustained economic pain and losses that their smaller private counterparts—and the broader economy—were enduring. In fact, some of the largest companies gained substantially more value, with seven companies gaining $3.4 trillion collectively in 2020. Plus, the overall market saw strong gains and a record number of IPOs. This all happened, to add insult to injury, after years of the Fed keeping interest rates artificially low and allowing big companies to take on low-cost debt—which they did in large part not to fortify their balance sheets but to buy back their stock and boost share prices.[2]

This brings us to the second idea we will investigate. The more government has done under the guise of protecting "us" from the "big, bad wolf–esque" corporations, the more powerful those corporations have become. This is a puzzle that takes time to sort through.

It begins with the reality that millions of small businesses across geographies, industries, and size are too hard for the government to control. They are decentralized. It is much easier and more effective for government to deal with a handful of big, wealthy, powerful companies and big, wealthy, powerful unions. This has always made small businesses a roadblock to a complete political power grab.

Though the stage was set long ago, the past two decades have seen an acceleration in the erosions of individual rights without meaningful pushback, creating a centrally planned government behemoth at all levels—city, state, and national—that is so large and complex that it is replete with incompetence, fraud, and inefficiencies. Frankly, it is a miracle that this hadn't happened sooner.

Most of us haven't thought about central planning since the USSR dissolved a generation ago. However, the desire for power never dies, and an easy route to consolidating power and wealth lies in directing and affecting the economy. The fewer the key players to regulate and the larger the portfolios of their executives, the more the government can direct via its spending and regulation. When you see politicians calling for new programs and bills, you start to realize how often both major political parties are calling for even more control via government.

This central planning, largely the opposite of free markets and entrepreneurship, has already sneaked in and replaced capitalism in large parts of our lives. The hybrid planning model now in place has created many issues.

The United States now spends more than just about any other

country on education but has poorer outcomes than many, courtesy of the big but ineffective government. Moreover, the federal government has nationalized large parts of the college lending business. This has created a younger generation among which many have been given basically predatory five-to-six-figure government loans for college educations sometimes worth not even half as much. It's no wonder their classes didn't teach them why capitalism is good and socialism is bad. Moving toward central planning has enabled the cronyism that favors big business and lessens competition. Ultimately, it has given brazen government officials the cover to think they can just shut down an individual's ability to transact business without fair and just compensation to the business owner and not suffer any consequences themselves.

Allowing central planning to invade America and create a hybrid planned economy has enabled the government creep, size, and scope that always was going to end badly.

The last financial crisis was caused by systemic problems causing certain institutions to be deemed "too big to fail."

This new financial crisis was caused by an infiltration of central planning creating a government-run system that is too big to succeed.

Ultimately, small businesses were deemed by government too hard to control. Small businesses are a nuisance at best, or a threat at worst, to politicians because they represent broad decentralized power.

In fact, during the last financial crisis, big banks were given a bailout and a slap on the wrist in the form of more regulation. The outgrowth of that regulation let the big banks not only survive but thrive, killing off their smaller competitors. The number of independent community banks declined by double digits and, post-legislation, the rate of new bank formation went from around a hundred per year to three. This had further consequences in terms of small businesses' inability to get loans; small business loan volume decreased while big business loan volume increased significantly. Truly, no "good" government deed goes unpunished for those who are not already powerful and connected.[3]

Small business presents a huge opportunity for any individual in America to change their lot in life. It is wholly intertwined with the American Dream. Regardless of their background and family or even if they arrive in the United States from halfway around the globe, entrepreneurship allows people to take control and build something. Owning a small business empowers individuals. It becomes not just their livelihood but a big part of who they are. And from Silicon Valley startups to a roadside hot dog stand, they embody decentralization and thwart government power, coercion, and control.

The government, big companies, and Wall Street have been waging battles against small businesses for decades. A piece in *The Atlantic* related that even back in 1938, "President Franklin D. Roosevelt hosted a conference in Washington, D.C., for 1,000 small business owners, hoping to gain their backing for the New Deal. But the beauty of the small business owner—a stubborn, sometimes radical independence—was also a political weakness. It was impossible to get the group to reach consensus on anything."[4]

Small business is synonymous with independence.

In 2020, as the opportunity presented itself, the government's battles turned into a full-out war on small business, with enormous consequences. People's livelihoods were taken away, and their souls and identities were crushed.

How did this happen? Can it be fixed before entrepreneurship and the American Dream are killed off entirely?

In this book, I will recount the framework of what happened in 2020, how it enabled total war on small businesses and individuals, and why the scenario was inevitable, even if not immediately predictable. I will also take you through some of the groundwork of the infiltration of central planning, working in conjunction with big business, that created this inevitability.

We will see how the United States has moved away from capitalism and why a return to individual rights, capitalism, and freedom is its best path to return to prosperity and avoid an even worse economic fate.

Though many people have fought for freedom and the decentralization that comes with it, massive central planning is already here in America and wreaking havoc; now there must be a fight to dismantle that centralized power, save small business, and preserve the American Dream for every individual.

CHAPTER 1

The Government Black Swan

An Unpredictable, Unprecedented Pandemic Reaction

"Black swan" is a term often used in the world of investing, popularized in a book of generally the same name by the noted author, professor, and former Wall Street quantitative trader Nassim Nicholas Taleb.

The phrase has been adapted in popular culture to talk about major, unpredictable, yet very severe events that ultimately have a grave impact.

In early 2020, I went on Cheddar, a streaming financial news channel targeted at millennial investors, to talk about the size of the US debt, earnings, and the possible impacts of the new coronavirus on global markets and the Chinese economy. The anchors asked me about my biggest concerns. I replied that one of the things that could most significantly impact the market was a black swan.

A short while later, a black swan hit America.

Though many people will argue that the black swan was the coronavirus, it was not. Though the particular strain of the virus was not known previously, other coronaviruses had existed. And though we didn't expect a pandemic in 2020 per se—it wasn't on my upcoming events calendar, for certain—many high-profile people, from scientists to Bill Gates, had been warning of and planning for a pandemic for years. In fact, the federal government had run a several-months-long series of pandemic preparation drills across a dozen states just the year prior.

Taleb, who was "irritated" about people calling the virus a black swan, told Bloomberg Television in late March 2020, "'The Black Swan' was meant to explain why, in a networked world, we need to change business practices and social norms—not . . . provide 'a cliché for any bad thing that surprises us.'"[1]

Because it was not a black swan, preparation for the virus could be undertaken. In fact, Taleb, who focuses his research in part on probabilities, coauthored a paper in late January 2020 saying that the virus's growth would likely be nonlinear and that behaviors such as what we now know as social distancing were prudent to take early on.

In his Bloomberg interview, he further said that governments "did not want to spend pennies in January; now they are going to spend trillions."

Though the pandemic itself was not a black swan, an actual black swan was born in its wake. What was that? The US government's reaction to the pandemic. The unprecedented decisions resulting in a historic, ongoing shutting down of a large part of the economy by direct order—that was a black swan. Nobody saw that coming. Government hadn't taken actions like that for other recent viruses; even in January, no one had been looking at the Chinese response and hoping to import it to the United States. In an era when information, technology, and resources are plentiful, no models or pundits were saying that at some point, the government's reaction would be to force people to stop working and doing business, let alone for months on end.

Yet the government did just that.

In terms of the virus, the government had a few paths to take. The first was early containment and eradication of the virus. That was blown by big government via a combination of arrogance, red tape, and typical bureaucratic confusion and inefficacy.

The second path was moving toward herd immunity, whether naturally or in conjunction with a vaccine. With vaccines known to take a long time to develop, even on an accelerated schedule, herd immunity via vaccination was not a near-term solution.

The final option was to suppress the virus.

The federal government suggested that people pitch in for just about two weeks—fifteen days—to ensure that hospitals wouldn't become overrun treating the new virus. Governors across the country mandated people to stay home and businesses to close. They locked down individuals and the economy. That is, unless they deemed your business "essential," leading to a game of the government deciding who would thrive and who would fight to survive.

Let me be clear: there was no full lockdown. In fact, there was no lockdown for large parts of the country, even in states and cities with a lockdown mandate. Notably, if you were a big or otherwise well-connected company, you were likely to get the nod to stay open, even if a competitive small business a few hundred yards away had to close.

The suppression "plan"—I put it into quotes because it was hardly a plan—was to lock down some people and businesses, not based on age, vulnerability, or other epidemiological evidence but at the government's whim.

There was no clear discussion of or communication about what length of time, cost, or other collateral damage would be acceptable for a lockdown strategy.

Fifteen days turned into hundreds of days with little reversal of course. The virus wasn't fully contained, and the costs—financially, individually, socially, and otherwise—were enormous and imbalanced.

Once lockdowns were initiated, those who were most vulnerable and needed the most protection received the least care. Small businesses were, unsurprisingly, disproportionately affected by shutdowns, as were lower-economic-status individuals and households, who bore the brunt of performing "essential" jobs and struggling through child care and remote learning challenges that didn't impact households with more resources similarly. People who were struggling with issues ranging from mental health to domestic violence were also largely disregarded.

The elderly, who were known to be the most vulnerable to the disease, were not given special protections or allocations of resources. At the same time, those who were at low risk for COVID morbidity weren't allowed to live their lives freely.

The inflexibility of government entities to adapt, admit their mistakes, and change course meant that this harmful policy went on for months on end, with no clear end point, compounding the damage.

A little more than halfway through the year, the review platform Yelp did an analysis of the companies on its platform. Although Yelp-listed businesses account for only a fraction of the overall businesses in the United States, they are a useful proxy for businesses in general. As Yelp's platform typically rates consumer-facing companies (stores, restaurants, home service providers, and so on), it is also a good proxy for the types of businesses that would be most directly affected by shutdown orders.

Though in April, 175,000 businesses had closed on the Yelp platform alone, as of July 10, Yelp's data showed that still more than 132,500 US businesses were closed either temporarily or permanently. Though some businesses were opening, bringing the overall number of closures down, the percentage of permanent closings was rising, accounting for a staggering 55 percent of all closed businesses. In the Chicagoland area, 4,400 businesses on Yelp reported being closed, and of those, 2,400 said they were closing permanently (aka, going out of business). As expected, in terms of overall closures as well as permanent closures, restaurants and retail outlets were the hardest hit, with beauty services, financial services, and home services as some of the other most affected industry sectors.[2]

In the restaurant sector, 60 percent of the businesses that were closed had posted that they were closed permanently.[3]

Though the Yelp data give a peek into specific industries, the reverberations from the closures of businesses such as restaurants and retailers affect the economy in a chain reaction. In addition to the direct jobs lost by the employees of those businesses, there is the economic activity lost—in whole or in part—by the companies that supply and service those businesses. From providers of produce and beverages to cleaning services and HVAC maintenance firms, other companies and their employees are impacted when their own clients are shuttered. This leads to fewer dollars spent in the economy, which ultimately affects other businesses as the cycle continues.

A report by the Hamilton Project, which looked at only the 6 million small businesses with employees (excluding the pre-COVID 24.2 million one-person businesses), found that more than 400,000 small businesses had closed permanently by June 2020. That means around 6.7 percent of all employer businesses in the country were forever shuttered by midyear.[4]

Ultimately, the small business closures, both temporary and permanent, played a substantial role in more than 40 million Americans' filing jobless claims by the end of May.

Meanwhile, the equity markets, which trade the stocks of larger companies, were seeing a different outcome. With many publicly traded businesses deemed "essential" while smaller businesses were not and others shielded from government actions by being technology based, plus an extra financial boost from the Federal Reserve, the stock market continued to soar. The Nasdaq Composite Index reached an all-time high on June 8, and the Dow Jones Industrial Average and S&P 500 were on the climb back toward theirs.

Though small businesses and individuals were struggling to survive, the second-quarter earnings cycle of 2020 saw blow-away numbers for large companies such as Amazon and Facebook, among others. On August 19, Apple hit a $2 trillion intraday market cap, making its market value greater than Canada's entire GDP.

Walmart blew past its second-quarter earnings expectations. A same-store sales increase of 9.3 percent and a near doubling of its online sales led the retailer to incredibly strong revenue ($137.7 billion for the quarter) and earnings.[5]

Target also reported a strong quarter, picking up around 10 million new e-commerce customers and increasing its profits by 80 percent, per its CEO and reporting.[6]

With people scared and out of work, small businesses struggling, and the number of unemployment claims making history, the government had induced an unfathomable recession and severe psychological damage. Yet the stock market, led by the world's biggest companies, was soaring to new highs.

This divergence of economic outcomes continued throughout the back half of the year, as the S&P 500 and Nasdaq Composite hit highs again in December, while many small businesses were forced by government to shutter once more.

How could this be? And was Taleb right—should this government action have been predictable?

Was this just another part of a long-standing campaign against small businesses and others too small to matter and in the way of consolidating power? What other damage lay ahead in 2020 and beyond?

To answer that, we need to start at the beginning.

CHAPTER 2

Hindsight Is 2020

*How Overreliance on Government Led to
History-Making Mistakes*

When 2020 is looked back upon in the history books, it will show that the government at all levels—local, state, and federal—made a set of inane, irresponsible, and costly policy mistakes, both economic and social, that changed the course of history for the worse.

It will also show that there was a direct consolidation of power among government, big business, and other special interests at the expense of decentralized small businesses and individuals.

A Deadly Distraction

A few weeks into January 2020, the most prominent business and political leaders in the world arrived in Davos, Switzerland, for the fiftieth World Economic Forum Annual Meeting. Billed as an ideas exchange and widely lamented as a fancy mutual flattery festival among the powerful, rich, and famous, Davos is where the elite go to be seen and to network against the backdrop of exchanging heady political and societal ideas.

One of the biggest topics of discussion was China.

However, those "thought leaders" were not bunkered down, strategizing risk management for a new mystery virus that had been discovered in China. Instead, they were discussing the first phase of the long-promised multiphase trade deal between the United States and China signed by President Donald Trump and Chinese president Xi Jinping on the fifteenth of the month.[1]

That deal, announced on the final day of 2019, had carried stocks up to end the year, making 2019 a banner year for US equity markets, with the Dow, S&P 500, and Nasdaq Composite closing up 22.3 percent, 28.9 percent, and 35.2 percent for the year, respectively. Overall, the US economy was still in the longest economic expansion on record, ending 2019 with only a 3.5 percent unemployment rate, the lowest since 1969 and reaching historic lows across demographic groups.[2]

Though the US-China trade deal had many people, including the CEOs at Davos, skeptical about its specific tangible benefits, it did stem the possibility of further trade tensions, which could have resulted in higher tariffs and other economically unfriendly outcomes and took one big economic issue off the table.

That optimism spilled over from Wall Street to Main Street. January's small business optimism reading was in the top 10 percent of the past four and a half decades, according to the National Federation of Independent Business (NFIB), which publishes the Small Business Optimism Index. NFIB's chief economist, William Dunkelberg, said, "2020 is off to an explosive start for the small business economy, with owners expecting increased sales, earnings, and higher wages for employees. Small businesses continue to build on the solid foundation of supportive federal tax policies and a deregulatory environment that allows owners to put an increased focus on operating and growing their businesses."[3]

Although the US economic signals looked strong and the signing of the trade pact with China was, at least optically, a big deal, its timing could not have been any worse. Whether it was an intentional distraction tactic by the Chinese or just a whole lot of bad luck, that seemingly good development likely blew the early opportunity to contain the virus.

The development likely led President Trump to tweet his support of China and its efforts regarding the new virus, posting on January 24, "China has been working very hard to contain the Coronavirus. The United States greatly appreciates their efforts and transparency. It will all work out well. In particular, on behalf of the American People, I want to thank President Xi!"

Where was the tough Trump? Had the signing of the Phase One trade deal less than ten days prior made the president and his administration feel less inclined to rock the boat with or increase its scrutiny of China? The trade deal timing was unfortunate from a macro standpoint and likely put blinders on what would have otherwise been increased attention, and possibly earlier risk management and action, on the virus and its implications. Instead of acting as disrupters, the president and his administration were behaving more like diplomats.

Fail to Plan, Plan to Fail

US lawmakers were so distracted by their own political antics that they were brushing off other potential concerns. Amid the political theater of the speaker of the House of Representatives, Nancy Pelosi, buying, distributing, and using souvenir pens to sign off on the resolution to send the two articles of impeachment against President Trump to the Senate and thereby initiating a Senate trial, the Centers for Disease Control and Prevention (CDC) was focused on the news from Wuhan.[4]

Although the Chinese had yet to confirm that there was a major coronavirus outbreak, and much was yet to be known about what was still a mystery disease, multiple deaths in China and the appearance of the virus outside China, including in Thailand and Japan, prompted the CDC, in conjunction with the Department of Homeland Security, to take action. They began screening passengers arriving in the United States from Wuhan, China, at two West Coast airports and one East Coast airport (Los Angeles, San Francisco, and New York's JFK).

Still, the US economy looked to be on a solid footing. Trade concerns had been slightly assuaged, the earnings season was off to a strong start, and existing home sales were up, so commentators were focused on "headwinds" (financial speak for things that could slow down the economy and market). These headwinds were centered around the possibility of slowing growth and the 2020 presidential election.

However, at least one senator was not feeling any goodwill toward China and raised red flags, contacting the CDC. Florida Republican senator Rick Scott asked the CDC in a formal letter, posted on his website, for information on "the agency's plan to combat the threat of the coronavirus" and urged "quick action to protect the health of American families." In his letter, he stated, "I am particularly concerned because of China's position as a global adversary and their general unwillingness to cooperate and share information with the United States and our allies. . . . Clearly, Communist China does not play straight with us."[5]

On the twenty-fourth, as Trump was tweeting his support to President Xi, Senator Scott publicly urged the president and his administration to declare coronavirus a public health emergency.

However, for the second time in four days, Dr. Anthony Fauci, the head of the National Institute of Allergy and Infectious Diseases who was a chief advisor and the top public health "expert," told a media outlet that the risk of Americans contracting the disease was low, downplaying the concerns and calls by Senator Scott to declare a public health emergency.

In the first instance, Dr. Fauci said, "It's a very, very low risk to the United States. . . . But it's something that we as public health officials need to take very seriously. . . . It isn't something the American public needs to worry about or be frightened about."[6] In the other instance, he also downplayed the risk, saying, "We don't want the American public to be worried about this because their risk is low. . . . On the other hand, we are taking this very seriously and are dealing very closely with Chinese authorities."[7]

Either way, in that moment, the Chinese government's history of being untrustworthy was discounted. Though the experts and administration were supposedly taking things seriously, they weren't taking enough preventive actions and certainly not creating any buy-in with or goodwill from the public, tactics that could have assisted in early containment and eradication of the virus.

While the US government was not moving quickly, if at all, on the new virus, in South Korea, government officials were meeting with top industry executives and medical experts, in some cases pulling people from their Lunar New Year celebrations to put together a plan of action. Having been more lackadaisical when Middle East respiratory syndrome (MERS) had emerged—the country had been hit with the most cases and fatalities outside the Middle East from the 2015 outbreak—this time, they vowed to do better and engaged the private sector to execute their plan. They agreed not to stand in the way of testing approval from a regulatory standpoint, and within a week of this meeting, South Korea had its first commercial test for COVID-19, the disease caused by the coronavirus.[8]

A Global Split

The Asian financial markets were the first to signal a problem. By January 27, the coronavirus outbreak had significantly rattled Asian markets, including the Japanese Nikkei 225, which closed down more than 2 percent on the day, a substantial one-day move. Those concerns sparked a sell-off in US markets as the three major indexes—the Dow, S&P 500, and Nasdaq Composite—all finished the day down between 0.6 percent and 0.9 percent.[9]

The markets were more concerned than the government seemed to be.

Seeing that the markets were unnerved, President Trump took to criticizing . . . the Federal Reserve, ostensibly seeing monetary policy as a silver bullet. He tweeted, "The Fed should get smart & lower the Rate to make our interest competitive with other Countries which pay much lower even though we are, by far, the high standard. We would then focus on paying off & refinancing debt! There is almost no inflation-this is the time (2 years late)!"

The markets, which were hooked on the Fed's meddling in the markets to investors' benefit, viewed this interaction and pressure favorably and recouped some of the previous day's losses.

The first look at GDP for the fourth quarter emerged with an estimate of 2.1 percent, which met expectations. However, this meant that for the 2019 full year, growth was slowing on a year-over-year basis, registering at 2.3 percent.[10]

As growth concerns percolated a bit on January 30, the director-general of the World Health Organization (WHO), Dr. Tedros Adhanom Ghebreyesus, declared the new coronavirus a public health emergency of international concern, or PHEIC. Despite the declaration, it seemed that the organization had less concern for the public's welfare and more for running interference for China. The WHO chief stated, "The main reason for this declaration is not what is happening in China but what is happening in other countries."[11] In its official statement, the organization said, "The Committee emphasized that the declaration of a PHEIC should be seen in the spirit of support and appreciation for China, its people, and the actions China has taken on the frontlines of this outbreak, with transparency, and, it is to be hoped, with success."[12]

The WHO provided few specific action steps and stated that it "does not recommend any travel or trade restriction based on the current information available." The organization's concern for China's feelings over global health was just one of many significant political "leadership" bungles that impeded the containment of the virus in the early days in most of the world.

Meanwhile, the CDC reported the first known person-to-person transmission in the United States in Chicago, the husband of a woman infected while visiting China. A CDC director reiterated his belief that the "immediate risk to the American public is low."[13]

The administration instituted a temporary travel ban on any foreign national who had been to China within the preceding two weeks, to go into effect on February 2. It was an extension of the previous screening efforts mentioned above. It redirected flights from China to the United States to a handful of airports set up as designated ports of entry, and the major airlines suspended flights between the United States and China.

By the end of the trading day on January 31, with the WHO announcement and concerns about the virus's potential impact on the Chinese economy, the stock market was upended. The Dow dropped 600 points (around 2.1 percent) to its worst day since August 2019, the fifth largest one-day drop on a points basis within the prior twelve months. The S&P 500 also logged its worst day in many months, falling around 1.8 percent, and even the tech-heavy Nasdaq fell 1.6 percent. This move wiped out all the Dow's gains that had been made by midmonth, when the year had looked to be off to a roaring start.[14]

There were a lot of big government distractions during the first month or so of the year, but that's the nature of expecting a centralized body to be able to do all things, let alone anything, well. Realistically, how can the same people who are managing trade policy, killing terrorist foes, pestering the Fed about the stock market, and representing the country at diplomatic events, not to mention dealing with an impeachment and an upcoming election, also focus all their energy on a health crisis? They cannot. It is impossible to make two things, let alone dozens of things, a number one priority. Unfortunately, in this case, the most important thing got lost among all the others.

The Roller-Coaster Ride Begins

As the Chinese stock market opened for trading on February 3 for the first time since its Chinese New Year closing, the Shanghai composite index dropped 7.7 percent.[15]

Despite this, in the United States it was a different story. The month began with market volatility but ultimately a big rebound and total reversal from just a few days prior. Larger companies saw different outcomes, as stocks like Tesla hit new highs, while Apple, which has substantial exposure in manufacturing and sales to China, bounced around. On the commodities front, oil signaled a bit of a concern as the price of Brent crude traded below $55 per barrel for the first time in more than a year off of fears that a coronavirus-induced global economic slowdown would impact oil demand.[16]

The next several days were upbeat on the hope of central bank intervention juicing markets worldwide, good earnings, decent economic data, and a fragile sense of optimism. On the fourth, the Department of Commerce reported a large increase in factory orders for December, a substantial reversal over the decline reported in November and the largest gain in around eighteen months. Even stocks directly impacted by the coronavirus, from the cruise ship carrier Carnival to major airline carriers, were up that day.[17]

The next day, February 5, on the back of the president's State of the Union address, the anticipation of the president's imminent acquittal by the Senate, and hopes that the coronavirus would be contained, the S&P 500 hit its new all-time record close.

The Senate ultimately acquitted President Trump of impeachment on both counts on the fifth.

Things were looking up, but that would soon change.

Generous to a Fault

Although it was not known until later, as testing at the time was limited and mostly contained to those who had traveled to China or had specific symptoms, the days that followed counted the first US deaths from COVID-19. However, instead of building up a preventive response to the virus and while private labs were trying to work around government red tape to get testing approved, US leaders were . . . sending critical medical supplies to China.[18]

The overhang from the newly normalized trade relations with China led to another US government misstep. Secretary of State Mike Pompeo announced that the State Department had

> facilitated the transportation of nearly 17.8 tons of donated medical supplies to the Chinese people, including masks, gowns, gauze, respirators, and other vital materials. . . .
>
> Today, the United States government is announcing it is prepared to spend up to $100 million in existing funds to assist China and other impacted countries, both directly and through multilateral organizations, to contain and combat the COVID 19. . . .
>
> The United States is and will remain the world's most generous donor.[19]

USA Today reported that it had analyzed US Census Bureau foreign trade data and found that despite the concerns and warnings about the virus, while the United States could have been building up its foundation of personal protective equipment (PPE) and asking companies to do the same, US companies had sold more than $17.5 million worth of face masks and $27.2 million worth of ventilators to China during January and February, far in excess of any similar period in the past decade.[20]

Why would the government be sending critical supplies abroad as more information was pointing to a pandemic?

Meanwhile, while most individuals—and government officials—were being arrogant in thinking that the virus would not spread broadly in the United States and those who were concerned were caught in a web of government red tape, South Korea already had approval for and begun COVID testing, and a couple of weeks later it was testing tens of thousands of people each day.[21]

Meanwhile, the stock market pushed ahead, shaking off coronavirus worries and anticipating a V-shaped global economic recovery (meaning that though the economy slides down sharply and quickly, it bottoms and turns around sharply to recover, like the letter V). At that point, about 70 percent of all S&P 500 companies had reported their fourth-quarter earnings, and more than 71 percent of them had beaten expectations. Even though the information was backward looking, the strong financial news kept investors focused on the Fed and company fundamentals instead of other global news.[22]

Additional solid earnings reports, a significant rise in the Bureau of Labor Statistics' Producer Price Index (PPI) in January, and the Federal Reserve's releasing its meeting minutes from January that reinforced its accommodative monetary policy stance pushed the S&P 500 and Nasdaq Composite to again reach record highs.[23]

On February 21, the tide started to turn in the United States. Dr. Nancy Messonnier, the director of the CDC's National Center for Immunization and Respiratory Diseases, said that the agency was working with state and local health departments and preparing for COVID-19 to very possibly, "even likely," become a pandemic.

These new concerns brought fear to the stock market, although not as severe as one may have predicted. Commentators believed that the virus and its drag on the economy would likely only last a couple of quarters before the economy bounced back and resumed growth later in the year.[24]

The WHO finally conceded that attempts to contain the virus, though still possible, were not likely, and Italy went into lockdown as cases spread throughout Europe and Iran.[25]

Seven and a half weeks into the year, the messaging ball was still dropped, and the CDC was still behind in its testing. There was not much being done about risk mitigation, other than the travel ban, presenting many missed opportunities.

Market Selling and Leaked Information

The ensuing week saw things unravel as the Trump administration and other agencies tried to ramp up their action. The CDC announced that the virus was spreading to people who had not been out of the country, leading to the assumption of person-to-person community spread of COVID-19. The president appointed a task force headed by Vice President Mike Pence and on February 26 assured the public that the administration and the country were ready and that "The risk to the American people remains very low."

The president also requested $2.5 billion in emergency funding, which was quickly rebuffed by Democrats in Congress as inadequate. Perhaps unsurprisingly, while congressional leaders were focused on the amount of money being inadequate for a response, they were entirely unfocused on any other steps that should be taken to help with the virus response.[26]

In fact, there was minimal proactive buy-in, advice, or direction for the public.

The week was a mess in the financial markets. Though markets are typically forward looking, they had been discounting any COVID impact and now were finally shifting their focus. On February 24, the Dow closed down more than 3.5 percent. Tremendous volatility ensued, and the week ended by seeing one of the largest weekly declines since the financial crisis (around 12.4 percent on the Dow alone), not only in the United States but also globally.

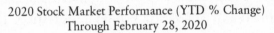

2020 Stock Market Performance (YTD % Change)
Through February 28, 2020

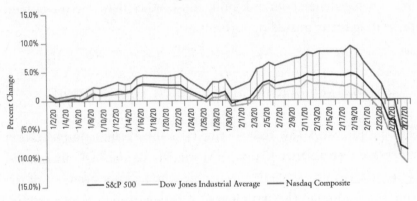

Data via Macrotrends, https://www.macrotrends.net.

The sell-off was a reading of the tea leaves, and also, apparently, an insider report. It was later reported that some attendees of private briefings and meetings between members of the Trump administration and the Hoover Institution had leaked their concerns, perhaps even in excess of what had been communicated to them, to members of the investment community, putting a further drag on the market. Of particular note was a document reportedly authored by a hedge fund consultant in attendance at those meetings that ultimately led to in-the-know investor selling. Wall Street insiders got out of their positions ahead of Main Street even knowing there was a problem.[27]

Masking the Message

Though the China trade deal clearly created a blind spot that affected the potential for early containment of the virus, messaging represented another missed opportunity.

The market was pretty clear about what it was seeing, but it was sending an entirely different message from the one the government and media were sending.

The US surgeon general specifically told the public not to buy face masks. He tweeted, "Seriously people - STOP BUYING MASKS! They are NOT effective in preventing general public from catching #Coronavirus, but if healthcare providers can't get them to care for sick patients, it puts them and our communities at risk!"[28]

The media ran interference on the "no mask stance." A sampling of media tweets and a headline:

February 26, *Washington Post*: "How to prepare for coronavirus in the U.S. (Spoiler: Not sick? No need to buy any masks.)"[29]

February 28, MSNBC: "Frequent hand-washing, not wearing a face mask, is the most important step the public can take to prevent the spread of the coronavirus, the WHO says."[30]

February 29, CNN: "Masks Can't Stop the Coronavirus in the US, but Hysteria Has Led to Bulk-Buying and Price-Gouging"[31]

Perhaps the misinformation from China and the WHO and the other historic events to contend with in January that might have put COVID on the back burner are forgivable, but by the time the United States declared a public health emergency at the end of January, it should have set up February to be a month of action. However, the month saw little coordination with the public and minimal testing, and instead of ramping up supplies in the United States, the government sent millions of dollars' worth of needed supplies to China.

Americans heard that there was a low risk of contracting the disease and were emphatically told they did not need to take precautions such as limiting their travel or wearing masks. The public internalized a belief that this was a passing issue that would be much like other global health issues before—such as SARS and MERS—that, although serious, wouldn't really affect them. There was no risk mitigation strategy or buy-in to take early action, despite many warning signs and red flags for a second entire month.

Those early mistakes were clearly on the shoulders of big government at the federal level and represented a complete bungling of the early containment and virus eradication potential path.

Testing, 1, 2, 3 . . .

Just as the government faltered on messaging, it also botched early testing. A congested, shortsighted, restrictive, and protocol-reliant government allowed precious weeks to pass without taking crucial action to test for and ultimately contain the coronavirus.

Trying to protect its turf and mired in its own web of bad regulation, the government failed to use the innovation, experience, and speed of the private sector that was available and had been ready from the start. Central planning thwarted capitalism.

MIT Technology Review conducted an interview with Keith Jerome, the head of virology at the University of Washington, who said, "The great strength the US has always had, not just in virology, is that we've always had a wide variety of people and groups working on any given problem. When we decided all coronavirus testing had to be done by a single entity, even one as outstanding as CDC, we basically gave away our greatest strength."[32]

That's a kind way of saying that centralization is bad and the government really messed up. That was a certainty, as the government embodies centralization and is therefore set up for failure.

How did it all happen? Well, shortly after the Chinese government published the genetic sequence of SARS-CoV-2 in January, the CDC designed a test kit that contained reagents (compounds that cause a chemical reaction, used in chemical analysis), in four vials per kit, to be used for testing patients for COVID. Pending FDA approval, the CDC, per protocol, intended to distribute the kits to public health labs to verify that the test worked.[33]

As you would expect the market to work, other scientific groups and companies were also working feverishly to develop a reliable COVID test. However, their efforts were stymied by the declaration of a public health emergency at the end of January. The declaration meant that the FDA would require that labs get what is called an emergency use authorization (EUA) before proceeding with test development. This is a fancy way of saying that the government would not let the market proceed with testing unless it said it was okay.[34]

The EUA is a scaled-down process meant to accelerate the cumbersome government approval process. Yet in this particular instance, when every moment was of the essence, it did the opposite, exacerbating the issue by significantly delaying the creation of the badly needed tests by organizations other than the CDC. Obtaining an EUA involved rigorous data production and extensive paperwork demands and proved to be very time consuming for the entities applying for approval. Almost a month after the EUA was invoked, no lab had yet received approval to develop tests aside from the CDC.[35]

With the government in control, the frequent outcome of central planning happened: rationing of resources. Former Food and Drug Administration (FDA) commissioner Scott Gottlieb explained in a tweet, "Since CDC and FDA haven't authorized public health or hospital labs to run the tests, right now #CDC is the only place that can. So, screening has to be rationed."[36]

Resources were scarce, and the government wasn't allowing competition; therefore, the government decided how to administer the tests and to whom. Such is the predictable outcome of progressive-style central planning.

The FDA finally approved the CDC's test on February 4, 2020, and it was distributed to around a hundred different state and local public health labs throughout the country to verify the CDC's results, per protocol. The majority of labs receiving the first batch of fifty test kits produced inconclusive results from one of the reagents. The CDC's test did not work, and no other lab had the authority to develop another test.[37]

Nancy Messonnier said that the verification problems experienced by labs were "part of the normal procedures," and until new reagents were manufactured, all COVID-19 testing would continue to go through only the CDC laboratories.[38]

That government decision would, of course, further slow testing.

The *Washington Post* reported that by mid-February, while officials from the FDA and CDC were meeting to discuss the test flaws, clinical labs tried to gain testing approval via devoting "hundreds of hours to the FDA's paperwork and data demands." The Mayo Clinic, for instance, created its first fifteen-person rapid response team, a third of whom spent fifteen hours a day for three weeks trying to meet the FDA's data and paperwork demands. " 'It's unlike anything we've ever done before,' said Matt Binnicker, a director of clinical virology at Mayo."[39]

The *Washington Post* also spoke with Alex Greninger, an assistant director of the University of Washington's clinical virology lab. He spent more than a hundred hours to comply with the paperwork for the FDA application, but the agency rejected it . . . because it had been submitted by email. It quoted a letter Greninger wrote to colleagues on February 14, saying, "The most pernicious effect of the current regulatory environment is that it kneecaps our ability for preparedness should a true emergency emerge."

While the government was messing around with protocol, other countries such as South Korea (which, as noted, had been through a similar process with MERS and knew the testing challenges) were using private companies to advance their testing capabilities.[40]

But with only one laboratory screening tests, the CDC, US testing was severely backlogged.[41]

Eventually, several labs discovered that if they didn't use one of the four vials in the CDC test kit, they could verify the CDC's results. That was enough for the labs to want to begin using the tests, but there was a snafu: the government. FDA regulations forbade doing that. Labs were required to use the test "as is," with no modifications.

Without a viable test and with no other lab having EUA, the government scrambled to find a solution. It took another three full weeks before the FDA finally announced that it would relax its rules and allow labs to modify the test or design one of their own.[42]

By the first week of March, just shy of 4,400 people had been tested for the coronavirus in the United States, compared with *The Atlantic*'s estimate that at the same point in its outbreak, South Korea had tested 100,000 people. South Korea had brought in the private sector early and relied on it to assist with testing instead of being mired in government bureaucracy. Though they had discovered the virus in their populations on the same day, by the time the much smaller South Korea had tested 290,000 people, the United States had tested only 60,000. Based on March CDC data on hospitalization rates for deaths and the overall impact of the virus, one can extrapolate that the United States likely had hundreds of thousands of undiagnosed cases at that point.[43]

The kits from the CDC were both faulty and unreliable. The *Washington Post* reported, "From mid-January until Feb. 28, fewer than 4,000 tests from the U.S. Centers for Disease Control and Prevention were used out of more [than] 160,000 produced." Compare that with the coordinated efforts of a small German company that produced and shipped more than 1.4 million tests for the WHO by the end of February.[44]

It was a battle of entrepreneurship and decentralization versus the cumbersome big government, and the government was not winning, to everyone's detriment.

The CDC's faulty test and the FDA's unwillingness to loosen the EUA regulations made it impossible for public health officials to gauge the spread of the illness—crucial to modeling it, assessing it, and containing it. That early blunder had a grave impact on the spread of the illness and the decisions made from it, including the economic implications of the government shutdowns across the country.

Industry participants begged the FDA to loosen its rules and formalities. On the last day of February, the FDA finally modified its regulations and allowed "certain laboratories seeking to develop diagnostic tests" to modify the CDC test kit or develop their own, "in order to achieve more rapid testing capacity in the U.S."[45]

Reports estimated that about 5,000 virology labs (out of around 260,000 in the country) had qualified. As testing began, they received positive test results for the virus.[46]

On the night before and the day of President Trump's declaring COVID a national emergency, several major health care companies received EUAs and were beginning testing.[47]

However, at the time of the emergency declaration, so few tests had been conducted that government officials did not have a firm grasp on any data around COVID. While South Korea had been testing 5,000 people per million, the United States was just coming up to testing 125 people per million. That lack of reliable data meant that government officials were making decisions pretty much flying blind.[48]

March . . . Forward?

Big government had missed messaging opportunities, sent critical supplies to China, and impeded testing progress. Only the Federal Reserve took decisive action.

The Fed rattled the markets by making a surprise emergency rate cut on March 3, its first since October, signaling to investors that the outlook for the virus was much worse than anyone had thought. That increased volatility in the markets and sent all the major averages (Dow, S&P 500, and Nasdaq Composite) down by around 3 percent—nearly 800 points for the Dow—despite the markets' having had a huge up day (nearly 1,300 points on the Dow) the previous day.

Though public market investors understood the signals, local governments did not. New York State was late to act, and New York City was still giving poor guidance—at least from a virus containment standpoint. On March 3, New York City health commissioner Oxiris Barbot said, "We are encouraging New Yorkers to go about their everyday lives"[49] and the following day, during a press conference, she said, "So, there's no indication that being in a car, being in the subways with someone who's potentially sick is a risk factor."[50]

The big-government proponent Mayor Bill de Blasio felt, with mistaken hubris, that instead of making commonsense decisions, people should look to him for behavioral cues. He said on the fifth, with almost two dozen confirmed cases in New York, "We'll tell you the second we think you should change your behavior."[51] He also took the subway that day to demonstrate that New Yorkers shouldn't be afraid of the virus.[52]

The glaring fact here is that there was no believable messaging or pushback to this particular scenario or others playing out around the country. Anything that was said had a political overtone; any coordination was based on political lies. Though people were doing their own prudent risk management, such as going out to buy supplies, including masks—that whole "personal responsibility" thing—they were being fed an entirely different and often conflicting narrative by various government representatives.

An Economic Crisis or a Health Crisis?

With the stock market reeling, on the evening of March 11, President Trump addressed the nation, saying, "This is not a financial crisis. This is just a temporary moment of time that we will overcome together as a nation and as a world." It is noteworthy how this was viewed in financial terms, perhaps due to fears of a systemic crisis such as the one we had seen during the "Great Recession" just more than a decade prior. Little did Trump know how easily the health crisis would be turned into an economic crisis by state and local government actions.

Trump's administration, mostly via Treasury Secretary Steven Mnuchin, worked with the Democrats to create a bill that would not be a full relief bill but would address some interim concerns. Given the urgency, Senate Majority Leader Mitch McConnell canceled the planned Senate recess.[53]

The Senate Republicans were not happy with the bill, but they went ahead with the vote believing that it was too urgent to delay further. McConnell said of his unhappy Senate colleagues, "My counsel to them is to gag and go for it anyway even if they think it has some shortcomings, and to address those shortcomings in the bill we're in the process of crafting."[54] The Families First Coronavirus Response Act (FFCRA) was signed into law by President Trump on March 18.[55]

The coronavirus situation—or at least the reaction to it—worsened rapidly. On Friday, March 13, President Trump formally declared COVID-19 a national emergency. He said that doing so would provide access to tens of billions of dollars in additional Federal Emergency Management Agency (FEMA) funding reserved for such situations and allow the Department of Health and Human Services to modify or waive regulations and laws, including for Medicare, Medicaid, and other programs and to deliver coronavirus testing more quickly.[56]

As the national emergency was declared, it marked a turning point in state and local authorities' actions.

It was also the day that everything changed.

Central planning had failed at every turn. It had failed to contain the virus. It had failed to shore up PPE. It had failed to expedite testing. But the next steps of central planning were not just a failure; they were an act of war.

CHAPTER 3

Fifteen Days to Slow the Spread

*Exploring Government Choosing
Winners and Losers via the Myth of
"Non-Essential" Businesses*

Shelley Luther is like many of the approximately 30.2 million small business owners in America.

An affable woman with a dimple in her cheek and blond hair cut in a bob, Ms. Luther is a symbol of the backbone of the US economy. She became a professional makeup artist and went the road of opening her own salon, Salon À la Mode, in Dallas, Texas, which provides a range of personal care services.[1]

As of March 2020, Luther's salon was the home base of the livelihood of not just herself but an additional nineteen people with contractor status, which is very typical in the personal services industry. As an entrepreneur, Shelley Luther isn't Amazon's Jeff Bezos or Facebook's Mark Zuckerberg. Still, her salon business helped support her family, helped stylists support theirs, and contributed to the local and national economy.

On May 5, 2020, her American Dream turned into a living nightmare. She was taken into custody after a court hearing and booked in the Dallas County jail.[2]

What had that woman of Main Street done? Had she committed murder, arson, or fraud? Did she have a feud with a neighboring stylist that came to violence? No.

What she had done was . . . drumroll, please . . . have the audacity to open and work in her own business.

Yes, Shelley Luther was thrown in jail, in America, in 2020, for working.

About a month and a half before, in the middle of March, Texas, as well as a slew of other states and local jurisdictions, had started putting all kinds of bans into place to deal with the disease caused by the new coronavirus, COVID-19.

Though the situation was uncertain, the mandates were unprecedented. Government entities, the same ones that were supposed to protect property rights and all individual rights, told many businesses, primarily small businesses, that they were considered "nonessential" and that they had to shut down, some in whole, some in part.

That was it: millions of businesses across the country received directives to close but nothing else. No compensation for helping the government or "society," no special provisions to safeguard their own or their staffs' livelihoods; just pack it in, shut it down, and go home.

Luther's salon was one of those businesses, and she complied with the order to shut down.

The same situation was repeated across the country, as small businesses shuttered their storefronts and were forced to tell their employees they had no jobs until further notice.

But two weeks became three, then four, then almost five, and Luther wasn't going to sit home anymore. She had a family to care for, as did her stylists. So on April 24, 2020, she decided to go back to work and reopened her salon. Noteworthy, at that time, was the fact that there were no unusual spikes in hospitalizations for COVID in Dallas County.[3]

As she later said in an interview, she didn't mind trying to help the health care workers on the front lines avoid being overwhelmed by closing her business for a couple of weeks, perhaps even three. Eventually, though, her hairstylists had decided to continue to see clients. Luther said they had told her, "'Look. I'm about to go to people's houses to do hair because I just don't have any money.'" She continued, "I decided to open because it's not safe for them, obviously, to be going to people's houses for them or their clients. I just felt like if I opened, I could create a sterile environment and make it at least a lot safer and follow CDC [Centers for Disease Control and Prevention] guidelines and regulations." She added that she "didn't want to be the reason why [the hairstylists] weren't making money."[4]

The disconnect between what was deemed essential by government was also glaring. Luther said, "When I have other businesses like the pet groomer next door that's been 'essential' the entire time, you could buy CBD oil, you could go to Home Depot and buy flowers, I mean two hundred people in the garden section, I didn't see why it would be any different for me to open up using much safer guidelines than what they were doing."[5]

Luther decided to stand up for herself via taking back control of her rights and her property and for other businesses through becoming active in the Open Texas movement, which advocated for the prompt reopening of the state.[6]

She ignored a citation from local authorities. She tore up a cease-and-desist letter, and she started using the hashtag #Rememberthealamode, a "punny" nod to her salon's name and situation.

In a social media video, she said she would be willing to go to jail to prove what government was doing was unconstitutional.

She also tried to work with the government, reaching out to them, often unsuccessfully. However, in an effort to expedite fully reopening the economy, Texas governor Greg Abbott's team reached out to her to get ideas on how salons could open safely.

In parallel with this attempt at collaboration, Luther received a temporary restraining order for her salon that she decided to ignore, as she had done with the other notices.

By May 5, she found herself in county jail.

It wasn't a scare tactic or a dramatic scene meant to prove a point. The reopening was treated as a serious crime, and Luther was brought before a judge to be sentenced.

Dallas district court judge Eric Moyé sentenced Luther to a $7,000 fine and a week in jail, an incredibly excessive penalty for disobeying an order that was likely unconstitutional. Moyé tried to get Luther to apologize, using that and an agreement not to reopen before government orders allowed her to do so as a trade-off to potentially let her avoid jail time.

Luther stood firm. She would not apologize for earning a living. "Feeding my kids is not selfish," she told the judge. "If you think the law is more important than kids getting fed, then please go ahead with your decision, but I am not going to shut the salon."[7]

Judge Moyé said Luther "expressed no contrition, remorse or regret."[8] Who among us would express remorse about wanting to work and earn a living—in the free land of America, no less?

Though the actual violation cited was civil and criminal contempt of court, the underlying story was that a small business owner in America was put into jail for trying to work (not to mention while plenty of other Americans were still working).

You might want to judge Luther in your own court of opinion because of political tribalism. You might say she was selfish, as the judge did. You might say that a hair salon visit isn't an emergency or that she didn't need the money. Though it is easy to judge when you are not walking in her shoes, remember that there were many businesses that remained open; not every business had to close, and Luther did not receive appropriate compensation for closing. In Texas, a slew of other businesses—especially big businesses—from grocery to home improvement retailers, were open. As Shelley Luther said in her interview, the pet-grooming business next door was open, so a "chosen" business could offer an animal a trim, but Luther couldn't offer her human clients the same. It was all so arbitrary, damaging, and an overstep of government authority.

Luther told the *Texas Tribune*, "Reopening my salon wasn't a political statement, it was a necessity for the people that rely on it."[9] But for many small business owners, she was the hero they needed to push back against unreasonable mandates.

With a situation so unusual, so tyrannical, and so un-American, as you can imagine, users of social media were quick to jump on it. Some people disapproved of Luther for being self-centered, but many others backed her cause as an important symbol of individual rights and freedom. One Twitter user, @rwm52, summed it up perfectly, tweeting, "The hair salon and barber shop were symbolic of protests to open businesses so people could pay bills, feed their families, avoid losing their businesses, and more. We weren't actually protesting to get a haircut."[10]

The social media buzz was also able to garner the attention of politicians, particularly high-profile Texas politicians. Republican senator Ted Cruz tweeted, "7 days in jail for cutting hair?? This is NUTS. And government officials don't get to order citizens to apologize to them for daring to earn a living."[11]

The already intense pressure on Governor Abbott to change his mandate was now heightened. Abbott has since modified his original executive order to say that local officials cannot jail people who violate the state's stay-at-home order. Previously, he had said that jailing offenders was an option for local officials but should be considered the last resort. "Throwing Texans in jail who have had their businesses shut down through no fault of their own is nonsensical, and I will not allow it to happen," he said as he announced the changes. "That is why I am modifying my executive orders to ensure confinement is not a punishment for violating an order."[12]

Texas attorney general Ken Paxton called Luther's sentence "outrageous and out of touch. . . . The trial judge did not need to lock up Shelley Luther," he said in a statement. "His order is a shameful abuse of judicial discretion, which seems like another political stunt in Dallas."[13]

Lieutenant Governor Dan Patrick even said he would volunteer to be placed under house arrest in Luther's place and pay her fine. After Luther was released, Patrick indeed paid her fine (which was a base of $3,500, along with $500 for every day her salon was open until the executive order was lifted).[14]

A couple of days prior to her sentencing hearing, Luther had, in fact, been approved for an $18,000 loan through the new federal Paycheck Protection Program (PPP). However, her brush with the government had bred further distrust, and she didn't know if because her stylists weren't employees but rented their space in the salon, using the funds on them would qualify her for loan forgiveness. She worried about becoming further indebted because of the loan, a point of concern for many small business owners regarding the convoluted program.

Strangers and friends alike contributed to a GoFundMe fundraiser for Luther's defense that raised more than a half million dollars in just a few weeks. It was so much that Luther decided to set up a nonprofit to help other small business owners.

Luther was far from the only Texan small business owner to rebel. In Laredo, Ana Isabel Castro Garcia and Brenda Stephanie Mata were arrested for allegedly violating the Stay Home Work Safe orders because they provided personal services from their homes. After Luther's case gained attention, the district attorney declined to prosecute them.[15]

In New Jersey, Ian Smith and Frank Trumbetti, the owners of Atilis Gym Bellmawr, went many rounds with their governor, racking up violations. They were also arrested and charged with contempt, obstruction, and violating the Disaster Control Act, vowing in late August to take their case all the way to the Supreme Court. By early December, their small business had racked up more than $1.2 million in fines from the state.[16]

Not every small business owner was jailed or fined, but many grew restless while others closed permanently. Some were able to furlough employees; others laid their employees off so the employees could collect unemployment.

But as the weeks dragged on into months, the United States surpassed 40 million jobless claims, and small businesses across the country, particularly in service-related industries, struggled to survive. Though these small companies and their employees were struggling, the share prices of big companies such as Amazon and Apple were hitting all-time highs and taking the overall market up with them.[17]

It was clear that the government had broken the backbone of America while selling Main Street out to Wall Street.

How did we get to a place where a small business owner was thrown into jail for exercising her right to earn a living and feed her family? Why were the biggest companies increasing in value while the rest of the economy was breaking down?

Though the wheels had long been in motion, everything came to a head with that black swan.

Just a Couple of Weeks . . .

On March 16, just a few days after President Trump declared COVID a national emergency and states started to announce school and other closings, the Trump administration rolled out an initiative called "15 Days to Slow the Spread."[18]

Though there was no official call for a national quarantine and the specifics were left up to the states, the idea was that if citizens came together (figuratively, very much not literally) and practiced social distancing measures, washed their hands frequently, stayed home if they were sick, limited their discretionary travel, and followed other basic practices, the spike in COVID cases could be flattened. The president also outlined measures specific to protecting members of the older population, who were more vulnerable to the new virus.

Though the measure let states decide on the specifics, additional administration guidance included suggesting that governors could consider closing schools if community transmission was taking place, as well as potentially closing other locations where people might congregate, including eating and drinking establishments, workout facilities, and similar locations of social congregation.

Though it was not thought that those measures would eradicate the virus, the stated and understood goal was to "flatten the curve" in terms of those who became seriously ill so that medical staff could handle the number of cases, in terms of both the medical personnel available to do so and hospital beds to accommodate them.[19]

The president also spoke the R-word—recession—but had an upbeat attitude regarding the country's ability to take on the new virus.

That upbeat feeling was not reflected in the stock market, which had a historically awful day. A second emergency rate move in two weeks by the Fed the day prior had fueled instead of quelled the market's fears and saw the Dow plummeting almost 3,000 points for the day; all the major indices were down by 12 to 13 percent for that one day. That kicked off a week of wild volatility in the markets.

Even though it stirred a hornets' nest and took a while to work, note that the first meaningful planned action was economic action to save not small businesses and vulnerable individuals but rather the stock market.

A big-government approach had failed to contain the virus early on. So now, faced with the remaining paths, the government was moving toward a suppression strategy. As noted in chapter 1, such a strategy typically comes with substantial costs and no end point.

So the United States undertook the "15 Days to Slow the Spread" approach. The president appropriately decided against a national approach, leaving the specifics up to the state governors. It hardly made sense to have a one-size-fits-all approach for a country so large and so varied in population and geography; one measure was not needed for everyone at the same time. Allowing the states more latitude was also consistent with how a smaller, decentralized government approach should work.

However, the guidance that suggested governors could enact measures that stood in opposition to civil liberties, such as closing schools and targeting certain establishments for closure in the cases of community spread (restaurants, bars, gyms, etc.), ended up providing a blueprint and cover for governors to create the next series of big-government mistakes and a veritable power grab with devastating consequences.

If you have only fifteen days of suppression, you don't have eradication. Then what? And at what cost?

The Closures Heard 'Round the Nation

Though it seemed clear to anyone who thought a few steps ahead that fifteen days would not be enough time to kill off a virus, it was plenty of time to kill the Constitution—and severely damage small businesses. The guidance, though it was supposed to give governors some tools for decision making and a little space to breathe, ended up providing the cover for far too many state and local government entities to put force ahead of collaboration, to put control ahead of common sense, and to stoke fear and panic that had costly—and deadly—consequences.

Near the time the initial "fifteen days" rollout at the federal level was coming to an end, thirty states had issued nationwide stay-at-home orders, and several others had issued hybrid orders or would issue orders shortly thereafter.[20]

In doing so, government entities acted like racehorses with blinders, not seeing anything else, only COVID directly ahead. They didn't reasonably consider the impacts of other diseases that would be back-burnered. They didn't materially consider mental health issues. They didn't appropriately consider the social and economic costs of shutting down some parts of the economy and not shutting down others. They didn't fully consider developmental issues in youth. Their assessment was entirely focused on the coronavirus. That is not risk management; that is maniacal behavior.

Whether you believe in doing what is "essential" or in preserving liberties, governments did neither successfully; thus, they found little upside and a lot of downside.

Central planning theory pretends that government knows better and will make better decisions, but in reality, governments can neither replicate the complexities of Adam Smith's "invisible hand" nor consider competing issues well at scale.

The solution to disasters caused by central planning is always more central planning. After years of thwarting small businesses with unfair and costly regulation and bailing out and giving breaks to their bigger competitors, a formal war on Main Street was declared.

The States Versus Small Business

Across the country, what had started out being sold as two weeks to "help society" became a severe maiming, and in some cases a death sentence, for small businesses. From bars to restaurants to personal care providers to small product retailers, local consumer-facing businesses were among the first and the longest targeted by cities and states across the nation.

In Ohio, one of the earliest movers, whereas smaller consumer-facing operations were shut down, many other businesses were exempted. The list of "essential" businesses was broad—from stores that sold groceries and medicine to food, beverage, and licensed marijuana production, as well as "critical" labor union functions and hotels and motels and funeral services, among many others. It was a pretty substantial list for a "lockdown."

This created a significant turning point in deeming who were the haves and who were the have-nots, making it difficult to discern why some entities could remain open and others couldn't, particularly when the latter were not compensated for the order. For example, marijuana sales facilities, which had been made legal in 2016 but had begun sales in the state only in 2019, were now deemed "essential," while other longtime local businesses were not.[21]

Ohio set the precedent of not having a full quarantine but not granting full liberty, either, a decision that, like many others that followed, created a drag both on combating the virus and on the economy.

The Ohio Restaurant Association reported that the closing of indoor dining for the state's estimated 22,000 restaurants was expected to affect some 500,000 workers.[22]

In Illinois, which was early and aggressively overreaching in its policies, residents became restless. As reported by Illinois Policy after a public outcry:

> Pritzker's office on May 20 withdrew his controversial rule that made a Class A misdemeanor out of violating his business closure order. The announcement came as the Illinois General Assembly's Joint Committee on Administrative Rules, or JCAR, was about to review the rule that imposed criminal penalties of up to a $2,500 fine and a year in jail.

> Pritzker created the rule after "Madison County declared its businesses could reopen May 13 as long as they maintained social distancing guidelines. About 80 retailers joined together to file suit against Pritzker and defy his closure order, saying he did not have the authority."[23]

Frustration grew as Illinois was hit during the spring and summer with substantial riots and looting and an overall increase in crime. That was particularly the case in Chicago, where Mayor Lori Lightfoot, who coordinated closely with the governor, treated protesters and rioters with less of a heavy hand than she did people simply gathering together and not wearing masks.

The severe response had substantial economic implications. Illinois Policy estimated that anywhere from 5,000 to almost 22,000 restaurants could permanently close in Illinois due to the economic fallout from the orders. Even the Michelin Star recipient Blackbird closed permanently.[24]

When the state eventually distributed grants via the Illinois Department of Commerce and Economic Opportunity with funds from the CARES Act (more than nine months after the bill's passage), only about 9,000 of the 50,000 businesses that had applied received any of the $290 million. *Crain's Chicago Business* noted that many restaurant owners were unhappy, citing some of the recipients and the low percentage of applicants receiving grants as issues. Ultimately, it was more government choosing of winners and losers. *Crain's* reported that a fine dining establishment, Acadia, had received $150,000 while others had received nothing, and that the owner of that business had reportedly moved out of state.[25]

In Michigan, when Governor Gretchen Whitmer extended her original stay-at-home order through the end of April, it included cordoning off garden centers and plant nurseries in stores that were larger than 50,000 square feet. "If you're not buying food or medicine or other essential items, you should not be going to the store," she said of her order, which was considered one of the most restrictive nationwide, given that it limited not only which stores could remain open but what one could purchase in those stores.[26] It was reported that "Along with prohibiting garden centers and plant nurseries, the order prohibits the sale of carpeting, flooring, furniture, and paint. It also blocks Michiganders from using motorboats and vacation properties."[27]

Whitmer used the "government tries to solve problems with more government" playbook. If you don't close Target because it sells groceries, why not stop it from selling baby clothes to keep people from browsing? Wouldn't that directive create more parity with the competitive stores forced closed by government that sold only baby clothes? This illustrates the cascade of rules and problems that always brings a Marxist state to its knees. The more government dictates what can't be bought and sold, the more bureaucrats and police are needed to monitor who is in violation of those rules. And if you don't think citizens would eventually start calling the police in Michigan to stop black-market baby clothes or plant sales out of jealousy or "virtue," you don't know your history and you didn't follow the news of citizens ratting out people gathering at restaurants, parties, and even holiday dinners.

Whitmer's directive created even more consistency problems. Though food is clearly essential, the order deemed that getting food for takeout was okay but growing your own food on your property is not. As Nick Sibilla, a legislative analyst at the Institute for Justice, pointed out in *Forbes*, though you couldn't buy gardening products at an open store, you could purchase lottery tickets and liquor everywhere they were for sale.[28]

The attempt at micromanagement was frustrating for many individuals and devastating for many businesses. The executive director of the Michigan Nursery and Landscape Association, Amy Upton, told Brownfield Ag News for America that Whitmer's order was destroying plants and devastating sales: "I talked to one greenhouse grower that sells Easter lilies. They threw out $125,000 worth of Easter lilies. They dumped them. He said they're in a big pile behind the greenhouses." The article noted that in the greenhouse and nursery industry, growers make most of their annual income within a six-week period, with Upton saying, "Mother's Day is another big time of year for us, and then with annuals, and if we are not able to sell those, we will see a lot of greenhouses go out of businesses [*sic*]."[29]

Despite growing outrage in the state, on April 24, Whitmer extended the stay-at-home order yet again—through May 15—but relaxed some of the previous provisions, such as the aforementioned nursery ban.

An op-ed by Thomas A. Hemphill and Syagnik Banerjee in the *Detroit News* questioned Whitmer's actions and categorization of essential businesses as not consistent with contact and exposure risk.

> First, according to the St. Louis Federal Reserve Bank, 21.6% of jobs nationwide are categorized as high contact-intensive, of which 67% are presently included in critical infrastructure categories, i.e. such as health care, food and groceries and transportation-related workers, etc. Hence, by labeling the majority of contact-intensive occupation workers as essential, the categorization does not sufficiently protect us from exposure.[30]

They further discussed the marginalization of industries and biases against smaller enterprises, noting, "Why small retail operations that provide similar products are required to be closed while larger, 'big box' retailers remain open to the public (operating under specific public health guidelines) and deemed 'essential' has yet to be satisfactorily explained." This is a critical question that I and many others have raised vis-à-vis actions taken across states.

Despite the havoc wreaked on the small business community, the state's Economic Development Corporation touted stats such as "94 Small Businesses Receive $565,750 in Support in First Round of Michigan Entrepreneur Resilience Fund," "58 Early-Stage Tech Companies Receive $3 Million in Support from State's Tech Startup Stabilization Fund," and "299 Michigan small businesses have been awarded $993,984 in grant funds through the Match-on-Main COVID-19 Response Program." When a state as large as Michigan (with almost 10 million inhabitants) promotes supporting only hundreds of businesses, it's hard to take its small business efforts seriously.[31]

Similar actions were taken by local and state governments across the country. Big chain stores stayed open, and there were no major death pools reported related to any of them, anywhere, but their smaller counterparts were out of luck. There was no rotation to spread out the closures among all businesses. Small entrepreneurs saw their customers flock to the biggest companies in the country, making those big companies stronger while they struggled to survive. As noted at the beginning of this chapter, there were instances, including in Texas, of small business owners being thrown into jail.

In North Carolina, which had a generally lighter-touch approach, small business owners questioned the science and pleaded for their livelihoods. After a month of closures, North Carolina Health News reported on a beauty shop owner, Keisha Lindsay, who runs the Beauty Shop in King, North Carolina, who started an online petition for "soft openings" that would allow cosmetologists to service one customer at a time. One petition signer commented, "I can do this safely. My clients need me physically and emotionally. This is my only source of income and what I have been doing for 37 years. I need to get back to my job to help support my family of 6." Another said, "people need to survive!! it appears that politicians and media don't have problems getting groomed nor social distancing. allow soft openings to get society back on track."[32]

In California, *The Sun* asked readers to grade Governor Newsom's response to the pandemic. Among several complaints about hypocrisy related to protesting, one in particular came from Suzanne Potter Zmudosky of Moreno Valley, who wrote:

For the first 30 days, I give Gavin Newsom's actions high marks. For the ensuing 30-plus days and counting, his plan and actions deserve a failing grade.

His pandemic executive order, "Resilience Roadmap" and pandemic-handling actions lack consistent, timely, objectively-measurable goals, indicators for roadmap progress or clear definitions of essential businesses, groups or permissible activities.

All progress beyond stage one has been sudden, capricious and solely a result of public protests or other group/legal pressure. His actions have failed to report or reflect current science and data differentiating risk among different age groups or health conditions.

He has failed to modify, rescind or replace the original executive order.

Above all, I give him failing marks for the fact that the majority of his actions, programs and orders are not pandemic-focused, but rather have an over-abundant focus on this "opportunity to reshape the way we do business and how we govern . . ."[33]

On the last day of August, California became a focus again. Though hair salons in California were still closed for business, San Francisco resident and Speaker of the House Nancy Pelosi was seen breaking the rules by getting her hair done at a local salon, bringing to light the hypocrisy of many big-government actions—and actors.

California's residents said it best, not just for that state but for many states across the nation: a prudent early effort had been transformed into a political power exercise. From lack of goal setting to prioritizing—or at least giving the appearance of doing so—to Newsom's own business, a large part of the efforts reeked of politics.

The States Versus the Elderly

In many ways, New York was the epicenter of everything that went wrong initially and what followed. Despite calls for New York to take action sooner, the state was a bit lackadaisical in terms of decision making, particularly in the emerging hot spot of New York

City, with Mayor de Blasio getting in his last workout at the gym very publicly instead of showing leadership on social distancing amid closure orders.[34]

On March 20, Governor Andrew Cuomo signed the New York State on PAUSE executive order, which shut down all "nonessential" businesses.[35] As noted by Syracuse.com, "Barber shops, nail and hair salons and related personal care services are specified as non-essential, and are directed to close."[36]

That drew the ire of people in many industries. For example, in dog grooming, smaller shops were forced to close while the big box retailer PetSmart remained open. Though the company—not the state—did shut down its grooming services at first, it reopened after just over a week, stating "regular grooming is vital to the health of so many dogs and cats." That didn't sit well with other animal groomers and small businesses that provided grooming services to people, including tens of thousands of nail salons throughout the state.[37]

Anyone over the age of seventy was advised to stay home under a law named Matilda's Law, after the governor's mother, and see only family and close friends in case of emergency, "to protect New York's most vulnerable populations, including individuals age seventy and older, those with compromised immune systems and those with underlying illnesses."[38]

Tragically, a few days later, Cuomo also issued an advisory that David Harsanyi of *National Review* referred to as "perhaps the single most deadly policy mistake in the entire crisis."[39] The policy directed nursing homes to comply with expedited admission of residents coming from hospitals. The advisory said, "No resident shall be denied re-admission or admission to the NH [nursing home] solely based on a confirmed or suspected diagnosis of COVID-19."[40]

That decision is often linked to the initially reported approximately 6,000 nursing home deaths that New York saw in just a few months from the virus's onset, as the order stayed in effect for forty-six days. It also skewed the overall death statistics for the state.[41]

According to the Associated Press, that horrific count was likely substantially, and perhaps intentionally, underreported. It said:

New York's coronavirus death toll in nursing homes, already among the highest in the nation, could actually be a significant undercount. Unlike every other state with major outbreaks, New York only counts residents who died on nursing home property and not those who were transported to hospitals and died there.

That statistic could add thousands to the state's official care home death toll. . . . But so far the administration of Democratic Gov. Andrew Cuomo has refused to divulge the number, leading to speculation the state is manipulating the figures to make it appear it is doing better than other states and to make a tragic situation less dire.[42]

Many other experts confirm that the number was likely underreported.[43]

Was it a mistake, or was it the government offloading risk to the private sector? According to a piece by Bill Hammond, a senior fellow for health policy at the Empire Center, in the *Wall Street Journal*, the nursing home fiasco may have been the result of prioritizing crony interests over the health of the most vulnerable residents of New York. Hammond says the Greater New York Hospital Association, which he dubs "the hospital and health-system trade group that is one of the most influential forces in New York politics," pitched the idea to Governor Cuomo, "In the name of easing a crisis for the association's members."[44]

The nursing home issues spilled over to Cuomo's alliance partners of New Jersey and Connecticut. By mid-July, New Jersey had 6,700 nursing home deaths, making it number one in the country for both reported nursing home deaths per thousand (120.3) and deaths per million. Connecticut was number three for nursing home deaths per thousand (98.5) and number four for overall deaths per million.

It is impossible to overstate how bad the tristate area alliance was for the United States' COVID situation. In addition to the staggering numbers of lives lost, it substantially skewed the early data that had created broad versus targeted forced shutdowns in other parts of the country, based on the fact that government officials in other states didn't know the significant nursing home contribution to the deaths from these three states at the time.

Later, Cuomo tried to blame his nursing home blunder on President Trump and the CDC, although no other governor did the same.[45]

However, by early March, scientific journals had already identified age, as well as comorbidities, as COVID mortality risk factors.[46]

Like New York and New Jersey, Michigan struggled with nursing home deaths. Somehow the severe, heavy-handed central planning missed the most vulnerable population, and Governor Whitmer's orders may have caused more deaths. As of August, about a third of all deaths in Michigan had occurred in nursing homes. That prompted the Department of Justice to make an announcement entitled "Department of Justice Requesting Data from Governors of States That Issued COVID-19 Orders That May Have Resulted in Deaths of Elderly Nursing Home Residents."[47]

The states in question: Michigan, New York, New Jersey, and Pennsylvania.

In a New York Minute . . .

Back in New York, Governor Cuomo announced a reopening plan, to take effect on May 15. He said, "This is not a sustainable situation. Close down everything, close down the economy, lock yourself in the home. You can do it for a short period of time, but you can't do it forever."[48]

It is a phrase that rings of truth, but unfortunately, a short-duration lockdown didn't become a reality for many small businesses. In fact, the nod to unions, including those in construction and manufacturing, in the first phase of Cuomo's reopening plan is notable. In 2019, New York had 1.732 million union members, as well as another 145,000 workers "represented by a union on their main job or covered by an employee association or contract while not union members themselves," which included around 22.7 percent of all employed workers in New York.[49]

As Mayor de Blasio announced Phase Two openings for certain businesses in New York City, it was too late for many of them. In mid-June, amNY reported:

> Some of those stores that will reopen include beauty parlors and barbershops, nail salons and restaurants. Many have been completely closed for more than 100 days and on the South Brooklyn Flatbush Avenue commercial corridor, a mostly minority-owned business district, already have "for rent" signs hanging in the windows or were doing clearance sales because they were closing for good.[50]

The state wouldn't reach Phase Four until mid-July, meaning that some businesses had been affected for four months, or a third of the year.

Despite having an early read and being a hot spot, New York not only messed up its own response but likely also did so for other states whose virus spikes followed. If it hadn't been for its early missteps, its numbers would have been better, and lockdowns across the country might never have happened, might have been shorter in duration, or might have focused on protecting the most vulnerable in the population, such as the elderly.

Additionally, crime in New York City was off the charts, with shootings and murders up substantially through the summer.

To make things worse, New York State "leaders" spent a lot of time acting hypocritically, not abiding by their own rules, and using arbitrary or crony metrics for other rules and choices.

Meanwhile, to add insult to injury, Governor Cuomo revealed that at the same time as he was supposed to be managing a pandemic and had engendered among the worst outcomes and likely impacted the panicked response around the country, he was busy negotiating and writing a book on his pandemic leadership.

State Outcomes

One of the takeaways is that the severity of states' lockdown approaches did not directly correlate to containing the virus. However, the heavy-handedness of the states' approaches did have an economic impact on them, along with factors such as the percentage of the economy that was consumer facing.

Through July, states such as North Carolina and Texas, which had taken a lighter-touch approach, had unemployment levels below the national average of 10.2 percent. Illinois's strict approach delivered a 11.5 percent unemployment rate, California saw a whopping 13.3 percent, and New York's unemployment rate was reported to be 15.9 percent.[51]

The impact on small businesses was outsized. In addition to the aforementioned closures, as of mid-November, it was reported that nearly a third of small businesses in New York and New Jersey had closed during the year.[52]

Nationwide, Opportunity Insights said that through the end of November, just over a quarter of all small businesses that were open in January were now closed.[53]

Clearly, central planning wasn't going to be able to contain a virus, but it would suppress the economy.

From 15 Days to 150 Days and Counting

When the public was initially told that it would take fifteen days to slow the spread and fifteen more days to flatten the curve, there was resistance, but the expectation was that people would pitch in and help make sure that the medical institutions were not overwhelmed. However, as is always the problem with government central planning, once citizens give up their freedom and choice for some "greater good," the politicians get intoxicated by their power, move the goalposts, and further overstep their bounds and individual liberties. Remember that even income taxes were originally meant to be temporary.[54]

It was clear to me at the time of the announcement, as I am sure that it was to many others, that there didn't seem to be a plan for after the first fifteen days, whenever the clock started ticking. It is one thing to say that you need to give the medical community enough time to get a game plan into place, but then what? As in 2019, many states had participated in a several-months-long series of pandemic preparation drills with the Department of Health and Human Services of this very scenario called "Crimson Contagion," they should have known precisely "then what."[55]

This is how central planning has been enabled and how it continues to cement more power in the hands of a few people instead of in the hands of "the people."

Appropriately, the federal government gave some guidance and left decision making to the states. However, many of the states stumbled in the same type of big, bureaucratic overreach that we expect at the federal level.

A stark reality is that even the states that had stringent rules in place at some time or for months on end didn't truly lock down. They kept only some people in lockdown. If your thesis is that you are going to shelter everyone "in place" for a short time to control the virus, you need to do it for everyone, not just some people.

There was a slew of people in all types of roles who were out and about, not just those in genuinely critical occupations. This is not to demean those workers, because everyone's work is vital and important, but is a person who works at a hardware store truly an "essential" worker? And if so, why is he or she more essential than any other small business worker? There should have been a better plan, and if government was going to advocate for a lockdown to reduce cases because of science, there should have been a full lockdown— not my strategic choice per se but at least it would have been showing some conviction.

If the government was going to attempt a partial lockdown, the focus shouldn't have been on who was "essential" but rather on who was at risk. Why were those who were elderly or had other health risk factors not locked down while everyone else went about their business?

Moreover, why was the "greater good" viewed only in terms of COVID? This all reads more like a case of intending to crush small businesses than of following science.

Though the science results didn't correspond with the lockdowns, what did result was a hodgepodge of winners and losers, and the smaller a business was, the more likely it was to be on the losing end. People who had to stay home versus people who were deemed essential. Businesses that were "allowed" to stay open versus businesses that had to close. Main Street versus Wall Street. Entire industries were targeted, even though there were plenty of other businesses open that catered to as many or more people or had similar contact levels. And there was no compensation plan for targeting specific industry sectors and keeping them shuttered.

The actions created a populace divided between those who were scared out of their minds and those who didn't believe anything because of the inherent hypocrisy in the way every aspect of the crisis was handled. The backbone of America was largely disregarded— or rather, highly targeted.

So, bottom line, whether you believe that things should be shut down or people should have freedom and risk management tools, neither of those was achieved.

State and local governments decided that they needed to appear to be taking action. Small businesses ended up as cannon fodder.

If local governments were going to cast small businesses and vulnerable individuals aside and disregard their rights, surely the federal government would step in to help and protect them? It had bailed out many big businesses and industries before that had gotten themselves into trouble. Small businesses hadn't done anything wrong; they had been forced to close by the government, so they should be more worthy of assistance than bailing out automakers or banks, right?

Well, back in Washington, just two days after the president signed the CARES Act, the White House extended its fifteen-day guidance for another thirty days. Fifteen days to flatten the curve ended up in the rearview mirror. And the financial "assistance" in the CARES Act measures, though taking care of Wall Street and the same big businesses that always get taken care of, was hardly enough to be a small business lifeline.[56]

CHAPTER 4

Breaking America's Backbone

More Than a Trillion Dollars for Cronies,
COVID Crumbs for At-Risk Small Businesses

The government forcing businesses to close—directly or indirectly— was an exceptional, historic, and severe action. As Cato Institute's Scott Lincicome noted, that action was similar to enacting eminent domain. When government enacts eminent domain, it is required to give appropriate compensation to those whose property rights it infringes upon.[1]

In layman's terms, if the government tells people they can't open their business for the "good of society," it needs to compensate them for subjugating their individual rights.

The businesses directed to close were due compensation. That wouldn't have been a bailout. It wasn't some irresponsible action of those businesses that had forced them to close and stay closed; it was the government's decree. Therefore, compensation was warranted for the government's infringement on property rights.

That compensation was needed both quickly and with specificity to ensure that small businesses stayed afloat and jobs were preserved.

Small businesses, as previously noted, make up more than 99 percent of all businesses, employ approximately half the workforce, and account for around half of the entire US GDP. Most small businesses are on the very small side (it is estimated that around 24.2 million of the pre-COVID 30.2 million were solopreneurs). Those that do have employees are typically strapped for cash. Because they are smaller in scope, they are more susceptible to volatility in their business. Plus, with thin operating margins and financial statements, including balance sheets, on a much smaller scale, they do not have the financial wherewithal to endure a closure the way a larger company in the same industry may. They also do not have the same access to investors and lenders that larger businesses do.[2]

As many small businesses are heavily invested in by their owners (many of whom also personally guarantee the loans and other liabilities of the business, meaning that if the business fails, they personally have to come up with the cash to cover those loans and liabilities), the financial implications of the business going belly-up mean personal financial ruin, not just a reorganization in bankruptcy court.

The government should have provided monies directly and quickly to any impacted business specifically to cover ongoing payroll costs and any other operating expenses they required to remain in business for at least a three-month period. With small businesses accounting for about half of the GDP and not every small business affected by shutdowns, around $1 trillion should have covered that need.

Helping companies to stay in business is not only about small businesses and their owner-entrepreneurs; it is also about keeping the workforce afloat. Helping the employees of small businesses retain employment was—and remains—a vastly superior tactic to sending checks directly to individuals.

Such a strategy would have prevented individuals from going on unemployment. When employees remain employed, even though they are sitting at home, they and their employer are still paying into Social Security and paying other taxes. Retaining them preserves the employees' access to health care. It puts them into the mindset that they are still earning and can therefore continue to spend freely (which is vital, as consumer spending makes up around 70 percent of the economy and consumer confidence had been fragile given the shutdowns and overall pandemic backdrop).

Most critically, funding businesses to keep employees on payrolls ensures that those businesses don't close permanently, so that the entrepreneurs will still have a company and livelihood and workers will have a job to go back to when the lockdown restrictions ease.

Why pay an individual to stay home unemployed when you can pay an individual to stay home as a worker and save their job and the small company for which they work?

The short-term costs, particularly those above what would otherwise be rung up in unemployment costs and offset by taxes still being paid, are far outweighed by the long-term benefits.

This tactic would also focus these emergency funds solely on those people who were impacted by the lockdowns. Many individuals' jobs or businesses were not substantially or negatively impacted. Some of the largest US employers actually increased their staffs. Other small businesses began to operate remotely or were deemed essential, so if the relief was meant as an emergency "eminent domain" type of funding, there was no reason to fund any of these other entities.

The funding should also have covered solopreneurs, gig workers, and other independent workers, looking at their earnings as their "payroll," if their ability to work was compromised, whether directly or via the smaller businesses that use contractors instead of employees.

The structure should also have been retroactive to allow any business to rehire employees they had to let go because of COVID-19 and provide appropriate payroll coverage.

In terms of a mechanism, direct small business payments should not have been done as loans, even forgivable loans. Without revenue coming in for several months, most small businesses don't make enough to service debt and would not be able to pay it back. Plus, applying for a loan requires substantial paperwork and time, and small businesses did not have the luxury of time.

For larger businesses in relevant impacted industries, such as travel and hospitality, that have debt capacity, any funding should have been a loan, if they showed they couldn't access the capital markets, which they should have been able to do. For larger businesses that couldn't service their debt, an equity stake would have been appropriate, and putting parameters on and limits to future uses of capital, such as limiting share buybacks until the taxpayers' money is repaid or a certain number of years has passed, would have been entirely appropriate.

As noted, this was an emergency situation, so the government didn't have time to enact means testing up front. What should have been done was to use the honor system for applying for relief due to the urgent nature of the situation. Parameters could have been clearly set to attest to and means testing could have been done via 2020 tax payments. If a business didn't keep its payroll or contractor usage intact, for example, and used the money elsewhere, or if it made more money than expected in 2020, that could have been adjusted for in its 2020 tax filing. Proof would be easy to provide by submitting payroll reports as backup, and given that so many of the businesses are microbusinesses, firms under a certain threshold of revenue or earnings could have had all paperwork provisions waived so that there would be no concern that "no good deed would go unpunished," such as being subject to an audit as a result of accepting due compensation.

Given that the federal government, via the IRS, requires all kinds of business verification information, including tax filings, it could have managed the payment disbursement directly—or used the banks or other intermediaries as helpers if that wasn't fast enough (as speed isn't something the government is known for).

As most of the closure mandates were done at the state level and a large portion of the states' budgets comes from the federal government, theoretically, the states should have been responsible. But given how much power and money the federal government has usurped, perhaps for now such funding was more appropriate federally. Either way, that is not something that needed to be sorted out up front. The federal government could have argued with the states later on about how the bill should be split, perhaps by the federal government shifting some of the funding it typically provides the states over the course of the year.

Ultimately, the priority was to ensure that businesses remained in business and people had jobs to go back to. Everyone was told, "fifteen days," which alone was a tremendous burden for smaller entities. Taking a three-month view with compensation would have alleviated that burden and also provided an appropriate time frame in which to plan and control the virus spread, as well as devise guidelines for ongoing business operations and best practices, knowing that the virus would not be stopped by then, that there would be no vaccine, and that the economy cannot—with any practicality—be shut down indefinitely to deal with a virus.

The bill to cover this should have been singular in focus (saving jobs and the businesses they are attached to) and highly focused on small businesses and vulnerable industries as the primary objective. COVID financing and other bills should have remained separate, and those most in jeopardy should have been treated as such.

This path would have saved small businesses and the jobs of vulnerable workers. As urgent and straightforward as such action was for the government to take, unfortunately, and also unsurprisingly, that was not what happened.

You Get a Trillion, and *You* Get a Trillion . . .

After giving up control of the first two more minor coronavirus-related economic packages, Senate Majority Leader Mitch McConnell took an early lead to draft the relief bill. He reportedly tried to work it out with his GOP cohorts first and then bring in Minority Leader Chuck Schumer and the Democrats. According to the *Los Angeles Times*, the original bill was for around $1 trillion, focused on direct payments to workers, and had a lot of pork in it.[3]

As the first effort was a no-go among his colleagues, McConnell reportedly pieced together another plan quickly to try to strong-arm a vote on it using the fear of a market crash as a catalyst. That didn't work, and the House decided to introduce its own bill, eating up precious time and eventually putting forth a $2.5 trillion counter-proposal.[4]

The time wasted by the Democratic-led House and the urgent backdrop of the relief needs put the Senate into a bind, one to which its members probably acquiesced too quickly. There was some back-and-forth but not enough. For example, most of the senators tried to do away with the expansion of the unemployment benefits "bonus," noting its likely counterproductive economic effects. They were unsuccessful in that and ultimately approved the bill with that provision. The CARES Act was passed 96–0 by the Senate. According to Adam Andrzejewski, the CEO and founder of Open the Books, in *Forbes*, "Twice during the first hour of Senate debate, two 'final' versions [of the CARES Act] were distributed. No one had time to read the final language."[5]

Representative Thomas Massie took to Twitter to criticize the entire process and outcome, saying in a series of tweets:

> The Constitution requires that a quorum of members be present to conduct business in the House. Right now, millions of essential, working-class Americans are still required to go to work during this pandemic such as manufacturing line workers, healthcare professionals, pilots, grocery clerks, cooks/chefs, delivery drivers, auto mechanics, and janitors (to name just a few). Is it too much to ask that the House do its job, just like the Senate did?
>
> I am not delaying the bill like Nancy Pelosi did last week. The bill that was worked on in the Senate late last week was much better before Speaker Pelosi showed up to destroy it and add days and days to the process. This bill should have

been voted on much sooner in both the Senate and House and it shouldn't be stuffed full of Nancy Pelosi's pork—including $25 million for the Kennedy Center, grants for the National Endowment for the Humanities and Arts, and millions more other measures that have no direct relation to the Coronavirus Pandemic. That $25 million, for example, should go directly to purchasing test kits. The number one priority of this bill should have been to expand testing availability and creation of tests.

This bill creates even more secrecy around a Federal Reserve that still refuses to be audited. It allows the Federal Reserve to make decisions about who gets what, how much money we'll print. With no transparency.[6]

Little CARES for the Little Guys

It was hard to disagree with Representative Massie. What was supposed to be an emergency economic relief bill ended up being a hodgepodge of crony helicopter money, other pork, and poorly structured relief, reaching the height of $2.3 trillion. To put that into perspective, the entire federal government spending outlay in 2001 was $1.9 trillion.

Despite that historic amount, very little of the money went to preserving small businesses or compensation for eminent domain–type action.

The bill was late as well. Though the Senate tried to get it passed quickly, the Democrats' posturing added time, heft, and more pork to the bill, which meant that it was not even signed by the president until March 27, 2020, nearly two weeks after many states and localities had shuttered small businesses.

Instead of enacting laser-focused bills, with more transparency and efficacy as I laid out above, Congress's megabill was a random collection of spending mandates. How much of the spending went to small business, and where else did it go? Below is a summary of some of the categories and items of expenditure that were included— good, bad, and ugly.[7]

COVID-Related Spending

Instead of dealing with COVID spending separately from economic relief, that funding was crammed into the megabill, which the Senate Appropriations Committee described as a "$340 billion surge in emergency funding to combat the coronavirus outbreak," with more than 80 percent going to state and local governments and communities. That included $117 billion for hospitals and veterans' health care, $45 billion for the FEMA Disaster Relief Fund, $4.3 billion for the Centers for Disease Control and Prevention, and $11 billion for vaccines, therapeutics, diagnostics, and other medical supplies, among other allocations.

State Funding

Additional funding was allocated to state and local governments to help deal with the virus and withstand the impact of anticipated lower tax collections.[8]

Individual Relief

Those who made less than $75,000 individually in 2018 (or 2019 if you had already filed your taxes) received a so-called stimulus check (formally called "economic impact payments") in the amount of $1,200 per individual and $500 for each child. Additional phaseouts were set for married couples and higher income levels, with a total cost estimated by J.P. Morgan to be $290 billion.

Because the check structure was based on past income levels instead of current needs, money went—in addition to some who needed it—to a slew of others who did not need it. I spoke with one individual off the record who said they felt guilty about the checks that their family members received, as they did not need them (they also did not return them). Another individual, off the record, who didn't need the payment, said, "I always get screwed in these things, so I don't need it, but I'm keeping it."

The processing was so sloppy that a substantial number of payments went to deceased people. With the bill's structure and retroactive timetable, the Government Accountability Office estimated that the Treasury Department had sent around 1.2 million checks totaling approximately $1.6 billion to people who were no longer living. By August, the Treasury said, almost 70 percent of that had been recovered, still leaving a lot of money outstanding and wasting resources and time. In November, the IRS admitted that it had also sent stimulus checks to non-Americans living in foreign countries.[9]

Unemployment

The treatment of unemployment was a mixed bag. One appropriate measure for those who did lose their jobs was that the time frame for payment of unemployment benefits was extended for thirteen weeks. However, that wouldn't have been as important if more weight and focus had been put into the small business portion of the relief and saving jobs from the get-go.

Additionally, there was an extended unemployment benefit payment of an incremental $600 per week. That proved to have disastrous consequences for certain small business owners as they tried to get workers back to work during "open" periods in their local economies; some small business owners claimed that with the extra benefits, workers were making nearly as much, if not more, staying home, which disincentivized them to return to the workforce and put additional stress and pressure on small business owners.

One thoughtful addition was a program put into place to cover independent contractors, gig workers, and other self-employed individuals, who would typically be excluded from qualifying for unemployment benefits.

Government Spending with Extra Bacon

One of the most controversial areas of the bill in terms of unnecessary funding was direct federal spending. Some spending arguably made sense as more people were likely to suffer unemployment and other issues, such as about $25 billion to the USDA Food and Nutrition Service to increase Child Nutrition Programs, SNAP benefits, and more—although it could be argued that if the bill had been structured correctly to preserve jobs, the existing spending on those programs should have covered what was necessary and no additional funding would have been needed.

Some of the questionable spending included everything from $20 million to the National Oceanic and Atmospheric Administration to "support continuity" of things such as the National Weather Service—it is unclear why the existing budget wouldn't have covered that—to $20 million that went to the Department of Defense's Office of Inspector General for additional personnel to audit their emergency funding. The Federal Building Fund was allocated $275 million for "coronavirus prevention and response in GSA-managed federal buildings"—that's a whole lot of hand sanitizer! Additionally, $80 million went to the Pandemic Response Accountability

Committee, $7.5 million to the Smithsonian, and $150 million to the National Endowments for the Arts and Humanities, among many other questionable to highly questionable spending endeavors.[10]

One tranche of funding that drew a lot of ire on social media was $25 million to the Kennedy Center. The first question was, why was the Kennedy Center treated differently from other small businesses or nonprofits that needed relief? Even if you could argue that it needed funds, why would it get a $25 million outright grant and not be subject to the same "hoop-jumping" provisions that small businesses were in the PPP program? Probably because its board of directors reads like a who's who of the wealthy, powerful, and connected.

According to the watchdog agency Open the Books, the Kennedy Center had received $68.3 million in federal grants between 2010 and 2019 and had total assets of $557 million. That is not the financial position of an entity in dire straits and is nowhere near the same situation that the struggling businesses of Main Street were in.[11]

Then, amid that cash grab, the Kennedy Center furloughed musicians and then 250 additional staff—so the justification that jobs had been saved couldn't even be made.[12]

Social media backlash ensued, pressuring some of the same GOP lawmakers who had voted unanimously for the bill to take a stand. Within a couple of weeks' time, the Kennedy Center musicians agreed to a pay cut instead of a furlough. The absurdity shows how the government's central planning enriches cronies, causes waste, and doesn't address actual issues. Millions of dollars that could have been going to save Main Street businesses instead were handed out to entities that did not need the funds for survival.[13]

The Education Stabilization Fund and Related Programs

Another area that caused an uproar only once it was noticed and picked up steam on social media was the $12.5 billion allocated to colleges and universities. A slightly larger lump sum was given to the Department of Education, which went about divvying it up by institution.[14]

Though about half of each allocation was supposed to be earmarked for emergency financial aid grants to students, the rationale made no sense. First, the colleges and universities had been paid in full for the school year by the students, so there was no need to collect any extra payments from them. Also, given the reduced operating costs due to not having staff on campus, the schools could have refunded a portion of their revenue to the students.

With large swaths of the rest of the country, including small business owners, taking pay cuts and sharing the burden of dealing with shutdowns "for the good of others," there was a backlash that the university executives, administrators, and teachers didn't do the same.

However, the biggest outrage came when it was pointed out that some of the country's wealthiest universities had been allocated millions of dollars by the DOE when they already had multibillion-dollar endowments. The poster child was Harvard University, whose endowment had recently been valued north of $40 billion but which was still allocated close to $9 million from the fund. It had just laid off its dining hall staff as well.[15]

On April 16 and 17, 2020, that news spread via social media such as Twitter like wildfire and even reached the attention of the president, who called it out in a press conference (despite having signed the law and having his DOE make the allocations).

Harvard was hardly the only rich university getting funds. The $12.5 billion included allocations to Columbia and Cornell for $12.8 million each, Yale for about $7 million, and the Louisiana State University system (excluding money allocated to its health and medical centers) for around $25 million. The University of Texas system, second only to Harvard in its endowment size, was allocated $165.8 million (excluding money allocated to its health and medical centers), the University of Arizona $31 million, and Arizona State University $63.5 million, among other allocations.[16]

That was all money that could have gone directly to saving small businesses and jobs, instead of going to nonprofits that already receive funding and tax breaks and in many cases have huge endowments. Plus, those institutions had already been paid for the school year (with, in many cases, loans to students originating from the government).

Notably, none of the funding was earmarked for the hardships endured by the college towns, which would bear a substantial blow as a result of the colleges' closing down their campuses. The closures

Top Endowments of US Universities[17]

School	Estimated Endowment (as of FY 2019; billions of dollars)*
Harvard University	$40.9
Yale University	$30.3
Stanford University	$27.7
Princeton University	$25.6
Massachusetts Institute of Technology	$17.4
University of Pennsylvania	$14.6
Texas A&M University	$12.6
University of Michigan Ann Arbor	$12.3
University of Notre Dame	$11.6
Columbia University	$11.0

*The University of Texas System's combined endowments are estimated at around $31 bçl²n.

impacted the towns' populations and in turn their businesses. NBC News reported that the "Financial strain from COVID-19 has been especially acute for college towns like Amherst, where the loss of students has meant the loss of money they poured into local economies. Undergraduate students—about 25,000 at the three schools combined—made up nearly three-quarters of Amherst's total population. That population largely left Amherst when the campuses closed."[18]

On April 21, Harvard, in a series of five tweets, doubled down on keeping the funds, explaining that they hadn't come from PPP but from the CARES Act in general (which was misreported by some media representatives who didn't understand the nuance). However, the larger point of outrage was that the relief bill was supposed to help the vulnerable in the economy. Money that could have gone to PPP or otherwise directly to small businesses had instead gone to institutions such as Harvard, which didn't have to do anything to receive the funds and, more important, did not need them for their survival.[19]

As Twitter user Helen Levinson (@HelenLevinson) pointed out, "They certainly don't need aid. Harvard had a surplus of $298 million in fiscal year 2019, up from $196 million in 2018. There are small businesses that only have a 2–3 week cushion of cash and have received ZERO funds."[20]

On April 22, among the buildup of negative press, Stanford University announced preemptively, in a series of tweets, that it had "contacted the Department of Education to ask that our application for relief funds under the Higher Education Emergency Relief Fund section of the CARES act be rescinded." Princeton University quickly followed suit.[21]

Under increased scrutiny, later that day, April 22, Harvard released a statement and a series of tweets that it would not be taking CARES Act money, primarily blaming the pressure it had received on politics.[22]

Though the users of Twitter had become the watchdogs and can take credit for bringing to light issues that the mainstream media didn't even report on, getting big universities not to accept emergency funds was a moral victory. But with that money likely reallocated to some other endeavor and $2.3 trillion spent overall, it was also a hollow victory.

Though Harvard and other institutions were appropriately shamed, the bigger shame lies with Congress, which does not receive nearly enough scorn or accountability. The CARES Act was meant as emergency relief money. Any entity, university or otherwise, that had not been put into an emergency survival situation by the government shutting it down should not have received money to begin with, and that was where the bigger problem lay.

It is also a travesty that journalists and the media, one of whose jobs is to hold the government accountable, spend too much time doing just about everything other than that. If it weren't for Twitter users bringing all this to light weeks after the CARES Act passed, who knows if it would have ever been reported on. Moreover, the journalists who had missed it to begin with still messed up the reporting by attributing the allocations to PPP instead of the CARES Act in general—a sorry state of affairs all around.

Big Business Relief

Despite small businesses being the most vulnerable, there is no doubt that government actions and the media-fueled hysteria around the virus led to specific industries and companies being disproportionately affected, including those in hospitality, travel, entertainment, and leisure. Therefore, there could be an argument for some assistance to help keep those businesses intact.

The CARES Act was heavily slanted toward big business relief. Tax breaks, in the form of adjustments to the way items such as net operating losses and interest deductions are treated, are estimated to be valued at around $280 billion by both J.P. Morgan and the Tax Policy Center.[23]

One of the biggest issues came around a $450 billion–ish "slush fund" that sent money to the US Treasury's Exchange Stabilization Fund. That was done through loans, guarantees, and other types of investments to back the Federal Reserve to prop up distressed companies (read: distressed big businesses). With leverage, it was expected to enable the Fed to spend north of $4 trillion to subsidize lending to big companies. That raised many eyebrows. Given the Fed's ability to "print" money, why would it need taxpayer funds at all? It's partly because of the structure designed to preserve secrecy and opacity around its transactions and investments.[24]

The bailouts for big businesses, including many questionable recipients, also drew attention. One such situation was a $700 million "relief loan" given to a struggling trucking company, YRC, that, according to KSHB in Kansas, the Defense Department had sued just two years prior, in 2018, "for overcharging the government for freight carrier services and making false statements."[25]

Another questionable expense was the bailout of the airline industry. There is no doubt that the stay-at-home orders created extra pressure on travel, including the airlines. However, the airlines were no strangers to mismanagement and bankruptcies. And, according to Fast Company, the industry has spent more than $350 million on lobbying since airlines were bailed out after 9/11.[26]

The airlines, according to Bloomberg, had spent 96 percent of their free cash flow over the last decade to buy back their own shares instead of creating a cushion for a crisis, something that, given the frequency of airline bankruptcies, they should know they need.[27]

The bailout of $60 billion, including to cargo transporters and contractors, could be argued as due compensation for the shutdowns if part of a larger program. However, in its current form, it looks more like the government propping up a few undeserving companies. As the airlines had valuable assets, as well as access to capital markets and bankruptcy courts, the real beneficiaries were their shareholders. This transfer of wealth to big businesses and their shareholders with big lobbying budgets is made even less palatable by the way the airlines frequently treat their customers.[28]

Though relief focused on the airlines, local economies were largely ignored. Take the local impact of business travel. Per the *Wall Street Journal*, "Domestic and international business travelers in the U.S. directly spent $334.2 billion in 2019, supporting 2.5 million jobs, according to the U.S. Travel Association." The *Journal* estimated that the total economic output and jobs supported by business travel before the pandemic had been about twice that.[29] So the airlines were taken care of directly and substantially, while local economies had to fight it out for scraps passed down from other programs.

A Small Lifeline: The Paycheck Protection Program (PPP)

With all of those giveaways, you might expect that small businesses would have also been taken care of by the government.

The amount of money required to ensure that small businesses stayed open, appropriately compensate them under an "eminent domain" scenario, and preserve jobs was probably in the $1 trillion range. Instead, what small businesses received as part of the CARES Act amounted to less than 20 percent of the overall relief package— again, a figure that makes little sense given that small businesses account for around half the economy and are the most vulnerable and most directly affected by the government black swan.

Instead of getting money to small business owners quickly and directly, which would have been the most effective tactic and consistent with the direct payments received by the likes of Congress members' cronies such as the Kennedy Center and universities, Congress cobbled together a shoddy, confusing "forgivable" loan program in the PPP.

The initial allocation and structure, which have been modified in part and generally improved since the plan's conception, forced small business owners to go through a series of hoops at commercial banks and other lending institutions to apply and compete for funds that initially covered eight weeks of payroll, rent, and utilities and would be forgiven if they kept employees on the payroll with at least 75 percent of the loan used for payroll expenses.[30]

Confusion and fear about whether taking the funds would lead to increased chances of tax audits and worries about the opacity of the forgiveness process and whether the loans would be forgiven at all led many small business owners to decide that the risk of applying wasn't worth it.

The structure of the program was also a massive problem. With few limits on the size (up to five hundred employees per applicant) and qualities that the businesses applying could possess and still receive the loans, many large entities that didn't need the funding for survival applied to their banks for the limited funds. As any other business would, the banks wanted to make sure that their best customers were taken care of first. Who do you think are the banks' best small business customers? Larger "small businesses"—not microbusinesses, which don't have the same access to capital.

Additionally, in terms of loan amounts, the program allowed for loans up to $10 million. If those loans were meant to protect payroll initially for two months or eight weeks, what kind of small business has a $5 million-per-month operating budget? Not a small, vulnerable one with limited access to financing, that's for sure.

The flawed structure of the PPP program left many of the smallest businesses out in the cold at first.

Ryan Hoover, a small business owner of a self-defense and fitness business in North Carolina, recounted his initial PPP experience to me. He was at first denied a PPP loan. His commercial banker sent him a note saying, "We had people applying for the PPP loans that were basically unaffected by the virus, and had no specific needs, but it was 'free money, so why not?'" Hoover said that although his business was in the system for the program, he never got to the submission stage, and his banker couldn't guarantee that he would get in for the second round. The banker told Hoover that the bank had received around 66,000 applications during the first weekend and that its employees had been told internally not to work on applications under the $100,000 threshold (i.e., the big customers were to be cared for first).[31]

According to the *Wall Street Journal*, when the program started in April, 92 percent of the 4,840 loans in amounts of $5 million to $10 million were approved, compared with 59 percent for all loans applied for in April.[32]

Additionally, many of the smaller small businesses didn't have any established banking relationships, which left them unclear about or unable to figure out who to turn to for help; online lenders helped some, but not all small business owners were familiar with those companies. Also, it was reported that newer startups struggled to produce the requisite paperwork.

Also, the PPP's eligibility structure made it difficult to impossible for some of the smallest businesses, including one-person businesses, to apply for relief, putting those small businesses, which often rely on their owner-operators' working with consultants, contractors, and other vendors, in jeopardy of survival.

The initial allocation of PPP funds was exhausted within thirteen days, reaching only about 1.6 million small businesses.[33]

It is not surprising that it went so quickly, with bigger businesses applying for and being prioritized for loans. *Forbes* estimated that seventy-one publicly traded companies took down loans in the first $350 billion tranche of the program.[34]

The blame rests mostly on the structure of the program, which had high maximum loan sizes and did not put in safeguards to ensure that businesses that were larger, that were not in danger of going out of business, and/or that had access to other capital did not get the loans. The program was structured more like a Las Vegas buffet, where VIP high rollers could skip to the front of the line.

The revelation, or at least publicity, of the abuse of the program forced Treasury Secretary Mnuchin to make a statement to help shame some companies into paying the loans back or otherwise forgo the funding. "It is unlikely that a public company with substantial market value and access to capital markets will be able to make the required certification in good faith, and such a company should be prepared to demonstrate to SBA, upon request, the basis for its certification," he said.[35]

With the Treasury secretary's statement and a fair amount of social media shame—which led to mainstream media shame—some recipients, including Shake Shack and Ruth's Hospitality Group, which operates the Ruth's Chris Steak House chain, decided to pay the loans back.[36]

Some recipients were even more shocking. *Forbes* reported that Hallador Energy, a coal producer whose 2019 financial statements showed $426 million of assets and $230 million of liabilities, secured a $10 million forgivable PPP loan. Companies that had foreign parent businesses also received loans. Singapore-based Wave Life Sciences and Canada-based CRH Medical both were among the seventy-one publicly traded entities that received multimillion-dollar loans.[37]

(*Forbes* also disclosed that its parent, Forbes Media LLC, had received a PPP loan of $5 million to $10 million.)[38]

Too Little, Too Late, Too Confusing

With the speed at which the program was exhausted and the PPP failing to reach enough small businesses, Congress allocated more funding. About a week before the end of April, another $310 billion was approved as part of a $484 billion interim stimulus funding bill.[39]

As an acknowledgment of failures in the structure of the original plan, reportedly $60 billion of the money was reserved for smaller businesses without existing banking relationships. However, that was very late in the game.[40]

Unfortunately, not all the small businesses that needed the money decided to take what was available during the second tranche. For some, it was just too late, and they decided to close up shop altogether. Moreover, the frequent rule changes and general distrust of government led some small business owners to decide that they didn't want to risk that the loan would not be forgiven.

According to the Associated Press, between March 31 and June 15, the SBA had "issued 35 changes to program rules and its frequently asked questions, according to a Government Accountability Office report issued last week." The loans' forgiveness was the biggest concern of small businesses and microbusinesses that didn't have the financial wherewithal to make up or withstand the lost revenue from the shutdowns and pay back the loan.

The first time the SBA and the Treasury Department released guidance on forgiveness was not until almost three-quarters of the way through May, and there was still a great deal of confusion among small business applicants, would-be applicants, and recipients.[41]

Additionally, the time frame for using the funding for payroll was a big hurdle for small businesses. It wasn't until the beginning of June, less than a month before the initial application deadline, that Congress extended the use period to twenty-four weeks. However, the initial structure, coupled with the too-late changes, kept many small businesses from applying altogether. It also forced small businesses to use up funds quickly that they otherwise would have been able to stretch out, for fear of not being in compliance with the forgiveness rules.

Too Small to Matter

It bears repeating: the companies that needed the money the most encountered the most obstacles to receiving the money. It isn't a surprise, but certainly a detriment and disappointment, that a government so big, so beholden to cronies, so opaque, and with so little accountability wouldn't do the right thing to save the economy. Crony entities got money directly, big colleges with billion-dollar endowments got money directly, Wall Street was supported, and small businesses got paperwork, headaches, and rules changes. This is how the government "helps" the little guy; this is democratic socialism in practice.

The Associated Press quoted some small business experts on the issues. Karen Kerrigan, CEO of the advocacy group the Small Business & Entrepreneurship Council, said, "We knew it was a problem a week after the legislation was signed, when we looked at the shutdown orders." Todd McCracken, the CEO of the advocacy group National Small Business Association, said, "It was too late for many companies" and agreed that the PPP had been "poorly designed from the start."[42]

It was estimated that banks would earn anywhere between $14 billion and $24 billion in fees for their role in processing the loans. The *Wall Street Journal* reported that several of the largest banks, including JPMorgan Chase and Bank of America, had stated their intention to donate any profits they made from PPP processing. However, it is unclear how program "profits" might be calculated after infrastructure costs and other allocated expenses.[43]

PPP's Mixed Results

In early July 2020, it was disclosed by the Small Business Administration (SBA) and the US Treasury that the government had allocated approximately $521 billion under the PPP, leaving more than

$138 billion on the table unclaimed. After a pressure campaign for transparency about who had received the loans, the names of the approximately 600,000 entities that had received at least $150,000 in loans under the program were also released.[44]

Overall, it was estimated that approximately 4.9 million small businesses and nonprofits had taken advantage of the program during the two "rounds" or tranches of funds. However, the biggest firms, those receiving more than $150,000 in forgivable loans up to the program maximum of $10 million, were also the biggest funding recipients. The largest 13.5 percent of program applicants accounted for approximately 75 percent of the dollars given out.[45]

In the July release, Treasury Secretary Mnuchin said, "The PPP is providing much-needed relief to millions of American small businesses, supporting more than 51 million jobs and over 80 percent of all small business employees, who are the drivers of economic growth in our country."[46] Those numbers may be a bit misleading. Perhaps the 4.9 million (which was also inclusive of nonprofits) is looked at as 80 percent of all employer businesses, but that would exclude the majority of solopreneur businesses. Looking at this across all small businesses, with approximately 6 million having employees and 24.2 million solo businesses (where the owner is the employee) at the time, the funds reached around 16 percent of the total number of small businesses. There's also no official way to know whether or not that was representative of the number of small businesses that needed aid, but based on what we know anecdotally, we can assume it was not.

John Arensmeyer, the chief executive officer of Small Business Majority, said, "Across the board, there are gaping holes and inconsistencies in the information." How much the businesses received was also at issue, particularly as larger businesses took down bigger loans. Arensmeyer said that many small business owners had received less than they had requested. "Nationally, a total of more than 21,800 small businesses, many with multiple employees, received a loan for under $1,000. To raise eyebrows even more, more than 1,200 of those businesses received less than $100—with some receiving loans as low as $1.00!"[47]

More Money, More Problems

Further disclosure by the SBA in early July 2020 revealed some of the well-known, wealthy, and frankly mind-boggling entities that had received forgivable PPP loans.

Not surprisingly, more than 33,600 full-service restaurants had, by that time, received federal loans of $150,000 or more, according to Yahoo! Finance analysis of the SBA data. Yahoo! Finance also found that around 21,000 medical practices and 14,310 law firms received large loans, with almost 300 combined receiving loans ranging from $5 million to $10 million.[48]

According to the SBA data, more than one-third of the funds under the PPP program were for loans of seven figures or greater. Again, I mention that this is undoubtedly not the several-month operating budget of the smallest, most vulnerable firms.[49]

On the sports-related front, Floyd Mayweather, who had reportedly earned close to $1 billion over the last decade, had applied for and received a forgivable PPP loan for his boxing promotion company, Mayweather Promotions, as had NFL football icon Tom Brady's TB12 company.[50]

A dozen Major League Soccer franchises applied for the small business relief; some didn't accept it, some did. NASCAR and Indy-Car teams also applied.[51]

According to the SBA, Yeezy, LLC, owned by Kanye West, received more than $2 million in PPP forgivable loans. During the same period, *Forbes* crowned West a billionaire with an estimated net worth of $1.3 billion, and West announced a major ten-year deal with the Gap. It doesn't sound as though his business would have gone under or didn't have the financial wherewithal to secure funding without emergency "small business relief."[52]

Elsewhere in Hollywood, forgivable PPP loans were made to a variety of entities. Judd Apatow's Apatow Productions, the International Academy of Television Arts & Sciences, American Film Institute, SAG-AFTRA Foundation, Motion Picture & Television Fund, Tribeca Film Institute, and GRAMMY Museum Foundation were just some of the entities receiving PPP relief.[53]

A slew of media companies received funds: The Daily Caller received between $150,000 and $350,000, while Media Matters for America, which showed $5.3 million in assets on its most recent IRS 990 (FY 2018), according to Open the Books, received between $1 million and $2 million in PPP lending.[54]

According to the Associated Press and Business Insider, Catholic Church entities, nonprofits that do not pay taxes, were among the top recipients of aid, for an estimated combined total of between $1.4 billion and $3.5 billion.[55]

More than a half dozen loans even went to companies owned, at least in part, by members of Congress and/or their spouses. The family of Transportation Secretary Elaine Chao (who is the wife of Senate Majority Leader Mitch McConnell) also received a six-figure loan.[56]

Family members of the president's son-in-law and White House advisor, Jared Kushner, including a media publication owned by Kushner's brother-in-law, were connected to companies that collectively received millions of dollars in funds.[57]

You can argue about any of these forgivable loan recipients individually and whether there was a legitimate need for them to get relief funds. However, going back to the original objectives of preserving jobs, overall, were these funds necessary and at what future cost, as we will all have to pay for them in time? Did the recipients have no ability to take a pay cut and share the pain the way so many other small business owners and contractors had to? Did the larger entities have no other access to capital, such as selling equity or taking out a loan? Did the big companies using up program funding early prevent legitimate struggling small businesses from being able to pay all their employees or even stay open?

Even the relief supposedly designated for small businesses was a wealth transfer to those who were well connected.

Money, Yes; Guidance, No

Though governors were busy picking winners and losers in terms of "essential" businesses and workers and Congress delivered helicopter money to big companies, another big miss from big government related to guidance.

There was so much focus on which businesses could and couldn't operate, parameters related to operations (such as New York's insistence that a business needed to serve more than chicken wings to be in compliance as an eating rather than drinking establishment), and lengthy shutdowns, and far too little focus on guidance and assistance on how a business could operate and create a safe working and customer environment. Of course, once the months of the government no-mask campaign was switched to a must-mask campaign, mask wearing was encouraged for businesses, and many complied and even made it mandatory. Other businesses adopted hand washing and marking off of floor areas to align with distancing guidelines, such as when customers were waiting for a checkout register. Some stores didn't allow more than a certain number of people to shop at one time or implemented shopping appointments. However, those actions were taken largely upon the initiative of businesses and in an entrepreneurial spirit, not due to excellent government guidelines or products to help make the transition easier, quicker, or less costly.

Despite the efforts of small businesses to operate safely—that is, if and when they could reopen and if they hadn't closed up shop for good—later government mandates and rules did not take into account track records or mitigation efforts to decide which businesses could open (and remain open).

It was almost as if the governors or mayors were rooting for businesses and the economy not to be open. How could that be? Did they expect federal funds for state bailouts and hope the economic woes would make their case?

At the federal level, small businesses remained too small to matter. Even though they represent half the economy, they are highly fragmented. The decentralized nature of small businesses stands in opposition to the mission of politicians, who seek to centralize power.

The government's actions at all levels are a playbook for precisely what you would do if you wanted to give the appearance of helping but actually wanted to crush small businesses. The government mandated the closures of some small businesses, and for those that remained open, it made the case that their survival would be based on government help.

The state governors made the official war declarations, and the federal government remained their allies.

Outcomes Halfway Through the Year

As the fifteen days to flatten the curve direction came about two weeks before the end of the first quarter, the shutdown's real effects were not seen until the second-quarter economic data came out. The first print of the GDP numbers, which came out at the end of July, showed a record contraction of 32.9 percent, which is a quarter-over-quarter annualized number (just slightly better than the 34.7 percent consensus drop expected), the first double-digit decline since 1958.[58]

Real Gross Domestic Product, Percentage Change from Preceding Period, Quarterly, Seasonally Adjusted Annual Rate, April 1947–April 2020

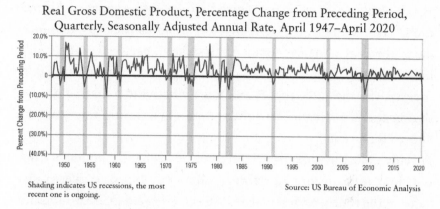

Shading indicates US recessions, the most recent one is ongoing.

Source: US Bureau of Economic Analysis

Source: US Bureau of Economic Analysis, Real Gross Domestic Product [A191RL1Q225SBEA], retrieved from FRED, Federal Reserve Bank of St. Louis; https://fred.stlouisfed.org/series/A191RL1Q225SBEA.

To compare this with the Great Recession, that financial crisis saw an 8.4 percent GDP decline at its trough in the fourth quarter of 2008—nowhere in the same ballpark as what happened due to the government black swan.

The US economy shrank in actual terms by 9.5 percent from April through June 2020, the largest quarterly decline on record.[59]

Personal consumption was down by 34.6 percent. A large part of that drop was the decrease in the consumption of services, which makes sense as service providers were among the first and most frequently targeted for closure.[60]

It was not a systemic recession. It wasn't a bug in the economy that was driving the United States to a bad economic outcome. It wasn't businesses or the market pulling back investment. It had been created and was owned by the government, which had forced businesses to close and their patrons to stay home, and prolonged by further bad decision making and a media that had created and supported additional fear. That, alongside the data, was also unprecedented.

Also, because of the government-forced recession, the stimulus did not have the same effect as it might otherwise have had in a systemic recession. As pointed out to me by the author and investor

James Rickards, Americans plowed money into savings at historic rates.[61] For example, in April, after the stimulus package announcement, the Bureau of Economic Analysis said, personal savings hit a historic rate of 33 percent. For context, that rate was mostly under 5 percent in the early aughts and mostly between 5 and 10 percent during the last decade. By July, the personal saving rate was still above 18 percent.[62]

However, the same day the second-quarter GDP numbers came out, four mega technology firms, whose combined market equity value at the time was north of $5 trillion, reported their earnings for the preceding quarter.

And although the economy had contracted at historic levels and personal consumption had shrunk by almost 35 percent, Amazon, Apple, and Facebook all posted incredible quarterly financial results. Though Wall Street had been expecting Amazon to generate about $81 billion in revenue and less than a dollar and a half per share in earnings, believing that it would be the beneficiary of Main Street closures and people in lockdown, the company blew that expectation away, posting $88.9 billion in revenue and $10.30 a share in earnings. So although consumption was down, what remained was shifted in large part to Amazon.

It should be noted that Amazon does enable more than 1 million small business sellers via its website. So those who could shift their business online had in some cases benefited. But the service providers, restaurants, and others that couldn't do so lost out.[63]

Apple, Facebook, and Alphabet (the parent company of Google) also posted revenue and earnings beats (with Alphabet being the weakest due to softness in its advertising business), generally posting monster results during the worst economic quarter of all time on record.

The big, publicly traded entities that were recording strong financial performances also benefited from the Federal Reserve spending

trillions of dollars to support the stock market. Who was supporting small businesses like that? Nobody in or affiliated with government, that is for certain.

Against that backdrop, the big takeaway from the GDP print
should have been recognizing the critical importance of small businesses in the economy and finding ways to ensure that the playing
field was level for them.

Unfortunately, that would not be the big takeaway for those with
the power to fix such things.

It was clear that small businesses were not the "chosen ones."

CHAPTER 5

Selling Out Main Street to Wall Street

*The Federal Reserve's Decades-Long Role
in Helping Government Transfer More Wealth
to the Wealthiest*

On June 5, 2020, the stock market was on fire. The Nasdaq Composite gained almost 200 points (around 2 percent) to close at 9,814.08 after reaching an intraday record. This turnaround happened after the Nasdaq Composite had lost about a quarter of its value—moving down to 6860.67—just a few months earlier. The Dow soared more than 800 points that day (more than 3 percent), and the S&P 500 gained around 2.6 percent in value, recovering around 43 percent of its losses from earlier in the year.[1]

2020 Stock Market Performance (YTD % Change)
Through June 5, 2020

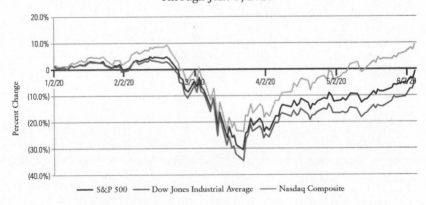

Data via Macrotrends, https://www.macrotrends.net.

One would think that would be a fantastic indicator regarding the economy's health, but the reality is that the economy remained in historically bad shape, with almost 21 million people out of work. Though the unemployment rate reported that day for the previous month (May) of a whopping 13.3 percent was better than the previous month's (April's) 14.7 percent, it was still firmly in double digits.[2]

On Main Street, many businesses were still mandated closed— entirely or in part—by state or local governments, while others weren't ready to reopen their doors. Other businesses had to make a difficult decision to close permanently after suffering months without customers. Some individuals decided not to return to work, whether it was for safety concerns, because they were making more money with Congress's stimulus unemployment bonus than they would at work, or both.

So it seems as though investors in the stock market, while perhaps being generous and believing in a recovery that would happen more quickly than some projections and models expected, still shouldn't be lifting the market to near-record or record levels.

How could there be such a disconnect between Wall Street and Main Street? A big part of that has to do with the complex actions taken by the Fed.

What Is the Fed?

The Federal Reserve System, also known as the Federal Reserve or colloquially as "the Fed," is the United States' central bank. The overarching purpose of the Fed, one could say, is to help guide the country's economic and financial stability. More accurately, in recent years, it has become a tool to prop up Wall Street and to enable capricious government spending.

Three key entities make up the Federal Reserve System: the Board of Governors, twelve Federal Reserve Banks that represent twelve districts, and the Federal Open Market Committee (FOMC). The Board of Governors, which is an agency of the federal government that reports to and—in its words but not in reality—is directly accountable to the United States Congress, oversees the twelve Federal Reserve Banks and provides input and guidance for the entire system.

Though the Fed derives its power and mandates from Congress, it is not truly accountable to anyone. That is intentional and by design. In fact, it may be the only entity in America not owned by or accountable to anybody else. Its independent status and guise of decentralization mean that it operates without the checks and balances essential to the rest of the government system. It is not audited. Though it releases "recaps" of its meetings, it doesn't release the full content of its discussions. It doesn't tell congressional representatives or committees about its behind-the-scenes undertakings, and it has little in the way of oversight.

The Fed's website tells you as much. It states, "Though the Congress sets the goals for monetary policy, decisions of the Board—and the Fed's monetary policy-setting body, the Federal Open Market Committee—about how to reach those goals do not require approval by the President or anyone else in the executive or legislative branches of government."[3] The Fed's secrecy and actions have been the cause of much ire and frustration on the part of many in the economic and financial communities.

It's said that the Fed primarily has a "dual mandate" from Congress, which has been reiterated by many Fed chairs, from Jerome Powell to Janet Yellen, when they hold press conferences and review the FOMC minutes. This dual mandate, established by the US Congress, is (1) maximum employment and (2) stable prices (that is, managing inflation).

The Fed conducts monetary policy (management and policy having to do with the supply of money, credit, and interest rates) meant to achieve specific economic objectives. This seems like an odd responsibility for an agency owned by and accountable to nobody. Monetary policy is differentiated from fiscal policy, which is typically done through legislation and is concerned with policies like taxes and spending, also to achieve economic (and often social) objectives.

The Federal Reserve System is not financed by congressional appropriations. It is financed primarily by receiving interest income on government securities that it purchases in the market. When the Fed has a surplus of money left over from its investment activities, it gives such surpluses back to the US Treasury.

The interest rate you often hear about on financial news is the Fed funds rate. It is a target rate that was historically meant to act as a guide for banks to lend to each other overnight to fulfill their reserve requirements, which has somewhat shifted in recent times.

Though the Fed funds target rate isn't a hard mandate per se, it has other broad-reaching financial implications, which is why you hear so much about it. It acts as a benchmark for other short-term rates, influencing how much banks charge for other products they offer, such as loans and credit cards. Lowering the Fed funds rate is associated with expansionary monetary policy, as it is supposed to spur more demand for credit by making it "inexpensive" to borrow, thus stimulating economic activity. (In layman's terms, the lower the interest rate, the more an individual or business can borrow while keeping the cost of each debt payment—and their overall cost of debt—lower.)

It also can affect the stock market in ways that are discussed in greater detail below.

The Fed also uses open market operations, or more simply, the buying and selling of government securities from banks and other investors in the market, to make adjustments to the supply of money and influence economic activity. As the Fed buys more securities and replaces them with "credit" in the selling banks' accounts, there is more "money" or credit available for lending and interest rates are also pushed downward (this is aligned with expansionary policy; contractionary policy would have the Fed selling securities and have the opposite effect).[4]

Moving Away from Its Purpose

This interest rate and money supply stuff may sound mundane and wonky, but it has incredible implications for what the Fed has become. Like many government institutions, the Fed has strayed far from its original purpose and mandates to interfere, as a quasi agency of the government, in the free markets.

Initially, the twelve Federal Reserve Banks were intended to be decentralized and operate independently. Like other functions that have been centralized, a centralized bank with national influence was something against which many critics warned. But over the two decades that followed the Fed's creation, centralized government creep took over and more national policy making occurred.

In actuality, much of the design was intentional and the outcomes unavoidable.

Dr. Murray Rothbard, in his book *The Case Against the Fed*, shared the story about the Fed's creation after several failed attempts at US central bank and national bank structures. He recounts that in the 1890s, the top Wall Street bankers wanted more control over banking.

The National Banking System structure at the time (also devised by those same financiers!) didn't have a mechanism for bailouts if the bankers got themselves into trouble. The bankers also wanted the money supply to be able to be increased more quickly, and they wanted to find a fix for their loss of dominance due to more competition in the market.[5]

So the financiers created a cartel and devised a long-term strategy to "revive" a central bank that would put them into control. They waged a propaganda campaign to convince the public that a central bank would "save" the public from big business interests. As we have seen repeatedly happen in modern times, including many times a day on social media, that simple propaganda trick worked.[6]

Though central banking was sold as an "impartial" restraint against the banks' tendency to inflate, the reality is that it was meant as a mechanism to allow banks to inflate and expand lending, and do so "without incurring the penalties of market competition." In layman's terms, the bankers wanted to be able to expand the money supply at their whim without being beholden to market forces.[7]

The one area of disagreement among the financiers structuring what became the Federal Reserve Act of 1913 was that some wanted a true central bank, whereas others felt they could sell the idea and gain more power if the central bank were to be "cloaked in the palatable camouflage of 'decentralization.'" Ultimately, that deceptive tactic won out.[8]

Today, although the Fed is technically "owned" by its member banks—part of the "decentralization" cloak—the banks do not receive any Fed profits; those go back to the Treasury. What matters is who controls it. What the banks receive is the benefit of covertly influencing decision making with no checks or balances or even proper accountability. Rothbard said, "In form as well as in content, the Federal Reserve System is precisely the cozy government-big bank partnership, the government-enforced banking cartel, that big bankers had long envisioned."[9]

To recap all of this, the Fed derives its authority from Congress, works with the Treasury, isn't owned by the government, but gives its "profits" back to the US government. It is central planning disguised as independence.

That all sounds very far from capitalism.

The Fed's Balance Sheet

Emblematic of the subject of straying from capitalism is the Fed "printing money."

When you hear that the Fed "prints money," it does so more figuratively than literally. Though the Fed directs the amount of currency to print and distributes it, the actual printing function happens via the US Treasury in the case of bills and the US Mint for coins. The Fed oversees the demand for currency in circulation on a worldwide basis, not just here in the United States. In fact, the Federal Reserve Bank of New York estimates that the majority of actual cash (bills and coins) in circulation is held outside the United States, with increasing interest in holding US dollars from abroad in recent years, ostensibly because the currency is deemed "safe" and "stable"; more on that below.[10]

The larger point of contention is the money printed "out of thin air" or "on paper." The Fed "creates" money to expand the amount of credit in the banking system and ultimately the economy. So when it buys securities, for example, it expands its balance sheet, but it does so with accounting trickery, by crediting the reserve account of the member banks it purchases from through an accounting or book entry. This creation of money and credit out of nowhere is obviously quite different in impact from value and wealth in the economy being created via innovation, sales, work, investing, or other activities.[11]

Also, as US currency is no longer backed by anything but the "faith of the US government," there is a lot of latitude for moral hazard (taking more risk because that entity does not bear the full consequences of the actions).

There were a few modern events that led to significant changes in Fed action and intervention. The first was in 1987, after Black Monday (the historic Dow sell-off of more than 500 points, which, at the time, accounted for a whopping 22.6 percent loss on the day).

The Fed stepped in, announcing that it was ready to be a source of liquidity to support the markets and the economy. It followed with what at the time was atypical intervention, lowering interest rates and increasing its open market operations, among other actions.[12]

The investor and pundit Peter Schiff, on his blog and in interviews, shared that when he was twenty-four years old, as Twitter had yet to be invented for people to yell at public figures, he did the old-fashioned (and quite proactive, I might add) thing: he sent a letter to Fed chair Alan Greenspan to share his displeasure with the Fed's intervention after Black Monday, seeing it as a mistake and as acting against Greenspan's long-standing free market stance.

Though Schiff didn't make copies of the letters he sent to Greenspan, Greenspan responded to him—twice—and he did keep those letters. In his second response to Schiff, Greenspan wrote:

My own belief is that, rather than resigning ourselves to the fate of a recession as a method of correcting the distortions in the economy, we should face the problems creating those distortions and attempt to solve them. A key here clearly is the effort to rein in the federal budget deficit; it is crucial that the Congress move quickly to enact the recent agreement in a manner that provides some assurance that durable deficit-reduction has been achieved.

Meanwhile, it is incumbent upon the Federal Reserve to do what it can to foster financial conditions consistent with sustainable, non-inflationary economic growth.[13]

Schiff's instincts were right, and Greenspan, though hopeful, fell into the trap that ensnares central planners and those of "good intentions" who want to "help" society. Greenspan believed that he knew better than the market how to fix things, that Congress would rein in its spending, and that the free markets would eventually be allowed to function normally and without intervention.

That took the already non–free market Fed and set it off on the path of no return. It moved more toward central planning and further from capitalism and took the financial markets with it.

Though Greenspan's actions were a first step, the giant leap happened more recently with the Fed's intervention during the Great Recession (aka the 2007–2009 financial crisis). Historically, the Fed's balance sheet wasn't a tool that was substantially used in a way that made anyone other than policy wonks take notice.

The Fed's actions during the Great Recession changed that. Prior to the crisis, the Fed's balance sheet had been less than $1 trillion to accommodate monetary policy. In times such as the Great Recession, when the Fed had already brought the target rate down and believed it needed more tools to enact its policy, it engaged in large, coordinated purchasing of securities in the open market to expand its balance sheet. This series of actions goes by the financial term you have undoubtedly heard many times over the last decade and a half, quantitative easing, or QE; the contraction of the balance sheet by shedding the securities from the balance sheet is known as quantitative tightening. As you can guess, QE was not a traditional activity of the Fed historically and introduced a significant amount of intervention in the markets.

Little "Interest"

The Fed funds rate had been lifted as high as 20 percent in 1980 as a tool to "fight inflation" and headed into the single digits in the latter half of the 1980s. After the dot-com bust in the early aughts, rates were brought down substantially as a means to spur economic growth. As the economy regained its footing, the Fed, as is the normal course of business when an economic recovery happens, began raising its rates. By June 2004, small 25-basis-point increases were occurring (100 basis points are equal to 1 percent; 25 basis points are .25 percent). The Fed enacted five increases in 2004, eight in 2005, and another four in the first half of 2006, bringing the Fed funds rate up to 5.25 percent by the end of June 2006.[14]

The Fed funds rate was then left alone for a year and a quarter until there were whiffs of instability due to what we now know to be the major financial crisis of the Great Recession. Starting with a 50-basis-point cut in September 2007, the Fed funds target rate was lowered all the way to 0.00 to 0.25 percent by December 2008.

What happened was unprecedented in both absolute numbers and duration. You'd have to go back around sixty years to find a Fed funds target rate as low as 0.5 percent. However, under the steward-ship of Fed chairs Ben Bernanke and then Janet Yellen, the Fed kept the historically, unprecedentedly low 0.00 to 0.25 percent rates for seven years. Let me reiterate that: seven years!

In addition to the interest rate maneuvering, the Fed's balance sheet was leveraged as a tool—or perhaps a weapon?

During the Great Recession, beginning in 2008, the Fed initiated a massive and increasing QE program, which at first targeted gov-ernment securities, such as Treasury securities, but then moved into buying other debt-oriented securities, including mortgage-backed securities.

By the end of 2009, the Fed's balance sheet stood at close to $2.25 trillion, more than two and a half times what it had been just sixteen months earlier. It's important to remember in this discussion that the Fed had bought those assets with money that it had gener-ated from an accounting entry.

Though people may argue that this Fed action was required to provide needed financial system liquidity during the crisis, even if you agree, the level and duration of interference remain unprece-dented and dangerous. As with so many other "good intentions," once you give up a principle, it is too easy for the ensuing actions to be abusive.

As it came out of the financial crisis under President Barack

Obama, the United States endured the most anemic job recovery since the Great Depression. As such, the Fed was not pressured to move interest rates. The Fed hid behind the shield of still needing to fulfill its mandate of maximizing employment, and with no signs of inflation, it kept interest rates near zero.[15]

The Fed's target rate was finally increased 25 basis points in December 2015 to a paltry 0.25 to 0.50 percent. After the election of Donald Trump as president in November 2016, with the hope for more business-friendly, pro-growth policies to spur the economy, the stock market increased by 4 percent in just over a month. With that movement, in December 2016, the Fed enacted another 25-basis-point increase, a full year after the previous one, to 0.50 to 0.75 percent.

Even though the economy seemed to be in the late stages of its expansion cycle, the new pro-growth agenda gave it some additional gas. The market received a boost, too, and with accommodative monetary policy, unemployment was brought to historically low levels without the economy seeing runaway inflation.

With the increasing steam brought to the economy, the Fed was able to inch the rates higher, both under Yellen's stewardship in 2017 and then under Jerome Powell's stewardship after being appointed to the post by President Trump in 2018. By September 2018, the Fed funds target rate stood at 2.00 to 2.25 percent; that was higher than zero but nowhere near the high of 5.25 percent seen before the financial crisis, which itself was far away from the types of rates seen in, say, the late 1970s through the 1980s.

After the Fed announced QE1 (aka the first QE program), it made north of $1.4 trillion in asset purchases. By March 2010, the securities on the Fed's balance sheet totaled $2.3 trillion. Though it was considered an "emergency" measure, the balance sheet never contracted during that period, with assets reaching more than $4 trillion in 2014. Once again, this meddling is more consistent with democratic socialist theory than with capitalism.[16]

The Powell Fed, 2018–2019

Though the economy was on a sound footing, the market and the president began to pressure Jerome Powell, after three rate increases, to hold off on continuing to raise interest rates. The arguments for pausing were thin and flimsy; the economy was growing moderately, and unemployment rates continued to trend down toward historical levels. Furthermore, the incentives of lower interest rates had been worn out by their duration. After seven years of 0.00 to 0.25 percent rates and a still historically low Fed funds rate of around 2 percent, the promise of low rates wasn't going to spur any substantial action. "Credit" wasn't a draw—its availability at low cost wasn't going to urge companies to make more capital expenditures or convince consumers to spend more if they hadn't done so already. Interest rates had already been low for a decade, so there was no pent-up demand for cheap debt.

Normalizing was, in my own opinion and the opinion of some market pundits and economists, the right thing to do. However, the market didn't like that one bit. They were addicted to the "easy money" provided by the Fed and didn't want it to stop. President Trump frequently and publicly weighed in on the Fed, despite being critical of the Fed having kept rates low under President Obama, the Fed's independent status, and the lack of historical presidential commentary on Fed decisions. This was likely because of the potential impact on the markets, a measure that Trump obsessively focused on—or perhaps his own history in real estate, which makes extensive use of credit and could have made him more focused on interest rate activity.[17]

As an example, in July 2018, the president told CNBC after the Fed announced one 25-basis-point rate hike, "I'm not thrilled. I am not happy about it. . . . I don't like all of this work that we're putting into the economy and then I see rates going up." However, that's exactly what should happen in a strong, stable economy, particularly a free market one![18]

When the Fed raised interest rates another 25 basis points in December 2018, the market went nuts. By going nuts, I mean that the Dow shed almost 1,900 points—nearly 8 percent—and the S&P 500 was down 7.66 percent over that day and the following three trading days, up to and including Christmas Eve. Criticism and bullying of the Fed by the market—and the president—continued.

Powell and the Fed stayed firm until August 1, 2019, when, inexplicably, despite record low unemployment (half of the dual mandate), a growing economy, and a healthy outlook set forth by folks in the administration, the Fed took what it couched as a "preemptive" step to quell concerns about slowing growth globally and lowered rates. Why would they do this when interest rates had been so low for so long? Additionally, the administration was saying that US growth was on a firm footing. I will discuss the implications of this action in greater detail below.

For three meetings in a row, inclusive of the aforementioned decrease, the Fed cut rates again, and by the end of October 2019, the Fed funds target rate was back down at 1.50 to 1.75 percent.

Critics worried that in addition to the bad implications for savers and asset bubble creation, this would give the Fed fewer tools, or, in financial jargon, "arrows in its quiver," should a real problem arise, such as a severe recession or some other global event that might require some monetary policy intervention.

Yet the market investors won and the president was happy. Well, actually, he wasn't. He didn't think it was enough, and with each rate cut, he further criticized the Fed for not doing enough. After the Fed lowered the target rate 25 basis points in September 2019, Trump tweeted, "Jay Powell and the Federal Reserve Fail Again. No 'guts,' no sense, no vision! A terrible communicator!"[19]

I will also mention that the Fed, the world's preeminent central bank (overseeing the dollar, the world's preeminent currency), and other central banks around the world were enabling a dangerous cycle. When worldwide central banks, including the ECB in Europe, lowered their rates, that gave the Fed cover to lower rates as well. However, that enabled more lowering abroad and so on, instead of the United States leading the way to interest rate normalization as the world's premier economy. This has led to prolonged negative interest rates in Europe (a simple explanation of negative interest rates is that banks don't earn money on their excess reserves; they are punished by being charged a fee for holding on to excess reserves, which is meant to push more lending and supposedly boost the economy—as you can imagine, this comes with downsides and criticism).[20]

During this period, the Fed's balance sheet, which had ballooned to $4.5 trillion at its peak, started to contract with securities sales under Powell, reaching $3.8 trillion in August 2019. However, that was short lived, and it started slowly climbing back up again as the Fed reversed course, hitting north of $4.2 trillion by the beginning of March 2020.[21]

2020—An Undue Emergency

After leaving rates steady since October 2019, on Tuesday, March 3, 2020, Jerome Powell and the FOMC undertook a surprise, unscheduled emergency rate cut of 0.50 percent, a move that hadn't been taken since the Great Recession financial crisis.

Though the move was made under the guise of strengthening the economy in the face of uncertainty from the virus, it read to many in the financial community that Powell was receiving pressure from the recent and violent market sell-off activity and badgering from the president to lower rates. However, given that the rate cut wasn't done concurrently with a scheduled Fed meeting (and particularly since one was coming up in a couple of weeks), instead of instilling confidence in the market, the market perception was that things were much worse with the virus and the economy than anticipated.

CNBC printed comments by Chris Rupkey, the chief financial economist at MUFG Union Bank, who said that the Fed cut "looks rushed to us and not properly considered" and that "Moving between meetings with a bigger than normal interest rate cut looks like Fed officials are panicking as much as stock market investors did last week. They did not need to be so aggressive and the Fed under Powell keeps responding wrongly in our view more to the financial markets than they are to the broader economy."[22]

Politicians, particularly those in the Trump administration, were thrilled—sort of. Trump said in a tweet that the cut wasn't enough, though Treasury Secretary Mnuchin said, "I applaud the Fed on this move."[23]

In the weeks that followed, the Fed increased its lending in what are deemed temporary or transitory open market operations called repurchase agreements or "repo" operations.[24]

The markets were in complete disarray. On both Monday, March 9, and Thursday, March 12, the post–opening bell circuit breakers at the New York Stock Exchange were triggered at Level 1, which occurs when the S&P 500 hits a 7 percent decline from the previous day's close and the markets are paused for fifteen minutes to realign.[25]

Later that day, the Fed announced its intention to make more than $1 trillion in asset purchases across a range of products. The very next day, the Fed accelerated its asset purchase announcement from just the day prior, and investors perceived it as bona fide QE.[26]

Investors and other market watchers warned that the Fed might be looking to appease the market (which is not part of its mandate) as opposed to having a real impact on the economy. Put more plainly, the Fed's actions were intended to boost the market, not help small businesses.

On Sunday, March 15, in the second emergency move in two weeks, mere days before a previously scheduled Fed meeting was supposed to take place, Powell announced that the Fed was dropping its target interest rate to 0.00 to 0.25 percent and "officially" launching a new round of quantitative easing, targeted at $700 billion and inclusive of Treasurys and mortgage-backed securities. While saying the Fed would not entertain negative interest rates, the announcement essentially took the last interest rate arrow out of the quiver. Futures, which act as after-hours/premarket indicators of market expectations, were down substantially. It was a precarious move vis-à-vis the state of economic activity.[27]

Fed Up?

The Federal Reserve Bank of Cleveland president, Loretta Mester, put out a statement saying that she had voted against the rate cut, making her the sole dissenter. She said:

> When markets are not functioning well, the transmission mechanism of monetary policy to the economy is disrupted, and any reduction in the target federal funds rate will have less of an impact on the real economy. . . . I preferred to stage our policy actions by first providing liquidity to improve market functioning, supported by a smaller reduction in the funds rate. This would have preserved the option of a further cut in the funds rate, if needed, for a time when market functioning had improved and such an action could be expected to be most effective in supporting the economy.[28]

In layman's terms, that means she was worried about not having any options for a rate cut as a tool in the future and doubted the efficacy of such a rate cut on boosting the economy (as opposed to the markets).[29]

The action didn't help the markets, at least in the short term. Monday saw a market bloodbath; in addition to the Fed stoking investor fear, Trump said that the coronavirus pandemic could extend to August. The Dow closed the day by recording another record drop of 2,997 points, or nearly 13 percent.[30]

As the drama around the virus unfolded throughout the country, the Fed kept intervening in the markets. It was an unusual economic scenario. As opposed to previous significant Fed interventions in the market due to systemic issues, such as the Great Recession, this economic halt was caused by governors turning off large swaths of the economy.

With the Fed funds rate already at zero, the Fed had to evaluate what tools it had. You could argue that no tools were necessary; monetary policy can't put people back to work who were out of work because the businesses they had worked for had been shut down.

That didn't stop the Fed. Its balance sheet swelled, again buoyed by money created from nowhere. It also included some unprecedented measures, including expanding the types of securities it was going to buy, putting into place emergency lending facilities, expanding the scope and powers of programs, and even adding a Main Street Lending Program. Though it carried the "Main Street" moniker, the program didn't really help the bulk of small businesses. The program was targeted toward larger small businesses and middle-market companies that had the ability to take on debt.

The program was not well received by either banks or customers because most companies that could service debt already had access to plenty and most smaller businesses were not in a financial position to take on more liabilities. Again, the small businesses that needed it most weren't helped.[31]

A Moral Hazard

Back in the end of March, the Fed made another unprecedented and highly cronyist move by hiring BlackRock, the world's largest asset manager, to manage a government bond purchase program. The *Wall Street Journal* said that BlackRock would purchase a number of different securities, including a

> vehicle for buying already-issued investment-grade bonds. . . . But the firm has latitude to buy U.S. investment grade bond ETFs—including exchange-traded funds of its own. Black-Rock is the largest provider of bond ETFs. . . .
>
> The tasks place BlackRock in a potentially controversial position of implementing the administration's response to the spreading coronavirus pandemic. The firm's roughly $7 trillion reach extends into everything from equities to bonds to private equity. The firm will face significant scrutiny on how it prevents conflicts of interests.[32]

The market commentator Jason Orestes broke down the implications for TheStreet, saying:

> The Fed also has now begun purchasing "risk assets" or securities that carry no such federal guarantees. . . .
>
> The Fed isn't legally able to do this by itself, and it's making it happen through some creative financial engineering. The Treasury is officially the one making the purchases with the help of BlackRock via special purpose vehicles (SPV) that are financed by the Fed. So the Fed is essentially acting as banker to the Treasury, which is employing BlackRock as its broker to carry out the effective nationalization of parts of markets.[33]

The move prompted thirty investor and watchdog groups to send a collective letter to the Fed, emphasizing the potential for conflicts of interest and the "lack of transparency and oversight" in the Black-Rock arrangement.[34]

Was that action truly a means to help the economy, or was it purely a means of not letting a good crisis go to waste in helping out Fed and Treasury cronies on Wall Street? I'll give you a hint: it wasn't designed to help the parts of the economy that were in the most trouble.

Here's another hint: The Fed scaled back what it calls "noncritical oversight" of financial institutions. It also made it easier for banks to invest in riskier assets, such as venture capital funds, and pared back some derivative trading rules, which came out of the post–Great Recession regulations.[35]

Sheila Bair, the chair of the Federal Deposit Insurance Corporation (FDIC) during the Great Recession financial crisis, said in an interview with CNBC that the move was "ill-advised" and that it increased risks to the financial system.[36]

As many small businesses on Main Street across the country continued to suffer shutdowns, the Fed continued to support Wall Street. By March 27, the Fed's balance sheet reached a record high, passing the $5 trillion threshold.[37]

Even the Fed's Main Street Lending Program went upmarket, in April increasing the eligibility ceiling to 15,000 employees. What small business has 15,000 employees? The minimum loan size was reduced from $1 million to $500,000. How many small businesses can take on half a million dollars of debt? Eventually, the minimum was lowered again, to $250,000. The program took several months to get going.

Though the most significant risks to the economy were to small businesses, the actions that were continually taken supported much larger entities, typical of big government and those enabling them or enabled by them. That helped Wall Street and the biggest companies consolidate more value and power.

By the end of May, the Fed's balance sheet had passed a staggering $7 trillion, equivalent to about a third of the 2019 GDP. For additional context, the entire US national debt at the end of January 2004 was approximately $7 trillion.[38]

That unprecedented increase, along with the means of enactment, brought more scrutiny to the Fed from those "in the know." Jeff Cox, an author and financial journalist who covers the Fed for CNBC, noted that as the Fed had been buying corporate debt in the market, it was supporting not just "struggling companies" struck by COVID but banner names such as Microsoft, Home Depot, and Visa and that "The Fed holds an expansive list of other companies indirectly, including names like Apple and Goldman Sachs, through exchange-traded funds it has purchased."[39]

Let me reiterate that while small businesses were struggling and looking for a lifeline, the Fed was buying Home Depot's and Microsoft's corporate bonds.

Cox further quoted Kathy Jones, the chief fixed income strategist at Schwab Center for Financial Research, who raised, as many had before, the issue of moral hazard. "I do think it's moral hazard," she said. "I think it's something they're going to have to deal with when things settle down. There will be accusations that they committed money in ways that didn't make sense and didn't help the average Joe." Cox also noted that Goldman Sachs saw the potential for moral hazard, misallocation of capital, and a diminishing appearance of independence for the Fed.

By the end of August, Powell announced during the Fed's annual symposium that it had in effect shifted their dual mandate and would focus on the unemployment rate, even if that meant letting inflation run up more than expected in the short term, as long as it averaged around 2 percent over time. Some investors took that as a clear signal that interest rates would not be raised at any point in the foreseeable future; others took it as a sign that inflation was already coming.[40]

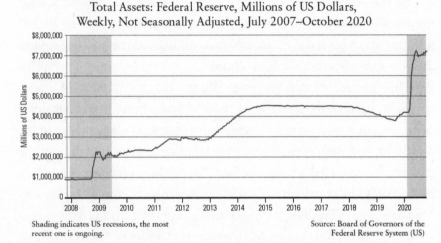

Total Assets: Federal Reserve, Millions of US Dollars, Weekly, Not Seasonally Adjusted, July 2007–October 2020

Shading indicates US recessions, the most recent one is ongoing.

Source: Board of Governors of the Federal Reserve System (US)

Board of Governors of the Federal Reserve System (US), Assets: Total Assets: Total Assets (Less Eliminat^{2}ns from Consolidat^{2}n): Wednesday Level [WALCL], retrieved from FRED, Federal Reserve Bank of St. Louis; https://fred.stlouisfed.org/series/WALCL.

The Market Isn't the Economy

Though investors were making money in the market, Main Street businesses were not faring as well. A report by the Federal Reserve Bank of New York said, "Nationally representative data on small businesses indicate that the number of active business owners fell by 22 percent from February to April 2020—the largest drop on record." It also noted that Black-owned businesses had fared the worst with a 41 percent drop and Latino-owned businesses had decreased by 32 percent. The report pointed to the lack of banking relationships and weaker financial positions, particularly in the most vulnerable communities, as well as their urban locations, which translates to blue states with heavy central planning.[41]

The business review platform Yelp released its September Economic Average report and found that on its platform—which, as noted, caters to small businesses and service and consumer businesses—by the end of August, 163,735 businesses indicated that they had closed, an increase of 23 percent over the previous month (covered in chapter 1). That was based on voluntary reporting and did not capture any companies that had closed whose owners had not taken the time to update their listing on Yelp.[42]

Yelp also reported that 60 percent of the closed businesses had indicated that they would be closed permanently. That data stands as a stark reminder, vis-à-vis the market reaction to the Fed, of the different realities of the 2020 economy. The economic recovery was likely to be what I call "E shaped." Imagine the horizontal lines that make up the capital letter *E*: those at the top, including big businesses, juiced by government and the Fed, directly or indirectly, stay on top and likely grow. Those in the middle probably aren't hurt or helped much in either direction. And those at the bottom, such as small businesses, workers in service industries, and others will have a long and painful recovery ahead.

In the fall of 2020, Alignable surveyed small business owners and found that 34 percent of small businesses that hadn't yet closed couldn't pay their October rent. Meanwhile, many of the biggest US businesses were getting larger.[43]

Main Street Versus Wall Street

This all sounds bad theoretically, but what does it mean in practice for you and me, as well as for small businesses and the economy as a whole?

I say this with the understanding that Wall Street, despite some of the political posturing, isn't just the "elites." The US markets are widely considered the most important in the world and have far-reaching implications for middle-class Americans, as many of their pension funds, 401(k)s, and other retirement funds are invested in them. A well-performing stock market often has a "wealth effect" that spills over into other asset classes, such as helping increase home values. So what happens there does have extensive reverberations across the economy.

That being said, 2019 data counted fewer than five thousand publicly traded companies in the United States, compared to the pre-COVID 30.2 million small businesses. The implications and outcomes for these categories of businesses are very different. The scale of big businesses allows them not only to access the public markets for capital, but also to take different capital allocation decisions than a small business without that scale can. A low interest rate may have enabled a small business owner to borrow at a lower rate to make a capital improvement in his or her business. But as the small business owner is probably still on the hook personally for the loan, he or she is perhaps less likely to take one out or at least will be more careful about doing so. The scope of their borrowing also has a much smaller impact than for a big corporation with a larger capital base, which can take on much more debt and use it to expand or buy back shares, etc.[44]

The Fed's long-term market intervention also drove even more short-term thinking, which was already a challenge on Wall Street. Instead of meaningfully increasing hiring, making capital investments, or saving for an emergency, companies made capital allocation decisions such as deciding to buy back stock, which, by decreasing the number of shares outstanding, increases the metric of "earnings per share" but doesn't strategically add value to the business— or directly help to grow the economy.

It also does not incentivize saving for an emergency.

Furthermore, by signaling their continued artificial support to the market with statements such as "We're not thinking about raising rates, we're not even thinking about thinking about raising rates" that Powell made in mid-June 2020 and supporting the debt of poorly managed big enterprises, the Fed did not create any incentives for large, publicly traded companies to change their behavior.

It also further increased the market's dependency on government intervention.[45]

Small businesses do not have that luxury. With small firms having limited capital overall, there are no special benefits or support for small businesses that result from Fed intervention. This means that a publicly traded company such as The Cheesecake Factory, even before the pandemic, had substantial access to low-interest-rate debt that allowed it more flexibility to grow (as well as buy back its stock and return capital to shareholders). The Cheesecake Factory took advantage of that; at the end of the third quarter of 2015, it had zero long-term debt on its balance sheet (excluding any lease obligations or landlord financing). By the same point in time in 2019, it had taken on $335 million in long-term debt. The small family restaurant down the street from you didn't have the same access to funding. If it were able to take on any at all, it would have been a small amount and likely personally guaranteed by the owner.[46]

Again, this is government (or government-approved) favoring of bigger companies over the small businesses of Main Street.

The Fed's measures also provided cover, whether intentionally or not, to the state governors. State pension funds, some of the largest investors in the market, were being artificially inflated, so their pension managers and cronies weren't pressuring their respective governors to change their myopic course of action.

Regarding the individuals of Main Street, the extended downward pressure on interest rates also had meaningful implications for those who depended on interest income because now their CD or money market account or bond was paying much less in interest than what they had expected. If you are a retiree and looking for income on your savings and investments with low risk, you now would receive a fraction of what you might have expected if interest rates were normalized. If you were planning to retire, you had to factor the lack of interest income into your plans and perhaps delay retirement to save more money to make up the difference.

Or if you, for the reasons mentioned above or otherwise, were looking to find an appropriate level of earnings on your investment (also known as "yield"), you might have to take on more risk, in either a riskier, interest-bearing debt security (such as a riskier fixed-income product) or via a stock that had a dividend that could provide you that ongoing earning level to substitute. At the time of writing, risky "junk" bond yields were at record lows. This means you don't get paid much more for taking the risk of buying a lower-quality security.[47]

It was not just retirees who were chasing yield. Because debt yields were down, people with money to invest chased after riskier assets with their money, including stocks. The law of supply and demand tells you that when more money is chasing stocks, it drives their prices up. The lower the yield and the longer the duration of the low yield, the higher the artificiality or inflation in the prices of riskier assets. Also, money returned to investors via stock buybacks now needs a place to go, so it gets deployed back into the market, even further inflating valuations. The same thing happened with a chunk of the individual COVID stimulus "relief" money that, because of the ineffective structure I previously discussed, many people put into the stock market.[48]

This creates an even worse situation for these investors because they are purchasing these riskier assets at inflated prices, exposing them to bigger potential losses when the asset "bubble" pops.

The Fed had fully disrupted risk in the markets.

This also led to a huge increase in the number of IPOs, as well as Special Purpose Acquisition Companies (SPACs). SPACs are entities that raise money publicly without having a business (because of this, they are also known as "blank check companies"), with the intention to go out and acquire a business later. Considered highly speculative, there were around four times as many of these vehicles created with more than five times the proceeds in 2020 versus 2019.[49]

So while Main Street small businesses struggled, the stock market indices continued to hit all-time highs. Amazon's value increased to record levels while your local restaurant went out of business.

This is not to say that Amazon and other big businesses aren't important. Indeed, the role Amazon played leading up to and during the pandemic has been invaluable. The larger point is that the Fed's intervention has created an even more unfair playing field and outcomes for large businesses and increased their values artificially.

In November 2020, the equity analysts Sophie Huynh and Charles de Boissezon at Société Générale projected that without the Fed intervention in 2020, particularly QE, the stock market would have been materially lower through the end of October. Their note to investors, as reported by MarketWatch, said, "In fact, without QE, the Nasdaq-100 . . . should be closer to 5,000 than 11,000, while the S&P 500 . . . should be closer to 1,800 rather than 3,300." This is value that has been transferred to Wall Street at the expense of Main Street. That is not capitalism.[50]

To recap, government shuttered small businesses, sending their customers to spend with bigger companies, and then the Fed's intervention added rocket fuel to make those big companies more valuable and powerful.

Consider additionally those individuals who are not currently invested in the markets. They are more concerned with having a job to go back to. Plus, strengthening the economy benefits the entire market, including the publicly traded companies, via consumer and business spending. Prolonged monetary policy like this only shifts value to those in the right position.

And that's the issue: this type of intervention by the Fed, which you can argue whether was necessary or not in the Great Recession, did not make any sense in 2020, given the state of interest rates and the Fed's balance sheet prior to the economic collapse, and the collapse coming from government and pandemic-related issues, instead of systemic problems. That leads to the conclusion that either the Fed was incompetent or it was fulfilling the crony duties aligned with its creation. Either way, that intervention interferes with capitalism in a nonbeneficial way.

Longer-Term Implications

There are other effects of the Fed intervention that are likely to play out over the long term, including the impact of "zombie" companies (which are already here), inflationary issues, the lack of "arrows in the quiver," and a potential for a future debt crisis.

No Arrows in the Quiver

Even if you believe that some central bank intervention is warranted from time to time, in emergency situations such as the Great Recession financial crisis, the Fed's actions over the decade-plus preceding 2020, and particularly the last several years, are still not justified. In fact, they jeopardize the Fed's ability to act in a systemic crisis. That jeopardizes the economy as a whole at the expense of kowtowing to the markets.

Had the Fed continued to increase rather than decrease interest rates (or at least leave them at their December 2018 levels), it would have some tools to utilize in the future. It would allow the markets to adjust naturally, something that at this point, after so many years of intervention, many investors can't even remember.

Inflation

Another impact that individuals have to worry about from the central bank's decade-plus expansionary monetary policy is the impact of inflation.

Whether we have already seen some inflation is up for debate. Though at the time of writing we could all agree that we were not in a period of runaway inflation, the veteran investor David Rocker said that inflation was here and had "just shifted from consumables to physical assets. Stocks and housing have risen sharply in response to the low interest rates. Further, it is not unreasonable to expect inflation to rise from here. Many of the forces that kept prices low are now reversing."[51]

Inflation is an increase in the cost of goods and services. In theory, there are more dollars chasing scarce goods and services, and therefore, every dollar you earn has less purchasing power than it did before inflation. Because of the expansionary effect of low interest rates and growing the Fed's balance sheet, those measures usually are accompanied by some future inflation. However, there is a lag between policy and outcomes. Inflation is one of many outcomes that investors and pundits have been waiting on over the last decade, and it is hard to predict and control once the horse leaves the proverbial barn.

The combination of Fed intervention and the high personal saving rate post–COVID stimulus, which I discussed earlier, could lead to inflation if those savings are spent and personal savings returns to a historically normalized level. This could also be exacerbated by an accommodative Fed in concert with more government stimulus and related spending. However, because of the unprecedented intervention by the Fed and the mix of factors such as capital supply and savings, as well as an uncertain global economy, the range of economic outcomes goes from substantial inflation to a contraction in the US economy.

Gregory Daco, the chief US economist at Oxford Economics, wrote in a June 2020 piece on The Hill that the most significant risk for runaway inflation comes from "the politicization of the Fed." We can make the argument that this has happened, at least in some part, and given the trends, if something doesn't change, his concern will become a certainty. He said, "An environment in which the central bank permanently monetizes government debt by keeping interest rates artificially low and maintaining QE indefinitely could lead to runaway inflation, as was the case in the early 1970s."[52]

Creating "Zombie" Companies

In a *Wall Street Journal* piece entitled "The Rescues Ruining Capitalism," Ruchir Sharma, chief global strategist at Morgan Stanley Investment Management, described the way the Fed's and other government actions have been saving companies not worth saving— the ones that capitalism should have killed off. He said:

> With more debt to fuel the same amount of growth, capitalism bogs down.
>
> Low interest rates are supposed to encourage investment in companies large and small, increasing productivity and boosting growth. Instead, as a recent paper from the National Bureau of Economic Research shows, low rates gave big companies a strategic incentive to grow even bigger, in large part because securing a dominant position in the market promises outsize financial rewards. . . .
>
> Government regulations, which expanded at an accelerating rate over the past four decades, created a thicket of rules best navigated by big companies with armies of lobbyists and lawyers.[53]

This is not capitalism; this is the government picking winners and losers and favoring the big guys once again. Sharma showed that this affected the distribution of companies, saying:

> Before the pandemic, the U.S. was generating startups—and shutting down established companies—at the slowest rates since at least the 1970s. . . .

Today an astonishing number of the survivors are, quite literally, creatures of credit. In the 1980s, only 2% of publicly traded companies in the U.S. were considered "zombies," a term used by the Bank for International Settlements (BIS) for companies that, over the previous three years, had not earned enough profit to make even the interest payments on their debt. The zombie minority started to grow rapidly in the early 2000s, and by the eve of the pandemic, accounted for 19% of U.S.-listed companies.[54]

That's approximately one in five publicly traded companies—before the pandemic even hit—that did not make enough money to pay for the interest on their debt, let alone the principal! Under normal free market circumstances, those businesses would need to be restructured. Today, because of the Fed's intervention in the market, they continue to be able to borrow money!

Zombie companies have several issues, including crowding out new entrants to the markets by providing resources to companies that otherwise wouldn't have access to them. This is backed by a 2017 OECD study cited in Sharma's piece that found that "zombie congestion" lowers productivity and reduces competition and startups.

This has a drag on innovation and the overall economy. Existing small businesses have to compete against larger zombie competitors that should be out of business. It also places smaller companies and other creditors at risk, distorting market signals regarding potential failure of the zombie companies. Often, zombie companies' creditors are smaller firms, who may find themselves getting pennies on the dollar—or no dollars at all—when the firms go through inevitable bankruptcy reorganization processes or entirely out of business.

Zombies eventually die; throwing money at a company that is structurally broken only prolongs the pain. In addition to the drag on innovation and the potential issues for small businesses and creditors, the zombie fallout could have other economic implications. It is estimated by Arbor Data Science that zombie companies control around 2.2 million jobs. Instead of the jobs falling out naturally in the past, when the economy had the ability to absorb them, they could be pushed to all collapsing around the same time, or in a time when the job market is soft, further dragging down employment and the overall economy.[55]

You could perhaps make the argument that stepping in to help companies during a broad economic crisis to regain footing makes sense. But keeping zombie companies alive for years on end is anti-competitive charity to Wall Street and other investors.

Future Debt Crises?

Obviously, the Fed indirectly influences the US government's ability to borrow at low rates, which helps them justify overspending. It tilts the playing field toward central planning and away from the decentralization of free markets. Even at low rates, more debt means more of future budgets paying for what has already been bought via increased debt service instead of spending on current endeavors. Pre-COVID, the Congressional Budget Office projected that net interest expense would rise to 11 percent by 2030, reducing the government's ability to pay for "nondiscretionary" spending. With the COVID spending, that is likely to be a conservative estimate.[56]

If there were no concerns about and adverse outcomes from monetizing debt and the government could just print to cover expenses, why should any of us have to pay taxes at all? That leads us to the concept of Modern Monetary Theory, or MMT, a fringe economic theory supported by democratic socialists that accompanies fiat money. It generally says that if the government can print its own money, it can basically do whatever it wants, with taxes being a means to control inflation. If printing money were left unchecked, most economists believe it would lead to hyperinflation and currency devaluation, as we have seen historically around the world.

However, though we may shake our heads at this democratic socialist agenda, we have to recognize that aspects of it are already here with the Fed expanding its balance sheet and the government racking up massive debts and deficits. Central planning's bad outcomes are seen in the Fed, along with the government at large; this should be a five-alarm warning that what is being done is incredibly dangerous.

Speaking of dangerous, what about other debt crises that may come out of this historical intervention? Is the worst yet to come?

Bloomberg reported that "U.S. nonfinancial business debt soared in the first quarter by the most in records back to 1952," and according to the Fed, total nonfinancial business debt stands at around $17.7 trillion at the time of writing.[57] Though debt is an important tool for business, it is only so when the business can handle the debt. Outsized debt, unserviceable debt (like that of the zombie companies), and/or slower growth that makes the debt loads of companies unmanageable could threaten the economy in the years to come.

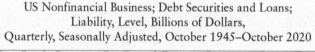

US Nonfinancial Business; Debt Securities and Loans;
Liability, Level, Billions of Dollars,
Quarterly, Seasonally Adjusted, October 1945–October 2020

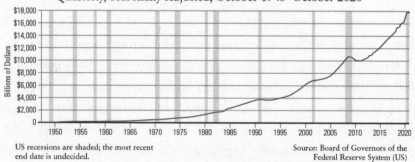

US recessions are shaded; the most recent
end date is undecided.

Source: Board of Governors of the
Federal Reserve System (US)

Source: Board of Governors of the Federal Reserve System (US), Nonfinancial Business; Debt Securities and Loans; Liabçity, Level [TBSDODNS], retrieved from FRED, Federal Reserve Bank of St. Louis; https://fred.stlouisfed.org/series/TBSDODNS.

The Fed's easy-money policy has also created concerns about debt securities called collateralized loan obligations (CLOs), which are securities made up of bundles of loans of various degrees of creditworthiness. They may sound familiar, as collateralized debt obligations (CDOs), which are similar but made up of mortgage debt instead of corporate debt, played a significant role in the Great Recession. CLOs have become big business, and though the credit rating agencies say that they are nothing to worry about, they also said that during the financial crisis.

The *Wall Street Journal* reported that a review published in the *Journal of Structured Finance* "found that ratings firms are inconsistent in how they apply their methodologies to CLOs and may be deviating from the criteria, which govern how grades are supposed to be assigned."[58]

How worried should we be? In June 2020, Fisher Investments said it was not concerned about CLOs, citing US banks' exposure as small compared to the fiasco of the last financial crisis. Things are different now, so while it may not be time to panic, the CLO issue, in conjunction with the other issues brought up or if the scope of exposure expands, could add fuel to the fire of a potential future debt crisis.[59]

Corporate Real Estate

The Fed's artificially low interest rate environment boosted the corporate real estate market, which was devastated in 2020 as governors shut down businesses and mandated stay-at-home orders. This could have a range of impacts, from defaults to lower property values, which would decrease state and local income tax revenues, the latter of which will undoubtedly tempt many government entities to engage in more taxation instead of pro-growth policies to make up the shortfalls. This cycle is poised to further drag down local economies.

Pensions

There is also a concern about what will happen to already floundering government pension plans. Ben Meng, then the chief investment officer of Calpers, California's public pension fund and the largest defined-benefit public pension fund in the United States, took the incredibly odd and unprecedented step of announcing the pension fund's strategy in a *Wall Street Journal* op-ed in June, saying:

> even before the pandemic, we knew that our goal of achieving a risk-adjusted return of 7% would require addressing the market's triple threat of low interest rates, high asset valuation and low economic growth. In late 2019 we mapped out an investment strategy to deliver sustainable results.
>
> The solution is based on "better assets" and "more assets" and will capitalize on Calpers's advantages. . . .
>
> "More assets" refers to a plan to use leverage, or borrowing, to increase the base of the assets generating returns in the portfolio. Leverage allows Calpers to take advantage of low interest rates by borrowing and using those funds to acquire assets with potentially higher returns.
>
> This approach is not without risk.[60]

This is the country's largest pension fund publicly telegraphing (1) that it needs cheap money to continue to get returns because of the Fed's distortions of the market and (2) that it is going to use it to pursue riskier investments. Government pensions, being defined benefit, as discussed elsewhere in this book, are a giant mistake, allowing government officials to make promises of future payouts they cannot keep and leaving future officials to clean up the mess. The Fed's actions create an even more uncertain investment strategy for these already underwater funds.

A Dangerous Path

The Fed had been on a long course of thinking it knew how to "control" the economy better than free markets. Alan Greenspan opened the door, but Ben Bernanke burst through it with reckless abandon, and there has been no turning back since.

Though artificially low interest rates gave big businesses war chests to prepare them to withstand 2020, most used them in nonproductive ways. The result is that the Fed, a quasi-government agency, picked winners and losers, transferring wealth to those who already have it and making it harder for those who don't to compete.

The Fed has slowed growth by propping up zombie companies, crowding out more innovation and small businesses. It has ensured that the biggest companies don't bear the same burdens that smaller, more vulnerable companies do.

It has thrown savers and retirees under the bus, all while propping up its cronies on Wall Street.

We do not yet know the full effects of the unprecedented actions of low rates and a $7 trillion balance sheet.

What we do know is that the establishment of the Fed was a ruse by the Wall Street elite to have cartel-type control instead of the free market, and today, that is still in place.

Though the central planning takeover of government, including the Fed, has enabled these damaging actions, if counteractions aren't undertaken quickly, the ruin of the US economy and its founding principles is certain to follow in short order.

The Fed is complicit in the war against small business, both directly and indirectly. It has overseen a tremendous non–free market transfer of wealth from Main Street to Wall Street. Failure to address this will mean more consolidated power and wealth on Wall Street and in big businesses, and ultimately economic ruin for those outside the power center.

CHAPTER 6

Social Justice and Social Costs

How Small Businesses Bore
Significant Costs Due to Government's
Economic and Civil Injustice

Across the United States, people were immensely frustrated, restless, and outraged at being told by the government that they couldn't work or their businesses could not open. Tens of millions of people were unemployed, children and young adults were out of school, and many individuals were wondering how a fifteen-day commitment to slow the spread of a virus had turned into months in lockdown.

That was coupled with a series of government-caused justice violations against individuals. The killings of George Floyd in Minneapolis and Breonna Taylor in Louisville, Kentucky, against the backdrop of the lockdown, led to widespread protests.

Though many legitimate peaceful protests occurred—a protected right that is vital and sacred—circumstances enabled those with nefarious intentions to take over and turn the protests into riots and looting. There was significant violence and destruction. Others, pushing an anticapitalistic, antifreedom agenda in favor of a coercive one, stood in stark contrast to the issue of big government infringing on people's rights via policing.

The indiscriminate nature of the chaos proved a double whammy for many small, struggling businesses. In Minneapolis, Korboi "KB" Balla, a firefighter who had dreamed of opening his own sports bar, had invested his life savings and "countless hours" into a new venture called Scores, which was planned for a March opening. Because of the state government shutdown of restaurants, Balla pushed his opening back to June. He made the news not for his new venture's opening but when he wept as it was burned to the ground during the rioting, a horrible irony for someone who had spent his life serving the public fighting fires. He was reported as saying, "To find out that the countless hours, hard work, late nights away from my kids, and family had all been for nothing was soul-shattering. It is not the material things, more so the time that cannot be reclaimed."[1]

Twyana Balla, KB's wife, posted graphic images of the aftermath on social media, along with a message that reiterated that they did not have insurance, saying also, "Let someone come run in your home and loot for the cause then and let's see you be ok with it! This is your neighborhood and if you have children you couldn't even walk them down the street because everything is burning or destroyed. You wouldn't understand unless you was in this position! Justice for George Floyd but not this kind of justice."[2]

Generous individuals, moved by the Ballas' story, contributed to a GoFundMe charity campaign set up on their behalf. At the time of writing, the fund had received more than $1 million in contributions. But while the Ballas' story made the media and they found kind souls to help, not every entrepreneur was that lucky. It was heartbreaking that many of the targeted businesses were owned by small entrepreneurs and people of color, as well as being located in underserved areas. Damaging these small, vulnerable businesses was completely inconsistent with "fighting back against the system."

A look back by Minneapolis's *Star Tribune* to assess the damage noted that restaurants and retail establishments were "the hardest hit" by the arson, looting, vandalism, and rioting that happened in the wake of the Floyd protests. It was particularly devastating for those industries because, as discussed, those businesses had been among the earliest and most stringently targeted by government

shutdowns, and they are owned in large part by small business owners. The *Star Tribune* estimated that the criminal acts in Minneapolis, St. Paul, and the surrounding communities had caused "millions
in property damage to more than 1,500 locations."[3]

That also included, as noted by the Balla family above, many communities that were lower-income and had people of color as their
primary residents.

The *Los Angeles Times* quoted thirty-year-old Liban Alin, a
resident who had grown up and settled in the Lake Street area of
Minneapolis, saying, "I agree with why people are upset, but don't
destroy the community. Who knows if the businesses are going to
want to come back?"[4]

David Allen, a forty-two-year-old resident of the neighborhood
who had engaged in peaceful protest himself, was reported as saying that the looting had become a distraction and the pub where he
worked had been closed and boarded up. "The message is getting
lost," he said, also noting that he and others had "lost confidence
in police and most political leaders," and that he believed that the
neighbors would come together to rebuild.

Eli Aswan, a fifty-year-old car salesman who had immigrated
from Tanzania nearly twenty years before, said that looters had sto-
len "more than $17,000 worth of auto repair equipment and titles,"
and after a couple of days, he had decided it was time to "close up
shop for a while."[5]

While chaos ensued in Minneapolis, peaceful protests took place
around the nation—and the world.

However, the nonpeaceful, illegal activities spread as well. By the
end of the month, twenty-six cities in sixteen states, including Chicago, Philadelphia, Los Angeles, Atlanta, and others, instituted cur-
fews (which were largely ignored).[6]

In Chicago, looting, which happened simultaneously with the
Floyd protests and continued throughout the summer, was another
hit to small businesses.

Small Businesses on the Front Lines

In addition to Chicago's, other local governments failed to protect small businesses just as they failed to protect rights and serve justice.

Near the Capitol Hill Autonomous Zone (CHAZ) in Seattle (later also known as "CHOP"), which was part children's backyard fairy tale–inspired play, part George Orwell's *Animal Farm*, and part *Lord of the Flies*, local government allowed even more damage to the already struggling small business community.

Businesses that had the misfortune of being located near CHAZ, including a slew of small businesses, were forced to close, many of them vandalized and robbed. The *New York Times* later portrayed a different story of what had happened there, quoting small business owners in the area describing "encampments overtaking the sidewalks . . . roving bands of masked protesters smashing windows and looting . . . men wielding guns" and detailing how difficult it was to do business. It was the worst block party ever. The business owners and residents also said that they believed many instigators were not part of Black Lives Matter (BLM) but rather were with antifa.[7]

Journalist Bowen Xiao reported that when an auto shop called Car Tender, located on the perimeter of CHAZ, was broken into, the owner and family members detained a suspect who attempted to rob and set fire to the store. However, they had to release the suspect as officers never arrived, despite their calling 911 several times. The son of the owner said he knew that officers wanted to help but couldn't, due to politics.[8]

With police activity being politically suppressed and a group of agitators occupying six blocks with no rules, not surprisingly, things went downhill further quickly and ended in lethal violence.

Following a weekend with multiple shootings that left one dead on June 22, the Associated Press reported a change in stance by Mayor Jenny Durkan. "The mayor says Seattle will move to wind down the city's 'occupied' protest zone following two shootings, including one that left a man dead." The block party was officially over.[9]

As the *New York Times* published regarding CHOP's aftermath, the outcome wasn't a good one. Its subhead was "What is it like when a city abandons a neighborhood and the police vanish? Business owners describe a harrowing experience of calling for help and being left all alone." The article went on to say that the abolish the police movement "has left small business owners as lonely voices in progressive areas, arguing that police officers are necessary and that cities cannot function without a robust public safety presence."[10] No protection of property rights means no businesses. No businesses mean no jobs, and so on. This was not an economic blueprint to be followed.

Ultimately, the progressive political "leadership" in Seattle demonstrated a government again not doing the very things that they were put in place for—protecting individual rights—and focused on everything with which it had no business being involved.

On August 11, Carmen Best, Seattle's police chief, a twenty-eight-year veteran and woman of color, resigned. As the *Wall Street Journal* said, "The city's first black police chief is out—thanks to progressives."[11]

In neighboring Portland, where small business owners had to deal with antifa, in addition to the negative social impact of the clashes, the economic impact was tangible and severe. Stacey Gibson, who owned five fast-food locations in the Portland area, told Fox News that "the coronavirus outbreak had already taken a 60 percent bite out of her overall sales—then two months ago the rioting and vandalism began, slowing sales by another 20 percent." Gibson also said that "she was initially supportive of the Black Lives Matter protests because she agreed with the underlying call for racial equality—but now believes the protests have been hijacked by violent opportunists

The War on Small Business   122

seeking to cause destruction for no reason. . . . 'It's just not fair that people can break laws and not have any kind of consequence. . . . It's terrifying as a business owner.'"[12]

The violence continued through the fall, with September protests featuring chants such as "If we don't get it, burn it down," just days after Oregon had endured horrific fires that were believed to be set by arsonists. The violence resulted in fatalities. There were no clear objectives other than political and social agitation, and again small businesses and vulnerable individuals suffered the most.[13]

The economic impact was felt for months after. *The Oregonian* said in December 2020 that Portland's small businesses were having a hard time finding insurance, and when they did, it was at a significantly higher cost, with higher deductibles and more caps and restrictions, due to concerns over looting and other unrest and damage in the city.[14]

Social Costs

Justice is an important cause and must always be a priority. We can appreciate that and also note that the timing of the protesting, made exponentially worse by the rioting, looting, and other illegal activity that happened simultaneously with the demonstrations by those who were peacefully and legally exercising their rights, created a more challenging path to recover from—including creating social and economic costs in many lower-economic areas of the country.

Overall, the economic impact is hard to assess fully at the time of this writing. What we do know is that on top of the mandated business closures and fear that made people stay home and spend less money, the rioting made some businesses close for longer, and other businesses that were already struggling consider that it might not be worth it to reopen at all.

The *New York Times* reported that the Lake Street corridor of

Minneapolis, "a largely Latino and East African business district," had a fundraiser that generated $9 million to help supplement the damage they had sustained to their businesses. However, when Allison Sharkey, the executive director of the Lake Street Council, which was in charge of the fundraising, asked the small businesses what the gap was between the damage incurred by the looting, arson, and vandalism and what their insurance would pay, the estimates totaled in the range of $200 million. Sharkey's own office, per the piece, was also burned down in the protests.[15]

In bigger cities, such as Chicago, the destruction meant the loss of not just small businesses but big companies as well, as retailers, restaurants, and other businesses sought to vacate their leases. Such business closures don't just mean a direct loss of jobs at those establishments but also at the neighboring small businesses and jobs they support. Those workers are no longer going to work, so the establishments that provided the workers with coffee, lunch, entertainment, sundries, transportation, and other goods and services also lose out. This means fewer amenities to entice and support new entrepreneurs. The city's tax base shrinks, and the cycle ends up draining money from the local and state economies.

As we wait for exact numbers, we can look at studies that were done on previous rioting and its impact as a proxy. Marketplace published insights by Victor Matheson, professor of economics at College of the Holy Cross, who had studied the costs of the Rodney King riots in Los Angeles in 1992. "'Economic activity in the areas affected didn't return for at least 10 years,' Matheson said. At least not to previous levels. He said those riots cost almost $5 billion in economic activity measured in lost sales over 10 years. 'If people don't feel safe where their businesses are, then they don't feel a need to rebuild.'"[16]

The analysis also looked at a major hurricane, Hurricane Andrew, that had hit Miami the same year and said that the economy had "recovered a heck of a lot faster." The analysis pointed out that government response to hurricanes was better and that some of it came down to mental state. It is one thing to deal with a natural disaster, but mentally it is more difficult to rebuild after the intentional acts of other individuals, not to mention overcoming the depression of consumer confidence.

Whether local shoppers or tourists, who wants to patronize areas that are deemed to be unsafe? Also, if you are worried about flare-ups of looting and violence, you may prefer to save your money instead of spending it—just in case.

In a 2004 study, "The Labor Market Effects of the 1960s Riots," William J. Collins and Robert A. Margo found that median Black family income had declined by 9 percent in cities where there had been substantial riots when compared with those that hadn't seen violence and found correlations between riots and an increase in African Americans living in high-poverty neighborhoods.[17]

On top of the direct business impact, there is the depression of commercial and residential property values. Another of Collins and Margo's reports found that the 1960s riots had "depressed the median value of black-owned property between 1960 and 1970, with little or no rebound in the 1970s."[18]

The business opinion writer Joe Cahill, in an op-ed for *Crain's Chicago Business*, talked about how looting is far worse than the pandemic in terms of long-term economic impacts, saying,

Anyone who remembers or has studied the postwar era knows the corrosive effect of fear on cities like Chicago. It's deadlier to urban health than any pandemic, or even the dire fiscal woes facing Chicago. And it can cripple a city's ability to meet those challenges.

It starts in real estate. A one-two punch of fear scares off buyers just as nervous residents put condos and houses up for sale. Economics 101 takes over, as excess supply and dwindling demand drive down values. And as values decline, builders who have been investing in city neighborhoods take their money elsewhere.[19]

Cahill then went on to talk about the interconnectedness of the local economies, which leads to fewer amenities and businesses, fewer jobs, then fewer businesses, and so on. In certain cities, such as Chicago, he notes, that can spill over to the convention and tourism businesses that are critical to those cities' revenue bases and overall economies.[20]

Not coincidentally, this has led to an acceleration of a trend that had already started: an exodus from big "blue" cities and states to "red" cities and/or states that have more freedoms and are less substantially impacted by overbearing government systems, policies, regulations, and, of course, taxes. Illinois, for example, saw a net population loss of around 80,000 people in 2020, with losses increasing every year for the last seven years.[21]

And, of course, as discussed elsewhere in this chapter, there is also a substantial impact on more impoverished communities, whose residents have fewer resources available to help rebuild and who end up being viewed as riskier investments as lawlessness prevails. Also, without the revenue base generated by those who are better off and are migrating out, there is left a smaller pool from which to fund everything from schools to other public services.

In May, the Congressional Budget Office provided an early analysis to Congress, estimating that the long-term fallout from the government's COVID reactions could impact the GDP to the tune of $8 trillion over the next decade, and that was before the impact of the rioting.[22]

Analysis later in the year, discussed in chapter 7, estimated total costs at double that.

Justice for individual rights is wholly intertwined with economic freedom. Suppressing economic opportunities and liberties and disenfranchising people to take risks required to reap economic rewards unfortunately moves that effort in the wrong direction.

Government's Economic Injustice

Layering the economic fallout of government pandemic panic and mismanagement with the additional economic blows of the rioting and looting created more dire financial situations. When small businesses saw the government stomping on their property rights, they turned around to find others destroying their property. That slowed the opportunities for recovery across the board. Some individuals won't ever be able to recover fully.

Small businesses were shut down, looted, and burned to the ground. There was no help. There was no meaningful financial lifeline. The war against small business was accelerating.

CHAPTER 7

A Couple Hundred Days' Worth of "Fifteen Days to Slow the Spread"

A Rapid and Historic Consolidation of Power and Wealth

July 23, 2020, also known as day 130 of "15 Days to Slow the Spread," was Opening Day for the 2020 Major League Baseball season. Though many small businesses around the country remained shuttered or were fighting for their existence and 16.3 million people were without jobs, professional sports were clearly essential, so much so that Dr. Anthony Fauci was recruited to throw out the first pitch for the MLB season opener between the Washington Nationals and the New York Yankees.[1]

The optics of that were bad; people were struggling. Businesses were being stymied while baseball was allowed to proceed. Fauci, who had made many mistakes and even outright shared known misinformation—"Right now, in the United States, people should not be walking around with masks"—was being held up as a hero.[2] It was partly politics, partly gaslighting, and partly a statement of who and what were valued.

Small business optimism was falling. A far cry from January's near-record optimism, the NFIB's Small Business Optimism Index for July showed a mere 25 percent of small business owners believing business conditions would improve within the following six months. "Small businesses are clearly still struggling from the coronavirus pandemic, whether through continued shutdowns, lower sales, higher costs, or troubles hiring," said William Dunkelberg, NFIB's chief economist.[3]

How could they not be demoralized? The hospitals weren't overrun yet; the health care system was not even taxed nearly everywhere; but businesses had been impacted for more than a quarter of a year without any clear benchmarks.

Earlier that month, California governor Gavin Newsom had ordered another round of business closures across nineteen counties in the state. Of note was the closure of wineries. In the words of *The Sun*, that had created substantial "sour grapes" because PlumpJack Winery and its tasting room, operated by a company cofounded by Newsom, was exempt from the order.[4]

Speaking of grapes, they were also at issue on the other side of the country. In New York, Governor Andrew Cuomo had put into place a rule that any bar that served alcohol must also serve food in order to remain open. That arbitrary rule was more closely aligned with control and cronyism than with science. Cuomo tweeted, "Let's be clear. Outdoor dining is now permitted statewide. Outside drinking is not."[5]

Different establishments got creative. Handshakes Bar & Grill in New York's Hudson Valley posted a "CUOMO" menu to Instagram, using the acronym to name it "Cuomo's Unnecessary Obligated Menu Options" and featuring a handful of $1 menu options of a few fries or a couple of onion rings with creative names. A bar in Buffalo called the Lafayette Brewing Company also threw together a $1 menu, mocking the mandate's absurdity with options such as "Grapes; Just a few grapes, not sure the color."[6]

When asked about it by reporters, Cuomo said, "they do not suffice in the existing law as a 'bar serving food.'"[7] According to WRGB in Albany, one establishment, Harvey's Irish Pub, received a call from a State Liquor Authority investigator, who said that chips wouldn't satisfy the order and would need to be served with salsa, dip, or something similar to comply. Where is the science or precedent in trying to control whether chips are served with or without dip, particularly as it relates to the big picture of the virus and the economy?

On the subject of dips, the dippy rules were generating real losses and waste. One entrepreneur said the mandate was causing him to throw away an unprecedented amount of food, as people were ordering the food to comply with the rule but not eating it.[8]

That political foolery was underscored by the performance of New York financially. That month, the state still had an unemployment rate of 15.9 percent, more than 50 percent higher than the national average.[9]

Yet New York State proceeded with more cronyism, favors, and control of what was deemed "okay" or "essential." For example, the MTV Video Music Awards were allowed to proceed without an audience but with a large staff, including performers and crew.[10]

In addition to vulnerable small businesses bearing a large part of the economic burden of the picking of "essential" businesses, younger individuals endured a significant toll, with youth unemployment rising more rapidly than for other workers, according to an analysis by Bloomberg. Youth unemployment for July, according to the Bureau of Labor Statistics, was still at 18.5 percent.[11]

More Problems, More Money?

As various states around the country opened their economies in part or in full, jobs came back. Though the media and economists were surprised (per headlines such as Business Insider's "US Shocks Economists by Adding 2.5 Million Jobs in May as Unemployment Declines to 13.3%"),[12] it was not rocket science; telling people to shutter their businesses had eliminated sales, sacrificed jobs, and more. When the government had let people go out of their homes and back to work, some of those jobs and businesses had returned.

As the economic depression had not been caused by a systemic issue, that result was reasonably apparent. Reopenings helped the economy regain some of the jobs that had been lost and increase overall economic activity.

However, what was looming was figuring out where the economic "wall" was. At what point would that switch flipping no longer work? Whether it resulted from entrepreneurs who gave up their businesses or industries that saw more dislocation, there was a point where the regaining of jobs would slow and stop.

Congress at first wanted to try to prompt economic growth with another major stimulus bill. Or rather, "buy" some votes in an election year. If its members had genuinely wanted to help the economy, they should have gotten out of the way; giving out money for which future generations will have to pay does not substitute for allowing people to return to their lives and jobs. It also doesn't eliminate hitting the economic "wall."

Yet Congress decided to try to do what it did best: spend. Several times, including in May and July, proposals were put on the table, but ultimately with little movement between the House and the Senate.

The two major parties tried to work on their proposals individually. At the end of July, the *New York Times* looked at the proposals, which were incremental to the $3.2 trillion Congress had already spent so far in 2020 on coronavirus relief. The Democratic proposal, which was for an additional $3.4 trillion, allocated more than a trillion dollars to state and local aid, $436 billion to individual stimulus checks, and a whopping zero dollars to direct small business aid. You read that correctly: nada for small business.[13]

To give context to just how massive that proposal was, should it have passed, it would have been $6.6 trillion on stimulus in one calendar year alone. As noted previously, that is just shy of the entire US national debt in January 2004 ($7 trillion). That would amount to around $51,000 per household in the United States, which seems crazy, particularly knowing that a large part of the economy, including many big businesses and their employees, weren't locked down and were not in need of any emergency relief.

The Republican proposal, which still clocked in at just over $1 trillion, allocated only 20 percent of funding to small business aid. That was still $200 billion more than the Democrats had in a bill a fraction of the size—and of course had about the same allocation for other "business tax breaks" (something the Democrats had allocated only $36 billion to).

The distance between the two sides was extensive, and although both parties and the Trump administration all signaled that they were working toward a compromise, investors started to feel that their achieving one was unlikely, at least before the election.

Though the political parties remained far apart on a "stimulus" package, the economic bounce-back "wall" was getting closer into view. September's job report showed some slowing. Job gains were only 661,000 (substantially fewer than the 800,000 predicted), and although unemployment fell to 7.9 percent, the decrease was due in part to people leaving the labor force.

Day 200 of "15 Days to Slow the Spread"

October 1 marked 200 days of "15 Days to Slow the Spread."

Individual rights retained a big win, courtesy of a landmark ruling by Michigan's Supreme Court against Governor Whitmer. The *Detroit News* reported that "the Michigan Supreme Court decided Friday that Gov. Gretchen Whitmer violated her constitutional authority by continuing to issue orders to combat COVID-19 without the approval of state lawmakers." The report said that Whitmer had overstepped her bounds and that declaring emergencies and keeping them in place without legislative input was unconstitutional.[14]

The report also unanimously ruled that another law didn't give the governor powers "after April 30, to issue or renew any executive orders related to the COVID-19 pandemic after 28 days without Legislative approval."

However, despite that small victory, people were restless. They were tired of the government playing terrorist, using COVID like the threat of a bomb to scare everyone, holding the American people hostage, and trying to force the population as a whole to alter their lives materially.

In October, job increases were stronger than expected as more businesses were allowed to reopen. Jobs increased by 638,000, and the unemployment rate dropped to 6.9 percent, both ahead of economists' expectations. Private sector job creation was even stronger—906,000 jobs—offset by government losses, including census workers.[15]

As reported by CNBC's Jeff Cox, based on the Labor Department report, those out of work because their employer closed (temporarily or permanently) was still 15.1 million people. Though down from the previous month, bringing the total payroll gains since May to around 12 million, it still meant that a lot of businesses and their employees remained impacted.

Meanwhile, as small businesses struggled to regain their footing, the biggest companies continued their dominance. Amazon reported third-quarter revenue up by 37 percent year over year to $96.1 billion, and Google's parent company, Alphabet, saw its third-quarter revenue increase by double digits (14 percent).[16]

By the market close of the day when the October jobs report was announced, four companies—Microsoft, Amazon, Alphabet (Google), and Apple—were now collectively worth almost $6.6 trillion, propelling the Nasdaq Composite up 32.5 percent for the year to date.[17] That enabled the accumulation and centralization of more power and heft among the tech giants, while the smallest businesses struggled to get themselves back on track—if they hadn't given up entirely.

Even from a stock market perspective, the small-cap indices, which represent publicly traded companies with smaller market values, struggled. On November 2, 2020, CNBC reported that for the year to date, small-cap stocks were down just a hair shy of 6 percent—a stark contrast to the soaring Nasdaq Composite.[18]

Of course, an expected fall wave of COVID case spikes was taking place, and governors were again contemplating lockdowns and continuing their power grabs, threatening the economic recovery. Despite previous orders being deemed unconstitutional, Michigan's Governor Whitmer was undeterred. She mandated that restaurants collect information on their diners, including names and phone numbers, creating huge concerns over privacy violations and liability issues for the already battered industry.[19]

In neighboring Wisconsin, the NFIB, a small business advocacy group, filed with the courts on behalf of Wisconsin small business owners, stemming from Governor Tony Evers's intention to release the names of small businesses with employees who had tested positive for COVID-19, saying that it "is not only illegal but will take a monumental toll on the financial health of small businesses in Wisconsin."[20]

The economy was furiously trying to get back to that wall where small business losses would create a breaking point—or perhaps climb over it, trading small business decentralized power and economic strength for government-led and Fed-enabled centralization of power among the largest companies.

And then all attention turned to the elections.

More Collateral Damage

Financial costs are often easier to measure, or at least benchmark. Social costs, which do eventually have both an economic impact and a huge individual impact, are also part of the collateral damage of the government's war on small business and individuals. These are vast and range from other areas of physical health, where treatment was rationed and in some cases unavailable, to the impact on mental health issues related to social isolation and the undue fear created by the government actions.

A friend recounted a story to me of an encounter in October 2020 in New York City's Central Park. He was watching a three- or four-year-old boy hit Wiffle balls with his father. The kid was having a great time, and another young boy, about the same age, approached him excitedly. As the second boy got near the first boy, the first boy's expression went from happiness to intense fear. He started screaming that the other boy was "too close" and "needs to go away" over and over until the second boy's mother came and took him away.

Imagine the psychological toll that the government's and media's pandemic messaging and actions have taken on both boys in these incredibly critical developmental years.

It is not just the young that endured a mental toll. By September 2020, military suicides in the United States increased around 20 percent during the pandemic from the same period the previous year. The CDC reported that nearly 41 percent of adults surveyed reported struggles with mental health issues or substance abuse. Experts remain concerned about long-term mental health effects, including PTSD, in all age groups. Drug overdoses were up by double digits percentagewise as well.[21]

With regard to American children and teenagers, the reaction to the pandemic may also create a substantial drag on learning. In August, EducationWeek said that students' learning would be impacted, noting, "What does seem certain is that it will be devastating—and that the effects are likely to be long lasting."[22]

In June, McKinsey & Company estimated that students could lose three to eleven months of learning, assuming that classroom teaching didn't resume broadly until January 2021.[23]

McKinsey & Company also noted that COVID could "exacerbate existing achievement gaps" for students of color, saying that "School shutdowns could not only cause disproportionate learning losses for these students—compounding existing gaps—but also lead more of them to drop out."[24] The government's decisions do not sound as though they were consistent with the goal of protecting the most vulnerable.

Were the costs and collateral damage—financial, mental, developmental, social, spiritual, and otherwise—of completely closing large parts of the economy and people's lives justified, on their own and/or in conjunction with the health outcomes they produced?

In October, former treasury secretary Lawrence Summers and Harvard University economist David Cutler estimated the cost of the pandemic in the United States to be $16 trillion, half due to direct economic loss from the shutdowns and the other half due to the long-term consequences of mental health, physical health, and other impairments at least partly attributable to the shutdowns.[25]

As we know, throughout history, estimates such as these are typically conservative, so that amount could well be the tip of the iceberg. The businesses that were killed may never come back, and replacing jobs lost could take years. Furthermore, why would a potential entrepreneur ever consider starting a bricks-and-mortar business again, knowing that his or her risk and livelihood are under the control and at the whim of the government?

Those costs are yet to be known. What is known is if the traditional mall dies and that land is converted, say into a warehouse, as Barclays predicts might happen, that will reduce property values an estimated 60 to 90 percent. Barclays forecast around 10,000 retail store closures for 2020.[26] As discussed in chapter 6, if the stores and amenities that make up a vital part of communities close, it can drag down everything else in the community and take years to recover.

Locking Down Again

As the year headed into its last few weeks, the situation was looking up for the haves but not so much for the have-nots.

It would seem that 2020, which saw the GDP tank to record lows, tens of millions filing for unemployment benefits, and small business closures, would have produced a challenging environment for capital raising. Astoundingly, by the close of the market on December 10, 2020, the day Airbnb went public and saw its stock more than double in its debut, 436 IPOs had been completed during the year. It was the same week that the S&P 500 and Nasdaq Composite hit fresh new all-time record highs.[27]

By the end of the year, according to StockAnalysis, 2020 had set an all-time record for initial public offerings, with around 20 percent more IPOs than the previous record in 2000 and more than double 2019's number of offerings. That means big businesses were accessing capital at an unprecedented rate at the same time as small businesses were struggling for a lifeline.[28]

On Main Street, governors throughout the country were mandating a new round of lockdowns and business closures. Despite all the time that had passed for government to figure out and communicate better risk mitigation strategies, that route was not pursued. Instead of its switching up which businesses were in lockdown, it allowed the big companies to remain open; most had never locked down or closed at all. The same small companies that had been targeted previously were asked to shutter once again, perhaps a final death blow to many of the small businesses that had scraped to survive at that point.

In New York, restaurants pushed back, to no avail; when after the state's own contact-tracing system attributed only 1.4 percent of all COVID cases between September and the end of November to restaurants, they were targeted for lockdown again. Meanwhile, the television program *Saturday Night Live* found loopholes to tape its shows, which were somehow deemed "essential."[29]

A special report analysis from Alignable's December 2020 small business survey highlighted the disastrous situation for small business. Forty-eight percent of the small businesses surveyed said they risked failure by the end of December, and only 43 percent had confidence that they would survive through June 2021. Eighty-five percent of the small business owners said they needed relief. How could they not? What entity, let alone a small entity, could survive like this?[30]

Yet Congress continued to play games and had yet to provide appropriate compensation for the government-mandated closures. They went to war against small business and wouldn't even send in a Red Cross equivalent to triage the damage.

Small business confidence at the end of November 2020, according to a CNBC and SurveyMonkey survey, dipped to an all-time low since they had begun the survey in 2017.[31]

Concurrently, two new vaccines were getting ready for approval and distribution in the United States, which had received approval and started to roll out in a handful of other countries already. However, with the supply issues and COVID cases and deaths spiking, getting to vaccine-led herd immunity would likely not occur for many months in a best-case scenario. This was made worse by government bumbling the eventual vaccine rollout. Of course, certain members of Congress, including those in low-risk age groups, "cut the line" and got vaccinated early, going to show that anyone who argues that the free market favors those who are wealthy or well connected is naive to think that the government doesn't favor those who are wealthy and well connected; it's just a (sometimes) different group of wealthy and well connected but with less choice and control in the case of the latter.

Congress, which has spent like a drunken sailor on all kinds of insanity for years on end, still couldn't get a "relief" bill agreed upon and passed until a few days before Christmas.

Though Congress had had more than nine months to figure out how to help those who were directly impacted by the government-mandated closures—just think, one could have conceived and birthed a human being during that time—the bill it ultimately passed made just about every mistake that had been made in the CARES Act in March. With nearly another $1 trillion in spending, there was no new means testing for direct aid—meaning that households that didn't need stimulus might receive it and those that did might not—there was still a supplement to unemployment creating a reason not to go back to work, crony interests received direct cash, and small businesses were relegated to another pass at PPP.

As the year ended, the Dow closed up 7.2 percent, the S&P 500 up 16.3 percent, and the Nasdaq Composite up an incredible 43.6 percent for 2020. Power and value were consolidated in several of the biggest companies at an unprecedented pace and with unprecedented scope.[32]

Apple's stock price increased by 81 percent for the year, giving it a market capitalization of $2.3 trillion. Amazon's stock price increased by more than 76 percent, while Tesla's increased by nearly 700 percent. As noted in the introduction to this book, seven tech companies amassed $3.4 trillion in incremental value during the year. The differential between the big businesses and many of the smallest companies by year's end wasn't a gap—it was a chasm.[33]

As the country headed into 2021, the war on small business caused many entrepreneurs to wave the white flag, all as more power was being concentrated in government and a handful of massive companies.

This is a giant neon sign for the need to save small business, individual rights, and the American Dream. To do so, we need to understand how this was enabled and what can be done to change things.

CHAPTER 8

Protecting the Smallest Minority

*How Individual Rights and Capitalism Set the
Foundation for Economic Freedom*

Why would the government, whether at the local, state, or federal level, declare war on small business? As discussed, with half of the economy in the balance, wouldn't killing a substantial portion of that create a problem instead of generating an opportunity?

Not in the context of central planning. Small business represents the ultimate in free markets and individual choice and freedom. They are an impediment to control that makes it difficult for politicians to gain and exert power. The more people who are entangled with the government, the better it is for central planners and their objectives. Small businesses do not fit into that plan.

To understand the war against small business and the battle tactics of 2020—as well as the groundwork laid well before now—it is critical to understand the concept of individual rights, what it means to Americans in particular, and how and why there has been a constant government campaign to erode those rights.

The concept of individual rights is what makes the United States unique and special. It is the only country in the world that enumerates and protects the rights of the individual and limits the power of the state.

Core to the United States' founding principles, enshrined in the Constitution, is the idea that humans are born with inalienable rights.

Though some Americans believe in putting the group interest over that of the individual, that stands in opposition to the Constitution. If you put the group interest first, it means that at any point in time, a man's existence, work, and other activities are at the whim of other people who have power by sheer force or numbers. As said in *A New Textbook of Americanism*, "The Constitution of the United States of America is not a document that limits the rights of man—but a document that limits the power of society over man."[1]

Though we can acknowledge that the Founding Fathers didn't always practice what they preached, whether toward women or people of color, the principle of protecting the individual is something Americans have worked to enact and defend. We should hold this vital principle as sacred, as the United States is the unique example of this in the world.

Though you may be tempted to think that majority rule is a good one, if a majority of people agree to something, even if it is not morally right or just, that ends up being the ruling law, and that can go very wrong.

Most important, the idea of whether or not the power of society is limited is an absolute. Either society's power is limited by individual rights, or it is not. If you believe in individual rights, you also cannot say that sometimes society's power is not limited over the individual. If you put on a qualifier, then you have erased the critical principle of individual rights. Note that I am not suggesting anarchy; rights are inherently limited by other individuals' rights and the laws that enforce those rights. More simply, your rights are your rights until they infringe on another's rights (which is where you get the protection from scenarios such as not being able to slander someone else, for example). Anything else opens the door to an unstoppable erosion of your rights.

Anyone who believes in the concept of individual rights will tell you that society is merely a collection of individuals. You participate in "society" at community, local, state, national, and global levels.

Imagine if you had to subvert your existence for the rights of any one of these groups? If you did, which would reign supreme? Buying into the idea of the group isn't a principle, it's a trick, and the goalposts can be moved to define the group by any means that meet the desires or impulses of those in the majority of the group.

That happened in 2020. There were no full lockdowns. Certain small businesses, their employees, and other individuals were told to give up their livelihoods for the "good of society," based on what government felt was "good." Many companies never closed and their employees had jobs, while a third of small businesses nationally were shuttered and their employees were sent home. We were never "all in this together"; there were the chosen and the not-chosen.

It is by design, not coincidence, that the most oppressive and destructive powers in history, including recent history, always begin by trying to sell the concept of the "good of society." It is an emotional ruse to rob you of being an individual and of your rights. Whether by the Chinese Communist Party or in modern Venezuela, the first step toward tyranny is convincing people that their own individual rights need to be set aside.

In 2020, many took the bait hook, line, and sinker.

Individual Rights and Capitalism

Capitalism requires the concept of individual rights to be upheld and enforced. Similarly, the only system that upholds, protects, and enforces individual rights is capitalism, which is why they are so fundamentally intertwined.

Small business is the ultimate example of capitalism. It allows anyone with an idea, regardless of their background and history, to come into the marketplace with a solution and prosper. Before 2020, that was the path for more than 30.2 million entrepreneurs and around half the US workforce.

Small business is the stepping-stone not only to innovation and the largest businesses, but for any person, anywhere to make their life better, their family members' lives better, their employees' lives better, and their customers' lives better and to increase prosperity overall.

That is, as long as the markets remain free and the game doesn't become rigged against them.

Property Rights

A subset of individual rights connected with capitalism is property rights. Though many people think of property in terms of real estate, your property includes anything tangible or intangible that you own, from your iPhone to your protectable ideas. For example, if you own a patent on a new technical innovation that enables cars to fly, that is an example of protecting your unique and valuable ideas and methodology; if you own the copyright for an article or book you have written, that is considered intellectual property because of its intangible quality (i.e., you can't hold the method of doing something in your hand). Nonetheless, it is your property.

Protection of property is critical for people to be incentivized to invest, create, and take ownership of tangible and intangible property. If there were no protection of your property, you'd have less incentive to work hard, to create wealth, to buy a home, to keep your home well maintained, and so on. People would not take the same type of risks if the output of risk taking could be seized.

Simply put, if property rights are not protected, you own nothing.

You cannot have capitalism without individual rights. Combining the freedom to interact with the protection of property is what creates what we know as capitalism.

In 2020, government infringed on property rights as a tactic in its war against small business and individual rights. These infringements, lockdowns without due compensation, begat a huge economic fallout.

Unicorns and Fairies

If you want to live among people in a way that is not based on the whims of a government or a group of people with numbers or force, you need to have a set of basic ground rules or principles. Politics should be based on principles (I know, try not to laugh), not the other way around. When principles become based on politics, rights get ignored and power becomes concentrated into the hands of a few. Force and coercion overtake freedom and choice.

Protecting the individual makes sure that his or her inalienable rights aren't taken away. It also doesn't rely on finding benevolent leaders to ensure the system's enactment; it limits leaders and their power.

This is where the ideas of central planning fall apart.

It is nice to think that some group of people wants what is best for you and others, and so you give up your rights and allow them to make decisions on your behalf, hoping they have your best interests at heart. But human nature includes self-interest and greed. In a free market, there are two ways that human nature is regulated. First is the explicit set of regulations that don't allow for the infringement of others' rights, which limits the ability to do whatever you want, including where you don't own specific property. The second is that actions are regulated by the desire to stay in business and make profits, as other market participants have the choice of with whom they want to transact. There is no such freedom, choice, or regulation with government. When greed and self-interest take over in the government—and due to human nature, they always will—

there is no marketplace or regulator to stop them. That is why giving them so much power and control ends up with the trampling of individuals' rights.

If you believe that monopolies in markets are bad, remember that the government is the ultimate monopoly, and it has the military and IRS attached to enforce their monopoly power!

Someone recently said to me that power has always been seductive, which is a problem we continuously have to fight against, as well as resisting those who use that power via deceptive tactics to push people to trade their freedoms for the perception of security.

In 2020, this central power played out for all of us to see; the government decided what it thought was best for "us." Whose interests did it really have in mind? In December 2020, a video went viral of the owner of Pineapple Hill Saloon and Grill in Sherman Oaks, California, Angela Marsden. She had worked and spent a reported $80,000 to accommodate outdoor seating required by local officials to comply with COVID rules. Still she was forced by officials to shut down.[2]

However, a movie company had gotten a permit not only to go into production but also to set up an outdoor catering and dining location for the movie cast and crew in the same parking lot as that of the Pineapple Hill Saloon and Grill, tens of feet away from the then-shuttered restaurant's door.

Los Angeles mayor Eric Garcetti responded, "My heart goes out to Ms. Marsden and the workers at the Pineapple Hill Saloon who have to comply with state and county public health restrictions that close outdoor dining. No one likes these restrictions, but I do support them as our hospital I.C.U. beds fill to capacity and cases have increased by 500%. We must stop this virus before it kills thousands of more Angelenos."[3]

What kind of science is behind one outdoor seating venue being granted the go-ahead and the other being shuttered? None.

This is pure politics staring everyone straight in the face. The movie filming was more "essential" than the ten-year-old community small business.

Those politics were highlighted when it was reported that California governor Gavin Newsom, who had been caught flouting his own COVID rules during a dinner at the French Laundry in November 2020, was seen dining with an entertainment industry lobbyist, whose own clients were able to avoid lockdown mandates.[4]

This is what happens when central planners say they are acting "in your best interests": it turns out to be in their own—and their cronies'—best interests.

Small Government Does Not Mean No Government or No Laws

Despite government's shortcomings, it does have a role to play in capitalism and freedom.

Capitalism is more of an un-system than a system. It is the collection of the actions, choices, and free will of all of its participants. But it still needs rules. For individuals to have agency to participate in the "system" and make decisions, whether regarding where to work, what to invest in, what to buy or not to buy, they need to have individual rights. They must be able to make choices freely. If someone or an entity can force or coerce them to make a choice, or even control their choices, the market isn't free. So despite people saying that capitalism has no rules, the enforcement of natural rights is critical to its existence and functioning.

A false criticism of capitalism and a critique of individual rights often come up around the concept of small government. People often conflate the desire for small government or limited government with the desire for no government or no laws.

As set forth above, that is not the case. Small or limited government means limiting the government to perform the role of creating and enforcing laws that uphold the rights of the individual. We need the government to enforce the rules of the game, as enshrined in the Constitution. There need to be laws against stealing and courts to bring those who violate others' rights to justice. We need the police and military to safeguard our property and lives. That is welcome until those entities themselves start overstepping the bounds of individual rights. The government plays an important role, but a limited role, in capitalism.

Though we need the referees to enforce the rules of the game, where it goes awry is when they throw the game or intentionally rig it to the benefit of one team. When they choose a movie production over Pineapple Hill Saloon and Grill. When they allow big box retailers to stay open but force smaller retailers to shutter. When they give perks to special interest groups but not to small businesses. That's what has happened with central planning creep: it's far easier for government to work out "deals" with a small number of big companies that are willing and able to play ball, such as those big box retailers and movie studios.

Economic Freedom Is Freedom

Capitalism is freedom, economic freedom, and it is inextricably intertwined with your rights; the middle right in the Constitution of life, liberty, and the pursuit of happiness is liberty, aka freedom.

People often say they are just trying to do what is good for society, based on whatever happens to be their own definition of "good" and "society." This is their prerogative—when there's no force. But as soon as one is forced to do something for someone else and at someone's behest, it violates their rights. Plus, what is the greatest good for society? Who decides?

It was "good for society" for Pineapple Hill Saloon and Grill to shut down its outdoor seating, but also "good for society" for the movie production company to have outdoor dining tens of feet away. That's what happens when government decides what's "good." In theory, it's simple to tell what's good for society; in practice, it's never easy.

A crisis always provides good cover for governments to violate rights; see, for example, the Patriot Act that came out of the fear and panic that ensued after 9/11.

It should be no surprise that when 2020 came about and emergencies were declared many people would look to the government as the supreme solution provider, some of whom would not only willingly give up their rights but lose their minds when others did not do the same.

Even the United Nations, which has a laughable track record on human rights, hit the nail on the head regarding rights violations, stating in March, "we urgently remind States that any emergency responses to the coronavirus must be proportionate, necessary and non-discriminatory."[5] The message was directed globally, but it reminded the only country founded on individual rights of what should have already been top of mind.

Governments on the federal, state, and local levels engaged in all kinds of violations of constitutional rights and liberties. These included, but were not limited to, the right to practice religion, the right to ensure that one's property isn't taken for "public use" without appropriate compensation, the ability to travel across state lines, and the ability to enforce certain contracts.

When it comes to forcing small businesses to close, a violation of property rights, many legal scholars and thinkers have reinforced the notion that eminent domain, the constitutional concept of fair compensation for taking over personal property, set forth in the Fifth Amendment, must come into play. Stephon Bagne of Clark Hill PLC wrote that when it comes to emergency powers under the Stafford Act and similar state legislation, "the acquisition of materials and facilities under this statute does not limit the government's obligation to pay just compensation."[6]

In addition to small business owners not being adequately compensated—or in some cases not compensated at all—for the partial or full closures of their businesses to support the emergency, the decisions were arguably arbitrary. Government let a PetSmart groom dog nails while a nail salon couldn't groom people's nails. Definitions of "essential" were all over the board and heavily favored larger businesses.

Many places of worship across religious groups sued local authorities for banning their gatherings over a certain size. That seemed arbitrary, as you could often find more people in a grocery store than in many houses of worship. It was further illustrated by the support many local and state government officials gave protesters throughout the summer while restricting small gatherings and businesses. If the Constitution protects both your right to protest and assemble and the right to practice religion, how are these differences being established and enforced?

According to the American Bar Association, in North Carolina, "non-resident homeowners sued local authorities after being turned away en route to their beach homes for fear they would spread COVID-19."[7]

Add those examples on top of a slew of others, from throwing citizens in jail or issuing excessive fines for violating orders to stop working to the fight over masks (which could be argued are protective of individual rights, but I will save that for another space), and the government clearly and repeatedly not only overstepped boundaries but fully stomped upon the rights of individuals, over and over again.

While you may agree with specific directives, you must always go back to the principle and ask yourself what the line is. Because once you concede it is anything other than what the Constitution enshrines and protects, that line can be moved. Would it be okay for someone to come into your home and remove you to a facility if you were suspected of being infected with COVID or anything else? What if government wanted to implant a tracking device in you—for the good of society, of course? When you build a monster, there is no controlling it.

What began under the guise of government "helping society" and "public health" predictably became a grab for power and an exercise in coercion, force, and control, applied with arbitrary standards and using fear tactics supported by the media.

The start down the road of not fiercely protecting individual rights was the first step in the journey toward more government and toward the outcomes of 2020.

CHAPTER 9

America's Worst Trade Deal

Why Central Planning Is Doomed to Fail

What do you think was the worst trade deal of all time for America?

The worst trade deal the United States ever made wasn't with China. In fact, it was not with Canada, Mexico, or any other trading partner. It was a trade internal to the nation: the trading of individual rights for a bigger, centrally planned government. This has happened gradually, over very long periods of time, at every level and even between levels of government, looking past state and local responsibilities to give the federal government more heft and size.

As Americans have put more trust, responsibility, and, of course, money into government, it has become bigger and more powerful, with little oversight, transparency, or accountability.

As it has become bigger, politicians have gotten a taste of power and become hungrier for more. As is human nature, they have sought more of it, and therefore pursued policies and actions that would lead to more power and centralization and less freedom and decentralization. This is precisely where government central planning differs from small business and entrepreneurship. It's also why central planners find capitalism and small business so inconvenient for them.

The more people who are dependent upon government and the fewer entities they have to negotiate with, the more power the central planning politicians wield.

This shift toward central planning has happened at an accelerating pace, and with its growth, government has a group of people managing exponentially more money, complexities, and activities than the largest companies in the world; its recruitment process is based on popularity votes or variations thereof—the same thing we did in high school to pick our student council.

Too Big to Succeed

From the time of the country's founding as a set of individualistic principles against a tyrannical reign to the slow creep toward central planning, government has become far too big to succeed. Even if you believe that the expansion was done in part or in whole with good intentions—which I tend to believe is magical thinking, but I will go with it for this example—the government's complexity makes it inherently inefficient. It is opaque, lacks accountability, and controls far too many different areas to be effective in any one of them, let alone all of them.

In May 2018, John Dickerson published a piece in *The Atlantic* called "The Hardest Job in the World" about how the presidency has become an impossible job. He noted that so many of the current responsibilities of the presidency were not part of the position's design or creation; the framers had intentionally limited the power and stature of the role.[1]

Being the commander in chief, charged with overseeing the largest military in the world, is a big enough job that requires constant attention and would be stressful in and of itself.

In addition to the scope of the military duties, the executive branch manages more than 2 million employees with a wide array of duties ranging from "regulating air pollution to x-raying passengers before they board an airplane," Dickerson said. Add to that millions more in contract and grant workers and the fact that the position, and its management staff, turns over every four to eight years, and it is truly unbelievable, let alone doable.[2]

Dickerson also laid out the scope of the expectations for the presidency, saying:

> The president must endure the relentless scrutiny of the digital age. He must console the widow of a soldier he sent into combat one moment, and welcome a championship-winning NCAA volleyball team to the White House the next. He must set a legislative agenda for an often feckless Congress, navigating a partisan divide as wide as any in modern American history. He must live with the paradox that he is the most powerful man in the world, yet is powerless to achieve many of his goals—thwarted by Congress, the courts, or the enormous bureaucracy he sometimes only nominally controls.[3]

Dickerson also pointed out that "No one man—or woman—can possibly represent the varied, competing interests of 327 million citizens."

That's where the issue loops back. No one man or woman can. No handful of men or women can. No legislative body can. That's why the United States was set up as a representative constitutional republic. That's why the government's purpose was to protect individual rights, because when a country is spread out across thousands of miles, with a diverse population with different wants, backgrounds, experiences, and priorities, the only thing that is unifying is their rights. That was what the US government was put into place to do: protect the rights of the individual. And the further it strays from that, the more issues it creates and the less effective it becomes.

This is not just about the presidency; it is about all of central planning, including by Congress, state government, and local government. Take Congress; its members have no expertise requirements to get their jobs—only that they are popular in their home state. Yet they are in charge of allocating trillions of dollars across every industry and function you can imagine—each year! They are supposed to oversee the Federal Reserve Board of Governors. They are charged with making laws in highly technical industries such as financial services, biotechnology, and technology. Even if you believe they should be doing more than the Founders and Constitution set forth, how can you expect them to do all of these things, let alone with any prowess?

If you think they can handle any of these issues, think about how ridiculously out of touch they sound when talking about any kind of common technology. That's how they sound on every issue to people who actually know what they're talking about.

In 2019, in a scene that could have come right out of a Mel Brooks comedy, Congresswoman Maxine Waters grilled the heads of the largest banks in the country about the size and scope of student loans. You may recall that Waters chaired the House Financial Services Committee, which oversees the entire financial services sector.

"What are you guys doing to help us with this student loan debt? Who would like to answer first? Mr. Moynihan, big bank," she asked the CEO of Bank of America, Brian Moynihan, who replied, "We stopped making student loans in 2007 or so."

She asked the same of the head of Citigroup, who responded that it had exited the business in 2009.

Finally, Congresswoman Waters got to Jamie Dimon, the head of JPMorgan Chase, who responded more explicitly, to either end or underscore the embarrassment. He replied, "When the government took over student lending in 2010 or so, we stopped doing all student lending."

Let's bring it to the bottom line: the head of the committee that oversees financial services did not know that the government itself had pushed the major banks out of student lending and had taken it over in large part nearly a decade prior.

Diseconomies of Scale

Economies of scale is a business concept that as a business gets larger, it becomes more productive, and its output or production becomes more efficient and/or less costly. Think, for example, of a small-batch ice cream manufacturer. It probably pays more for ingredients and has less money to invest in equipment. So it produces fewer ice cream pints each hour with a higher cost of goods than a mass producer of ice cream that obtains deals to buy ingredients in bulk and has state-of-the-art equipment that churns out—pun intended—more ice cream pints per hour.

Also, as you have scale in a business, that business can spread out other costs over a bigger sales base. With fewer ongoing fixed costs, this is how technology firms, for example, end up becoming so valuable.

However, after a certain point, a business can no longer derive benefits by increasing its output or production. Costs start to rise, and inefficiencies occur. In economics, this is referred to as diseconomies of scale. This is typically explained by economists noting that as organizations get to a certain size, individual workers don't always have the same scrutiny (good or bad) vis-à-vis decision makers, and so they don't work as efficiently. Also, as companies become larger, there are more layers of decision makers, approvals, rules, opacity, and other bureaucracy. This adds to costs and decreases efficiency.

Does that sound familiar?

This underscores why there is a life cycle to businesses and why almost three-quarters of the existing Dow Jones 30 composite stocks have been added since 1991. In fact, fourteen have been added since 2000 and only one stock remains from prior to 1976. It is also illustrated by the fact that those companies that get very big and diversified have a hard time managing and being effective over time.[4]

In government, there are few efficiencies from scale to begin with, as they are mostly not producing a product. Though government has few economies of scale, it does have the problems that come with diseconomies of scale. Government becomes bloated in size, scale, and scope.

The bigger the government, whether that be in scope of functions, amount of spending, or otherwise, the less efficient it becomes. The complexity creates opacity, and it is hard to see where money is spent and measure the outcomes of such spending. Even if you can follow the money and outcomes on a small scale, the government is doing too many things to keep track of and has little accountability for doing them poorly or even allowing fraud. Though its programs may be labeled as progressive, their outcomes are regressive.

Additionally, the more that goes to the federal government as opposed to state and local governments, the further removed you are from the decision making and ability to keep tabs on government. In capitalism, the market works because the interested parties are actively engaged with the payments and outcomes. The government purposely complicates that intention and related outcomes.

How can something so disorganized and disparate be "power hungry"? First, it's made up of people, and seeking power is human nature. Second, think of it as a blob slowly spreading in every direction. It doesn't always need someone directing it to grow and take over. It just does if no one stops it.

Bloating, at Scale

Often the government, including Congress, is criticized for doing nothing. That isn't exactly accurate; it may seem that way because it doesn't do things well or effectively or things that are seemingly important, but it is busy. In fact, it is too busy, as we have traded the protection of our rights for the government being our babysitter, benevolent benefactor, and fairy godmother.

Looking at laws, I would love to tell you how many laws there are in the United States, but nobody has produced accurate, sourceable data because the laws are virtually impossible to count. You would think there would be some economies of scale to lawmaking—as more are passed, fewer are needed—but that has not happened. As the members of Congress believe that their job is to create laws, lots of laws are passed, very few are repealed, and the outcome is a hodgepodge of far too many rules and regulations.

Dave Kowal of Kowal Communications said on his blog, "When federal laws were first codified in 1927, they fit into a single volume. By the 1980s, there were 50 volumes of more than 23,000 pages. And today? Online sources say that no one knows. The Internal Revenue Code alone, first codified in 1874, contains more than 3.4 million words and, if printed 60 lines to the page, is more than 7,500 pages long."[5]

The report "Government Unchecked," from the Center for Judicial Engagement, notes that Congress passed 15,817 laws from 1954 to 2002. The Supreme Court struck down 103—or just two-thirds of 1 percent of those. Plus, the federal government adopted 21,462 regulations from 1986 to 2006. The Court struck down 121—or about a half of a percent.[6]

When it comes to crime, the American Bar Association's Task Force on Federalization of Criminal Law stated, "So large is the present body of federal criminal law that there is no conveniently accessible, complete list of federal crimes." Best guesses from various sources put the estimated number close to 4,500.[7]

Building the Spending Monster

In addition to the laws and generally unruly size of the government, the government's spending has also continually increased, exploding in recent times. Much of that has to do with morphing from a protector of individual rights to a redistributor of money and a benefactor of crony interests.

According to *Welfare, the Family, and Reproductive Behavior: Research Perspectives*, public assistance morphed from the responsibilities of local areas (townships, counties, etc.) with states "becoming more and more involved over the last half of the nineteenth and the early twentieth century."[8]

The federal government did not get involved until the "New Deal programs of the 1930s established a precedent for federal responsibility in this area. Even so, such programs remained relatively small in the immediate decades after the 1930s, with only small numbers of recipients and small costs."[9]

Once you create a monster, it becomes impossible to control. And so we Frankensteined the government.

Spending on entitlements and other non-rights-protecting initiatives blew up from the 1960s onward, never reaching economies of scale. For example, on the jobs front, according to the Office of Management and Budget, the federal government has forty-seven different employment and training programs managed by fifteen disparate government agencies. Their spending in 2019 alone was $18.9 billion. However, employment ebbs and flows more based on fiscal policy and the government getting out of the way of businesses, which create jobs, and not meaningfully as a result of any of these programs.[10]

In his book, *Punting Poverty: Breaking the Chains of Welfare*, Damon Dunn explained that there are so many different programs that focus on poverty, it is hard even to know the count. He said:

The Congressional Research Service estimates that there are 102 separate federal programs. . . . Heritage Foundation estimates cover 93 different programs.

. . . Federal anti-poverty efforts list 104 programs for economic, community, and regional development based on the current Catalog of Federal Domestic Assistance. A search for

training programs brings up 599 different ones. While not
all are broadly available . . . these numbers illustrate how
a basic concept—the need to help the poor out of poverty,
exploded into hundreds of bureaucratic and often competing
divisions.[11]

Regardless of the program, there are very few changes resulting
in the betterment of people's positions and outcomes. It is not that
there is too little money or effort going into poverty; it is purely centrally planned government failure. That's the system that has failed,
not the capitalistic un-system that has lifted many others out of poverty worldwide.

It seems as if government is more incentivized to keep people on
these programs, thus keeping their power base, than to structure
effective programs.[12]

Even the way government names and accounts for spending is
backward vis-à-vis what government was set up to do. When you

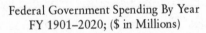

Federal Government Spending By Year
FY 1901–2020; ($ in Millions)

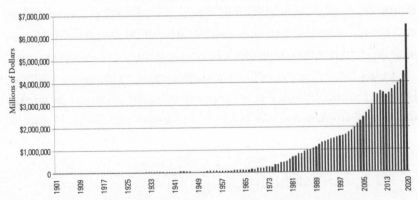

Source: "Historical Tables," Office of Management and Budget, The White House, https://www
.whitehouse.gov/omb/historical-tables/; "Fiscal Year 2020 Budget Summary Through September
2020," Bureau of the Fiscal Service, US Department of the Treasury, https://fiscal.treasury.gov/fçes
/reports-statements/mts/budget-summary-with-adjusted-differences-report-september-2020.pdf.

think of mandatory spending, you might think of things such as the military to protect your security and your rights, but that's called "discretionary" spending. What is called "mandatory" spending includes things that have nothing to do with enforcement of rights, such as entitlements like Social Security and Medicare that redistribute funds, not something set forth in the Constitution and not consistent with the protection of rights as the government's primary or sole function.

Spending has exploded over time. At the time of writing, federal debt (aka the amount owed as a result of cumulative federal government spending in excess of money—primarily taxes—taken in) was more than $27 trillion.

In 2019, US federal government spending increased to a record of more than $4.4 trillion, while in 2020, with the stimulus plans, it reached approximately $6.6 trillion.

The increase has proliferated in the past several decades. In 1981, the federal government spent $678 billion. By 1991, that was more than $1.3 trillion. A decade later, that was $1.9 trillion. In 2011, on the back side of the financial crisis, spending had exploded to $3.6 trillion, and government added almost another trillion in the last decade (before the COVID stimulus).

The explosion in spending is not justified by population growth. If you look back at the population change, it had grown only 15 percent or so since 2001, while spending increased by nearly 140 percent (pre-COVID). Now the US population's makeup is trending older, so that adds additional costs when government becomes involved in entitlements.

The State of the States

As individuals have given up their rights to the government at all levels, the states have likewise given up power to the federal government, but that doesn't make the states idle in their endeavors. At the state level, the "Government Unchecked" report cited previously noted that during the same period (1954 to 2002), state legislatures passed a whopping 1,006,649 laws![13]

Moreover, as state budgets have exploded, there has been a convoluted, cumbersome flow of money from individuals to the federal government back to the states in many forms. Think about how inefficient, not to mention weird, that is. Instead of paying for government at the local level directly, your tax dollars are sent to the federal government. Then Congress plays its games to figure out how much your state of residence gets back, which works out well for some states and poorly for others.

The federal government is involved in all kinds of things at the state level from a budget standpoint, from job training to health care to education. The funding for such endeavors exploded from $154.5 billion in 1991 to $318.5 billion in 2001 to nearly three-quarters of a trillion dollars in 2019. With the CARES Act aid, 2020 reached new records as well.

According to a May 2019 Congressional Research Service re-

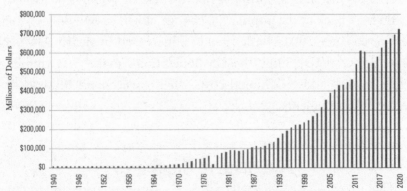

Federal Outlays to State and Local Governments
FY 1940–2019; ($ in Millions)

Source: "Contents of the Historical Tables," Table 12.1, The White House, https://www.whitehouse.gov/wp-content/uploads/2019/03/hist-fy2020.pdf.

port, "Federal Grants to State and Local Governments: A Historical Perspective on Contemporary Issues," and consistent with other research, the federal government, on average, accounts for about one-third of total state government funding but also more than half of state funding for health care and public assistance programs.[14]

What is also staggering at the state level is the extent to which some states subsidize others. A 2017 study by the Rockefeller Institute of Government analyzed how much residents of each state pay to the federal government compared with what they get back in terms of grants. Though states such as Virginia (coincidentally, perhaps, home to many people who work for the federal government, but probably not, as Maryland was also in the top ten recipients) received $10,301 per resident and Kentucky received $9,145 per resident, other states were at a substantial deficit. Illinois received $364 per resident less than was paid in, New York's deficit was $1,792 per resident, New Jersey's deficit was $2,368 per resident, and Connecticut's was a colossal $4,000 per resident. In total, New York's deficit was $35.6 billion in 2017, and New Jersey's was $21.3 billion, meaning that those states' taxpayers subsidized other states by their money being funneled through the federal government.[15]

This system is not what was envisioned in terms of a republic focused on preserving individual rights. It has the centralization of power and lacks the freedom Benjamin Franklin and his counterparts warned about hundreds of years ago.

Even if you buy into the notion the government should be involved in some of these things, based on its size, scope, and outcomes, you can tell they are not done well. It's impossible to do so at that size and especially when you remove the free market tenets and replace them with a behemoth central planning structure.

This has been demonstrated more than just anecdotally. Ruchir Sharma, chief global strategist at Morgan Stanley Investment Management, wrote:

The problem is that growing government involvement in the economy typically leads to lower productivity and weaker growth. A 2011 European Central Bank working paper found a "significant negative effect" of bigger government on per capita GDP growth in a set of 108 countries over the previous four decades. A recent report from BCA Research found a similar link in 28 major developed economies, including the U.S., over the last two decades.[16]

The scary reality is that if you define "democratic socialism" by how much of the economy the government provides or controls, "democratic socialism" is already here. It is estimated that, after backing out intergovernment transfers, such as between the federal government and the states, the government at all levels in the United States spends between $7.3 trillion and $8.2 trillion. With approximately 128.6 million households in the country, the government, in total, spends somewhere between $56,765 and $63,763 per household. In 2019, the median household income was $61,937. So the government is spending the equivalent of the full median household income per household every year. The Trojan horse of "democratic socialism" has been pushed right into Washington, DC, as well as every state of the union.[17]

We, the People

How have we, the people, allowed this to happen?

In July 1775, Founding Father John Adams wrote in a letter to his wife, Abigail, several lines that perfectly described the battle between emotion and reason:

Your Description of the Distresses of the worthy Inhabitants of Boston, and the other Sea Port Towns, is enough to melt an Heart of stone. Our Consolation must be this, my dear, that Cities may be rebuilt, and a People reduced to Poverty, may acquire fresh Property: But a Constitution of Government once changed from Freedom, can never be restored. Liberty once lost is lost forever. When the People once surrender their share in the Legislature, and their Right of defending the Limitations upon the Government, and of resisting every Encroachment upon them, they can never regain it.[18]

That's the issue. Many other entities can solve problems; communities and charities filled voids before big government existed in the United States. Free markets are always an option. We each can solve many of our own issues if we are not lazy. But turning over freedoms to government is a fool's errand. And since it has been done so often for so long it will take a lot of fighting and pushback to undo the damage that has been done.

The government is supposed to protect individual rights, not guarantee individual outcomes.

2020: Trading Much for Little

With the systematic and continued creep of government and the simultaneous weakening of individual rights, it is not a surprise that many people looked to government entities to have solutions and execute them vis-à-vis the coronavirus pandemic, nor that the government used the crisis as cover to ignore rights and make decisions in a centrally planned fashion.

In a country as big and diverse as the United States, and as the country is a republic, this is an arena in which some general guidance should have immediately led to decentralized action. However, the states became too comfortable with looking to the federal government while the president was trying to empower the states, which produced a gap in the timing of decisions. There was also a lot of passing the buck, finger-pointing, and lack of leadership.

Almost none of that was focused on empowering Americans to assess their own risk properly and take action. That was borne out of the decades of a progressive push to look to government instead of to personal accountability, which turned into a catalyst for individuals to follow the government like sheep to the economic slaughter and allow it to topple the economy at any and all costs. Shut down the economy? Sure, no problem. Spend like drunken sailors, funded with debt? As long as I get my stimulus check, why should I care? Let the Federal Reserve manipulate the markets, suppress interest rates, and bloat its balance sheet? Man, I don't even know what that means.

As Britt Raybould, a former state representative in Idaho, told me after her firsthand experience with government, "People are too willing to overlook all of the bad in the system so that they don't have to forgo the small benefits that they receive."[19] Sadly, this is the case even if the small benefits are greatly outweighed by the costs incurred by letting the system stay in the status quo.

Financially, the implications of turning to government have become disastrous. Based on estimates, it could take half a decade or longer to recover in parts of the economy; that is, if the country can get off the spending train. Otherwise, the United States may never recover.

As Ruchir Sharma wrote in "The Rescues Ruining Capitalism":

The world economy went into this pandemic vulnerable to another financial crisis precisely because it had already become so fragile, so heavily dependent on constant government help. Governments have offered increasingly easy credit and generous bailouts not only to soften the impact of every crisis since the 1980s but also to try to boost growth during the good times. . . .

The idea of government as the balm for all crises is appealing in the short term, but it ignores the unintended consequences.[20]

This leads to a game of groups and businesses banding together to lobby for benefits, maneuver for special treatment, and give up power to central planners in return for the game being tilted in their direction. It gives nobody a fair chance and only means more government, which enables more lobbying, begging, and maneuvering in a vicious cycle.

That enabled government in 2020 to send out helicopter cash, much of which went to those who weren't in need or, in the case of big businesses, saved companies that were already dying before the pandemic, without doing the basic work that would have preserved the economy.

That led to more small business closures, more zombie companies staying alive, and more government spending than the world has ever seen.

During the Great Recession, the United States saw the largest deficit in history in fiscal year 2009: government intervention led to deficit spending of 9.8 percent of that year's GDP. In FY 2020, total spending reached $6.6 trillion, with deficit spending of almost 14.5 percent of the prior year's GDP. Government accelerated the economic crisis, intervened in the crisis, and spent at historical levels, generating a $3.1 trillion deficit.[21]

That debt is a trade, burdening young people and their future ability to prosper and enriching big, connected cronies at the expense of smaller entities and individuals. But it is just one piece of the awful trade. Just because government isn't openly nationalizing industries, it doesn't mean it isn't slowly taking control of every industry. It's crushing small businesses and moving their employees to big businesses or onto the government dole, both outcomes that help increase the size, scope, and power of central planners.

As Americans have sold out to government and traded their individual rights for more central planning, the country has begun to look less like the United States of America and more like China.

CHAPTER 10

Losing the Branding on Capitalism

How a War of Words Led to Weakened
Individual Rights and Centralized Power

In the long war against small business, one of the biggest attacks has come in the language around business and capitalism, creating intentional misunderstandings, bad feelings, and a full-out campaign against the decentralization that stands in the way of more government power. АН

A bomb was dropped in this war on July 13, 2012, by then president Barack Obama, who said in a famous speech, "If you were successful, somebody along the line gave you some help. There was a great teacher somewhere in your life. Somebody helped to create this unbelievable American system that we have that allowed you to thrive. Somebody invested in roads and bridges. If you've got a business—you didn't build that. Somebody else made that happen."[1]

Aside from the fact that every taxpaying American pays for education, roads, and other services and not everyone builds a business, aside from the fact that things such as roads are part of the government-mandated protection of property rights, and aside from the fact that all of those things can be funded privately (and probably more efficiently) outside of government, imagine telling a small business owner who invested his or her life's savings, took on debt, worked the equivalent of two full-time jobs a week, and had the stress of his and others' livelihoods in the balance, that the government did more to make that happen than he or she did.

And with that, the leader of the country that is supposed to be synonymous with capitalism dealt capitalism and small business another substantial and unfair blow.

That sentiment gets absorbed into all kinds of rhetoric. When small businesses were largely damaged during the 2020 rioting, as discussed in chapter 6, those perpetrating and backing the looting made claims that it wasn't violence, or that it didn't matter because the businesses had insurance or more available funds (which is not only still immoral but in many cases for small businesses untrue).

For example, after coordinated August lootings that targeted various stores in Chicago's downtown and other shopping districts and vandalized restaurants, including many small businesses, Ariel Atkins, a BLM organizer in Chicago, told Chicago's WBEZ, "A lot of people are really attacking our pages. They're like, 'Oh, you support the looters.' And yeah, we do, 100%. That's reparations," further saying, "The whole idea of criminality is based on racism anyway."

She continued, "The fact that anybody gives a s*** about these businesses over what is happening in this city right now and the pain that people are in and the suffering that is taking place, I don't care."[2]

Envy politics ignores the reality that, other than the critical principle of equality in the eyes of the law, "fairness" in a free society is an emotional concept, not a rational one. If one person has more than another, regardless of the choices he or she made to secure that outcome, the far Left will argue that it isn't "fair" or "just" or that "you didn't build that." And as that happens, the concept of what capitalism is and what it stands for takes a hit.

Good System, Bad Branding

For all of its great successes, capitalism has found itself under attack largely because it has become the victim of consistently inaccurate branding.

Despite unparalleled wealth being created in the countries that have historically embraced elements of capitalism fairly well (such as the United States), wealth evaporating in those that have abandoned it (such as Venezuela), and incredible, positive changes occurring in those that have moved further toward it (such as China and India), capitalism itself has been widely and increasingly criticized.

Politicians, pundits, and even billionaires who have succeeded because of capitalism are putting aside concrete realities, including the fact that as millionaires and billionaires have been minted, their innovations have improved people's lives worldwide both directly and indirectly. Simultaneously, we have seen extreme poverty drop from half of the world's population in the 1970s to less than 10 percent today.

The criticisms of capitalism are vast. Capitalism is broken or flawed, we hear. Others complain that wealth creation is unequal. Some say that capitalists are "greedy" and the wealthy don't pay their "fair share"—or worse, that they "exploit" workers. People today don't have a fair shot at getting ahead!

These criticisms are usually empirically untrue or entirely misguided, so what is going on? In almost every scenario, people are blaming capitalism for problems created by central planning.

Language Matters

When people don't understand capitalism, they tend to be less willing to embrace ideas that are built upon it and more willing to embrace government-driven policies.

Though "free markets" sounds like something good, "capitalism" can sound as though someone is negatively capitalizing on something. That easily gets twisted by both bad actors and the generally misinformed into the concept of capitalizing at someone else's expense or even exploitation, both of which have no part in true free market capitalism.

The bait and switch on words continues. Phrases and concepts such as "greed" and "seeking profits" have turned into rallying points for a tribal war, provoking the masses to want to "eat the rich." Again, this is intentional. The ideas that stand against capitalism are inferior to it, so trying to paint capitalism as something that it isn't and creating misdirection and confusion are all part of a carefully crafted strategy.

If you ask people if they support small business, they will likely say "yes." However, if you ask them if they support what small businesses engage in—capitalism—there has been an increasing trend toward saying "no." A 2019 study conducted by YouGov found that 36% of millennials viewed communism favorably, and 43% of millennials thought that *The Communist Manifesto* better "guarantees freedom and equality" than the US Declaration of Independence or weren't sure.[3]

The YouGov poll also found that only about half of millennial and Gen Z respondents had a very or somewhat favorable view of capitalism, and 70 percent of millennials said they were extremely or somewhat likely to vote for a socialist. And a Gallup poll found that "nearly 50% of millennial and Gen Z respondents held a positive view of socialism."[4]

This bleeds into popular culture. If you have ever read *Teen Vogue*, a media site that reads more like communist propaganda than anything adjacent to fashion and lifestyle, you have undoubtedly stumbled onto one of its many anticapitalistic gems. They send out tweets like "Can't #endpoverty without ending capitalism!,"[5] ignoring the fact that capitalism has lifted more people out of poverty than any other force in the world, that it has shrunk extreme poverty from half the world in the 1970s to less than 10 percent today, and that socialism has failed—and caused misery, death, and famine—everywhere it has been tried. But don't let facts get in the way of a sassy tweet! Absurdly, its propaganda is displayed online next to advertisements for Walmart and Amazon, as well as a "style" section featuring articles such as "How to Have the Perfect Night In with These 7 Outfits" and "Ariana Grande Is Releasing a 'R.E.M.' Perfume. It'll Be Her Sixth."[6]

Cognitive dissonance seems to be a rampant issue. It's like the rapper Cardi B, known for a successful career that allows her to style herself luxuriously with matching Hermès Birkin bags worth thousands of dollars to her outfits. She even gave her husband $500,000 stacked inside a refrigerator for his birthday in 2019! However, despite being the poster child for capitalism and even posting online in 2018 a note to the government, "Uncle Sam, I want to know what you're doing with my f—ing tax money," she ultimately vocally supported Bernie Sanders and his socialist big-government policies.[7]

The disconnection and lack of understanding of financial and economic principles ultimately empower young people to believe and promote garbage that is further removed from reality. Another *Teen Vogue* piece lamented having to work, saying, "Selling your labor in a capitalist marketplace so you don't end up on the street is horrible and unnatural, and we shouldn't have to exist this way."[8] It's hard to know what the writer expects should happen or believes has happened since the beginning of time in some shape or form; perhaps that goods, services, and housing should be delivered by magic fairies while you lounge around doing yoga?

When this kind of drivel appears in *Teen Vogue*, young people start to believe that it must be fashionable to think this way.

Pop culture has, for years, been creating the delusion that productivity and income shouldn't be connected. It's why you see more and more proposals such as for universal basic income (UBI) and calls for "free" everything. It is also why when the government closed so many businesses, there was a whole group of people who didn't bat an eye or question how that could possibly work; they just demanded to be well paid to stay home.

It should also be noted that this is an attitude that isn't typically seen among immigrants, more among those raised in the United

States who have no context of what bad policies—or reality around the world—are like. It should be no surprise to find that around 43 percent of all Fortune 500 companies were founded by first- or second-generation immigrants to the United States or that immigrants overall are quite successful in pursuing the American Dream.[9]

Imagine escaping from a socialist regime to come to America and pursue freedom and opportunity, only to discover a bunch of naive Americans who want to push the country further toward central planning, force, and control!

What Is Capitalism?

Before I can talk through what has happened due to losing the branding around capitalism, it is crucial to define what capitalism is and isn't. At its core, capitalism is a method of distributing scarce resources based on the free choice, interactions, and free will of millions of individuals. It is contrasted to centrally planned economies, which means that the government takes control of the means of production and distribution of those same resources and/or a small number of people make the decisions regarding what's bought, what's sold, how it is distributed, who works where, and more on behalf of the masses.

When you think about resource allocation, political systems, and the interrelationships between them, I want you to think of a spectrum. On one side of the spectrum are individual freedom and choice. As you move along the spectrum with less freedom and choice, you move toward force and control at the other end.

Free-Market
Capitalism

Central Planning
Socialism
Communism

Freedom, Choice   Force, Coercion

The individual freedom and choice side is free market capitalism. When you think of capitalism, you should think of liberty.

As I noted above, capitalism is shorthand for free market capitalism and analogous to free markets. So you can use the terms interchangeably and think of them as the same.

Capitalism is an un-system rooted in freedom—a collection of individual actions made of free will. There is no central, coordinated design.

Under capitalism, every participant chooses how to participate, how much to participate, and how often to participate, in terms of production, labor, risk taking, or consumption. As millions or billions of participants do this, resources are allocated toward their best and most efficient uses. If there is a lack of demand for one good or service and a ton of demand for another, more resources move toward the item in demand.

The understanding of capitalism and free markets has been blurred by lack of financial literacy, political power grabs, and envy politics, causing people who in actuality embrace capitalism via their actions and benefit from it to dismiss it, to potentially dangerous effects.

Capitalism versus socialism and other government planning is truly a battle of the ideals of choice and freedom versus force and control.

It is also a battle of growth versus allocation. Capitalism focuses on continually "growing the pie" so that no matter what your slice is, how large it can become is never capped, and your piece is never dependent on someone else giving up some of theirs. Government and systems that focus on central planning are concerned with allocating one fixed pie.

Capitalism is also, at its core, a battle of human nature. Most people who hate capitalism don't hate the "system" of free exchange; they hate human nature. However, capitalism leverages and harnesses the power of human nature while socialism and other central planning pretend human nature doesn't exist.

Free Markets and Individual Rights

Though capitalism means freedom and choice, it doesn't mean that there is perfect information available at every moment in time, that every person or entity participating in the market acts rationally, or that human beings are not sometimes bad actors. However, over time, capitalism self-corrects based on individuals' choices in the market based on their own free will. It allows people to do what they want and desire—and reap the outcomes, good, bad, or otherwise, of those decisions. It doesn't assume that any group of people knows better than a given individual what will work for him or her and doesn't force the individual to comply with someone else's mandates.

A capitalist economy doesn't prevent a company at a given point in time from making goods or providing services that nobody wants to buy. However, the market corrects for that: a company won't be in business long if it doesn't adjust to demand. In a centrally planned economy, a country can end up with *all* the companies making goods or providing services that no one wants to buy, based on the decisions and directives of one or a few powerful people! (Such as the government stockpile of 1.4 billion pounds of cheese, to be discussed in the next chapter.)

Though there are different degrees of freedom in markets world-wide and even in different industries, the reality is that there is no pure capitalistic "system" in broad existence (i.e., countrywide) to-day. Yet we pursue the ideals of the free markets and capitalism not only because they are the founding ideals that are uniquely Ameri-can but also because we know that the closer we get to capitalism and free markets and their basic tenets, such as transparency and accountability, the better off we will be. The further away we get from them, the worse off we will be. This has been shown true over substantial data sets and time periods, at scale. Of course, a small cooperative may work for some time, but as a means of organizing an entire economy at scale, individual freedom and choice always win.

As stated above, in central planning, a small group of people believe in taking the power of decision making away from the individual and, instead, letting the powerful and connected in the government make decisions for millions of people. Whether they are put into those positions of power by a popular vote or by coup, it doesn't matter—they still take the freedom and choice away from individuals and centralize it. Maybe those government actors narcissistically believe they know better or perhaps they just use socialism as an excuse to try to sell their power grab, but in either scenario, history has proven they are wrong. There has been nowhere in history, regardless of time or geographic location, where, at scale, a handful of people making decisions led to better, more efficient allocations of resources and general outcomes over reasonable time periods than putting that freedom into the hands of individuals.

Though not all central planning is pure socialism (in terms of owning the means of production), central planning again creates force and shifts control for decision making and leads to the government choosing winners and losers.

Wherever and whenever socialism has been tried, it has failed. Though it has cemented power and corruption for its leaders, it has ended in poverty, hunger, and death for everyone else. As the economics professor and scholar with AEI Mark J. Perry said in his 1995 article "Why Socialism Failed," "Socialism is the Big Lie of the Twentieth century. While it promised prosperity, equality, and security, it delivered poverty, misery, and tyranny. Equality was achieved only in the sense that everyone was equal in his or her misery."[10]

Although progressives try to dress up socialism by sticking "democratic" in front of it, force and control that you vote for is putting lipstick on a pig.

Unfortunately, when people see a problem they believe needs

to be solved, they rarely ask, "Does this problem need widespread solving, outside of each individual tackling the issue?" and if the answer is yes, "Is government the only solution, or is there a better one?"

Do you think that people who are the smartest, most thoughtful, most benevolent, and any other qualities that make up the "best" people are politicians in government positions? Do you expect that you will always have the best people in government? Congress's approval rating hasn't been over 30 percent in more than a decade, and in 2019, the Pew Research Center found that only 17 percent of Americans trusted government always or most of the time.[11] From the political turnover in the United Kingdom to the utter decimation of Venezuela as a leading economic force, you can look to other countries to see that it's not just an American issue. So, if you don't have the best people, why give them more power and control? If you design a system that works solely if you find the best people to run it consistently, the system is flawed. The ultimate system should work regardless of who is in government.

That's precisely why understanding capitalism and its roots is essential. If, at a minimum, you do believe that some central planning is necessary for whatever reasons, at least recognizing the issues and limitations should help you to think through the downsides and work to minimize them. It is this level of strategic thought that is absent from the discourse.

There Are No "Versions" of Capitalism

It has become en vogue for those who want to push a social or political agenda to start talking about capitalism in stages. We are in late-stage capitalism, they say; our current version of capitalism is flawed, or capitalism today is broken. However, there aren't versions or stages of capitalism. Capitalism is something very concrete.

As noted above, regardless of where you live, even in the United States, you don't live in a pure capitalist system, but you should aspire to move toward one. Any perceived failures of economic organization don't come from free trade; they come from government interference, intervention, and/or cronyism, none of which are features of capitalism.

When we conflate this with capitalism instead of calling it what it is, we don't solve any problems and we get people hating what works due to confusion. We need to move more toward capitalism, not toward the government power and interference that causes these problems.

The Branding of Inequality

Concurrent with losing the branding on capitalism is the rise of branding around flawed concepts. For example, when the media, politicians, or progressive activists push the idea of inequality, they try to get you to buy into an emotional framing that defies common sense.

If it is automatically immoral for someone to have ten times as much money as you, why isn't it immoral for you to have ten times as much as someone else? The average annual income in Indonesia is approximately US $4,050 per year, or about 6.2 percent of the average annual income in the United States. The median net worth in Venezuela is zero (notably, before moving to central planning, the country's GDP in the mid–twentieth century was fourth in the world). Are you planning to donate 90-plus percent of your money to Indonesians or Venezuelans to make things more equal? Why should that obligation (or lack thereof) change simply because you live within the same landmass as someone else?[12]

When you use a comparative measurement such as "equalness," you are saying that a difference between two things is the relevant measure that needs to be paid attention to: disparity is bad, sameness is good.

Though the comparison of equality is a very relevant measure in terms of the treatment of people under the law and for the purposes of each of our rights, it is not for wealth or income. This is, among other reasons, because you have different inputs, and different inputs will get you different outputs—by choice. It is also not a relevant measure where you have the freedom and the infinite ability to create value and wealth, and where you are not trying to divide up a static amount (such as under a dictatorship, for example).

Let's dig into the notion of financial equality as a measurement. People in a certain area could all be rich but have wildly different amounts of wealth (millionaires versus billionaires). Or they could all be equal in wealth yet all in poverty (everyone has no retained wealth). Indeed, the highly unequal first scenario is preferable to the latter scenario, in which everyone has nothing yet there is no inequality.

Another example: people who make a million dollars a year and spend it all can have no net worth, while those who make the same amount, save, and invest their income could become worth tens of millions over several decades. Those differing behaviors and choices produce a ton of inequality—no net worth versus multimillionaire status—among people who make the same seven-figure income.

When you focus on inequality in the context of financial metrics, it not only makes little sense but takes the focus away from the problem. If you believe that poverty is a problem, it's something worth discussing and addressing, but it is not a problem related to not being equal in a free society. "Equal in poverty" is not an objective to pursue.

This is relevant to the branding around both capitalism and equality because inequality is a feature, not a bug, of capitalism. When people interact freely in a system, they will have different values and objectives. This will lead to different inputs and ultimately different outputs. Depending on your level of education, how much you devoted yourself to earning good grades in school, the type of work you choose, the hours you work, where you live, how you spend, how you invest, how much risk you take on in your investments, whether you produce a vast life-changing innovation or prefer to spend more time with your family—all of these decisions and more will produce different outcomes. Moreover, money is only one form of currency and one store of value; people value health, time, relationships, hobbies, and other factors that all contribute to one's quality of life and ultimately their income and then wealth in some way. However, we never talk about or measure those nonfinancial metrics, probably because they are difficult to quantify because they lack the homogeneity of money.

Because many people do not grasp the aforementioned concept, inequality of financial measures becomes exploited. Though inequality itself isn't a problem, it becomes a problem when translated into envy. Inequality porn is a calculated ruse used by media, politicians, and others to create class resentment and leverage envy politics for their own power, as they work to shift the focus from poverty to envy-based class warfare.

So the branding of inequality inappropriately ends up impacting the branding of capitalism, which ends up hurting the small businesses that embody capitalism.

Freedom Is Choice

It is also important to clarify another element of capitalism and its branding. We often equate capitalism with money instead of freedom and choice. For those who don't want to chase financially oriented goals, having free choice is also the American Dream. Whether you want to be an engineer or a dance teacher, it's your choice. If you choose to pursue a different set of wants than purely financial success, you are better off than in other systems that don't afford you that choice.

The choices are all still available to anyone. You can choose to work in a job or profession you love and are passionate about, live in the moment or reside in the big city and perhaps not have much in savings, knowing it is your freedom to make those choices that align with your priorities. However, if your goals are different, you can't lament that you aren't living the dream based on your own decisions and actions.

The opportunity to pursue freedom of choice and enjoy your own standard of success is why people from every pocket of the world clamor to come to America and participate in the American Dream.

The American Dream is alive and well; however, it's not a fairy tale, and as one of my Twitter followers pointed out, it's not a guarantee, either. Yet it still presents the best opportunity in the world for those who embrace it.

If you want to have a better financial life, you engage in delayed gratification. You work extra hours early in life. You don't take on debts unless they will help you earn more. You get a job that will lead to earning more money. This may mean doing things you don't want to do, but that's life and that's the same sacrifice that every previous generation had to make. However, in a capitalist system, you could also work part-time in the arts, live frugally with a bunch of roommates, and spend the rest of your time volunteering.

Having choices is capitalism, and that is beautiful. No other system allows you the same range of options.

Capitalism and Economic Mobility

Another way we have lost branding around the concept of capitalism is through the myth that the top 1 percent—or even the top 50 percent—is always the same people.

Though some people complain that the wealthiest were born with silver spoons in their mouths, inherit their money, and therefore nobody else has a chance, the numbers say otherwise.

Business Insider shared statistics showing incredible economic mobility in the United States: "over 50% of Americans will find themselves in the top 10% of earners for at least one year of their lives. More than 11% will find themselves in the top 1%. . . . And close to 99% of those who make it into the top 1% of earners will find themselves on the outside looking in within a decade."[13] This means that people at the "bottom" and the "top" of earners change frequently.

Additionally, in the United States, 80 percent of all millionaires are first generation. In 2018, 675,000 brand-new millionaires were created, and that's just in one year.[14]

On the small business front, pre-COVID, the average small business owner was able to make more than $71,000 a year, and nearly 4 million small business owners built their way into making six figures or more a year.[15]

Has every rich person truly earned every dollar of their wealth? Of course not. But for many of the richest, they did so with the assistance of the government, whether by protecting their pricing, their market share, or, in the case of Elon Musk, via billions of dollars in special government subsidies. That's all a problem, but not with free markets. It's a problem with government.[16]

Because capitalism enables growth, capitalists have an abundance mindset. There is more available for everyone. Capitalists want other people to do well (or who else will they exchange with in the market)? Socialists and central planners have a scarcity mindset and focus on division and redistribution instead of growth.

Of course, that is with the exception of the magical unicorns and fairies crowd, who, in opposition to their own arguments of the game being rigged and limited, also delusionally believe that money grows on trees and that despite all evidence to the contrary, prosperity is a natural state of being. These folks believe that everyone could stay home, get UBI, free health care, and free school or that companies could be forced to pay everyone six-figure wages, and there would still be food, cars, new iPhones, and more.

2020: A Spotlight on Restricting Freedom

Losing the branding around capitalism extends to capitalism's core principles. The debate around school openings during 2020 is the perfect example of how capitalism and its tenets can work, even when there is some government intervention.

As people have bought into giving more powers up to the government, we have seen more poor outcomes, as centralizing political power always stands in opposition to free choice, free will, transparency, accountability, and other free market, capitalistic concepts.

Take the city I live in, Chicago; the Chicago Public Schools (CPS) system spends almost $17,000 a year per student for school instruction and operations, not including capital expenditures or long-term debt payments. However, its output has been horrible. Union control, in concert with the political power the unions wield, has created a stranglehold that has shifted schools away from any benefits associated with capitalism.[17]

In September 2019, EducationWeek noted that "America's public school system today costs taxpayers over two-and-a-half times more than it did half a century ago—far outstripping changes in enrollment over that time. When federal, state, and local spending is taken together, it stands as one of government's most-expensive endeavors."[18]

In fact, the United States spends more money per student on education than just about any other country in the world, 51 percent higher than the global average. Even the "democratic socialist" countries that you hear about from progressives—America has outspent them, but not with better outcomes, mind you, according to the Organisation for Economic Co-operation and Development's annual report of education indicators.[19]

According to the National Center on Education and the Economy (NCEE), US students rank sixth in math, a half year to three and a half years behind Germany, Canada, Finland, Singapore, and South Korea. The average student in Singapore is ahead of his or her US counterparts not only by 3.5 years in math but also by 2.5 years in science and 1.5 years in reading. According to a 2018 analysis by *The Guardian* of those data, US students rank behind those in countries such as the Netherlands and Estonia in overall education. *The Guardian* also spoke to Marc Tucker, the NCEE president, who noted, "The issues are systemic . . . and getting worse."[20]

Not only is the United States lagging behind other countries in education, but it also isn't keeping up with its own metrics. In a 2013 study for the Friedman Foundation for Educational Choice (now EdChoice), Benjamin Scafidi noted that the academic outcomes of K–12 education in the United States have not increased in lockstep with the growth of teachers and administrators, saying, "Public high school graduation rates peaked around 1970, and government data show reading scores on the National Assessment of Educational Progress (NAEP) fell slightly between 1992 and 2008. Math scores on the NAEP Long-Term Trend were stagnant during the same period."[21]

How is the United States spending more than almost every other country on the planet and not getting the right outcomes? This is a not-surprising result of large-scale government intervention and union cronyism that could be fixed by capitalism.

Now, under pure capitalism, the government wouldn't be involved in education at all. However, I am a pragmatist and not an absolutist like some others. I realize that such a transition is not likely to happen soon, if at all, and that at least in the short term, taking government out of education could create an absence of opportunities for those who live in disadvantaged areas or were born into a family that doesn't value education. However, that doesn't mean that capitalistic principles can't apply.

In the realm of education, that can mean more school choice, reducing union power, and other shifts to give more freedom to the "consumers," the families and students of each school. It is preposterous to think the only way someone has the ability to take their business elsewhere and have choice in the current education system is to bear the burden of moving (a very high barrier), homeschooling, or, for the wealthy, sending their kids to private schools or alternative learning arrangements at an additional cost to taxes.

Take what happened in July 2020, when the CDC put forth the guidance that schools should open in the fall. That proclamation was immediately politicized. Those who were in opposition to either the Trump administration or sending their kids—or themselves—to school thought the government was too heavy-handed and was putting them in danger. Others who supported the Trump administration or the notion of sending their kids or themselves back to school argued that the government should force teachers and students back; if nurses were essential workers, if big box retail cashiers were essential workers, why were teachers not essential workers?[22]

However, if free market forces were at work in education, people could make the right choices for themselves and their families. Why should anyone, from social media pundits to a bunch of government politicians, be able to make that risk call for you and your family?

If free market forces were at work, instead of teachers' unions tied to government officials directing negotiations, teachers who wanted to work in schools could and those who wanted to teach remotely also could, to the extent that there was a demand for each. Moreover, these activities would likely be at different pay scales.

Likewise, as a parent, based on your family's circumstances, you could send your child to school or set up remote learning from home. Or perhaps you'd prefer to take the dollars allocated to your child and pay for a tutor, private schooling, or some other educational option.

Options. Freedom. Choice. That is what capitalistic principles would bring to education, and people would never be in a situation where a government entity could force students or teachers to either work or stay home at their whim. It's the perfect illustration of how the too-big-to-succeed government was structured for failure; it was apparent before, but 2020 illustrated it with bold font and an exclamation point.

In fact, while the government-run schools struggled in 2020, private schools thrived. According to a study conducted in late November 2020, reported on by The Hill, despite the general economic upheaval, independent private K–12 schools were "flourishing." Many parents who were able to go to the free markets exercised that option. Seventy percent of the independent schools surveyed had seen their enrollment increase or stay the same, and at the time of the survey, none of them was on a fully virtual schedule; 75 percent were fully open, and the other 25 percent used a hybrid model. The schools reported having detailed COVID protocols that they were able to quickly put into place.[23]

This example also illustrates the danger of losing the branding around capitalism. Central planners use these tactics to create power and a stranglehold of bad policies. Because of the size and power of the government, and in turn its cronies, such as the teachers' unions, it becomes incredibly difficult to unwind these bad policies once they take hold. We need to do more dismantling, not set up more challenges and roadblocks, if we want to get the country back on track, from its heart to its economic foundation.

A Dangerous Cycle

Whether it is selling inequality porn, the greed narrative, or any other branding meant to soil the name of capitalism, this bad branding keeps people focused on symptoms instead of root causes. For example, when you focus on the meaningless differential measure of wealth instead of poverty, you approach the issue with a scarcity mindset and misdirect the concern toward what other people have. This creates a blind spot for solutions and begets more government intervention.

You end up believing that some magic entity will put your interests ahead of its own and take better care of you than you would or could yourself. But that's far from the case and is not rational behavior. As Damon Dunn of Pacific Research Institute said in his book, *Punting Poverty*, "Is Mark Zuckerberg teaching his kids that the best they can expect in life is a government handout? No. And no parent should. Otherwise, we will doom our children to a life enslaved by government-imposed limits."[24]

When the focus is shifted away from free market solutions to more government, you end up with more government dependency, a bigger government, and a lack of initiative for people to lift themselves out of poverty. And thus, the big-government cycle continues— lather, rinse, repeat—until we get more and more government from which we can't get away.

As fewer people understand the tenets and benefits of capitalism, it is easy to get further away from it.

How to Win at the Branding Game

Until branding is fixed around concepts such as capitalism, the masses won't understand those concepts and principles. They will fight against the free market and push for more big government, even when their principles say otherwise—like the same people wanting to "defund the police" for individual rights violations who don't understand that they are pushing for more free market intervention and principles.

To take back the branding around capitalism, talking more about free markets or free market capitalism and working to associate capitalism with free choice correctly can help.

I also suggest eliminating the use of crony capitalism and calling out its misuse while replacing it with cronyism and the reminder that cronyism is a government function, not a free market function.

In addition to shifting language, it is important to point out where people have benefited under free market capitalism by choice, particularly if they have decided to trade financial metrics for other ones. If someone is pursuing a passion or vocation that pays less because they enjoy it, that's their choice to participate in the market by putting nonfinancial objectives first.

Free market capitalism needs to be decoupled from politics because free markets are antipolitics. Though Democratic policies lean more toward big government in general and in principle, both major US political parties bear responsibility for the ballooning size and scope of the government, cronyism, and non–free market legislation.

It may come to the point where words and concepts need to be rebranded fully (heck, that seems to be working for the far Left these days, when words no longer mean anything); so if that's the strategy, maybe classical liberalism needs to be reengaged, or new terms and concepts need to emerge.

We need a push for more people who not only say they are in favor of small government, fiscal conservatism, and related principles but who actively work to make those happen. Honesty is important. Republicans have hugely expanded government under their leadership while preaching fiscal conservatism; at least the Democrats are honest about their intentions.

Creating wealth, which capitalism has done worldwide, is an

infinite opportunity and dividing up wealth, which is a government function since they create nothing, is a finite exercise. That needs to be said over and over again.

More on Language, Greed, and Profits

There are other branding issues related to capitalism to address. One of the biggest criticisms of the free market, capitalism, or capitalists themselves relates to the label of greed. We are told repeatedly that the system itself and its participants are "greedy" by those who oppose it. But is the opposition to greed a criticism of capitalism or human nature? And does the obsession with greed and capitalism provide another objection that obfuscates the ills of central planning?

Greed is often defined as an intense and selfish desire for something, including wealth, status, power, food, material goods, and so on. The connotation is that people are pursuing and keeping more of those items than they need.

There are two critical issues with this being a criticism of capitalism. Unless you are coming to the argument in bad faith or finding the exception-to-the-rule saints among us, pretty much everyone acts in their self-interest; this is not particular to capitalism. To pretend that isn't the case is denying fundamental human nature that dates back to the beginning of time.

In terms of pursuing and keeping more than you need, again, that is human nature and is rampant in every facet of life. In developed nations, people typically seek to live in more square footage than they need, eat more than they should, have more clothes and shoes than are necessary to keep covered, and so on. This isn't any moral failing but a reality that keeps people productive.

Given that a propensity to act in self-interest exists and that the citizens of all developed countries have more than they need, the inherent benefit of capitalism is that it harnesses that greed for the benefit of all in the "system," while socialism pretends that human nature and greed don't exist, to the detriment of all but those who are in power.

Business Greed Is Good

I will channel my best Gordon Gekko from the classic 1980s movie *Wall Street* here and say that the pursuit of profit and avoidance of losses in capitalism is what makes the system work so well, and if that is considered greed, then greed is good.

Going back to the famed economist Thomas Sowell's definition of economics as the allocation of scarce resources, in capitalism, pursuing profits helps to allocate resources efficiently and it keeps companies competitive with one another. Thinking about this on the most basic level, if a company (aka market participant) is not serving its customers appropriately via the right products, services, pricing, and so on, customers will go elsewhere.

What does that mean in everyday terms? Let's say we have the Evil Chocolate Company (ECC), which makes an industry standard 6 percent profit on its chocolate. So for every $1 in chocolate products it sells, it makes six cents of profits. If ECC sells $1 billion worth of chocolate in a year, it will make $60 million a year. The owners of ECC and its management would like to make more money (they are greedy). However, the market will let it maximize its profits only if it aligns with customers' benefits. If it raises the price of a chocolate bar from $1 to $2 to try to increase its profits, customers may say, "Well, the chocolate is good, but not two-dollar-a-bar good—I'm going to buy my chocolate from Joe's Chocolate instead." If ECC uses an inferior ingredient that costs less to boost profits, customers will notice that the chocolate isn't as tasty. ECC can't keep increasing its profits infinitely because at some point, customers will start to say, "I'm out." Losing customers is not a profitable business strategy; if that happens, the company will make less money or possibly go out of business.

As there are always other companies also seeking to be greedy— i.e., make lots of money—Evil Chocolate Company must continually innovate, service its customers well, and maintain fair prices to compete with the existing and new entrants into the market. If its pricing, offering, service, or any other facet of its business isn't up to snuff, a competitor will be able to lure its customers away. Competition, a cornerstone of the free market, serves to lower prices and increase quality for the consumer. So the greed of the new and existing entrants of the market creates checks and balances under capitalism.

The same thing happens with pay. If ECC doesn't pay enough money to its workers, it won't attract good workers or employees will leave for another job and the quality of its products or customer service will suffer. Then, as I said before, if that happens, customers won't buy the products and there will be no excess profits for the company. The company management wants to maximize profits, so they are greedy until the point where being so stops benefiting all parties.

Because you are not forced to buy chocolate from ECC—or anyone else, for that matter—and because you may choose to eat chocolate or substitute a multitude of other foods, any company you want to support, you can, and those you don't want to support, you don't have to. These individual, free choices, multiplied by millions of people in the market every day, impact everything from which companies stay in business to the products they offer.

This may seem trivial, but balancing company operations with market feedback is quite hard to do, and it's why the most profitable companies find it a challenge to stay at the top. This, again, self-regulates corporate greed.

It is also worth noting while there are always new entrants in a free market competing, the government has no competition. This lack of competition takes away any incentive to do the best for its "customers": the citizens.

Government Greed

Having a free market allows for an incredibly efficient distribution of goods and services. This is very different from any kind of government planning, which doesn't allow for the free choice of all individual market participants to provide information on resource allocation. Instead, a few people decide how many—if any—chocolate bars are made. Moreover, there is no mechanism to ensure that pricing or quality is up to snuff or that resources are allocated efficiently and appropriately.

Our greedy human nature is also present in not just companies but also consumers, who naturally want the best product for the lowest price. Greed also presents in workers who want to make more money or get other benefits for their labor. When all of these forces work together, greed creates the perfect balance to ensure that all participants in the system benefit.

Socialism—or any type of central planning that moves away from free choice—misses the mark. Even with the most complex financial models at their disposal, individuals lack the ability to replicate what the market does. This is why in so many socialist regimes people starved to death, not because food wasn't available, but instead because lack of market efficiency stopped the food from getting to those who needed it. (I suggest you read Sowell's book *Basic Economics* for a full understanding of this and other economic concepts.)

If you want to see incompetence in action, have you ever used government services? How do they compare to the services of those who must compete for your business? It is not difficult to see the difference that motivation provides.

The Company Is Greedy, but I'm Not!

Greed always seems to come from the perspective of "not me but thee." If you were to ask a room full of people if they have ever dealt with a person or company that is greedy, they would undoubtedly say they have. Ask the same people which of them is greedy, and you are likely to hear crickets.

A frequent objection is that companies are greedy and take advantage of circumstances. For instance, take Uber, the ride-sharing app and service used throughout the world for rides on demand. It works by incentivizing individuals to want to drive, so there is enough supply of drivers to meet the user riders' demand.

Sometimes there are more prospective riders available in an area than drivers who are willing to provide rides. This often happens at times such as rush hour or on certain holidays. So what does Uber do to solve this? It raises the price, which in its app is called "surge pricing." I have heard many people complain that Uber is greedy for its surge pricing practices. It isn't greed but rather a mechanism to solve the imbalance of supply and demand. Or, if you want to call it greedy, greed is again good!

On the supply side, a driver who might not be willing to work during rush hour or New Year's Eve—lots of traffic and drunk passengers may not be worth it for a standard fare—may be enticed to work for the higher fare. The extra money makes it worth it to him, and that brings more drivers into the market.

On the demand side, some riders who were willing to take an Uber at regular pricing will find the increased pricing not worth it and instead take a taxi or a bus, carpool, or walk. This decreases the number of potential cars needed to service riders at the time.

Ultimately, the change in pricing helps those who value the ride at that particular time get a ride. It's not greed; it's the genius of the free market.

Funny enough, if things were slow at a specific point in time, when Uber had many available drivers but not enough riders, it could offer you a coupon or other discount to incentivize you to utilize the service. That would give you not the regular market price but a price below that. If you accept it, does that make you greedy? I mean, you are considering only your own interests and not how it might affect the company or the driver, right?

The answer: no, it doesn't. It makes you human, and that interaction is captured in the free market appropriately as well.

Just be clear about one thing: it is no more greedy for a company to raise prices in periods of increased demand than it is for you to use a coupon to take advantage of slower demand. And remember, everyone benefits. If there is no benefit to one party, they will not participate.

On the government side, while people label the pursuit of profits or market adjustments for high demand as "greedy," those same people bafflingly never think that the government is greedy or that advocating for taking one person's hard-earned money to be transferred to someone else at the whim of an elected official is greedy, either.

As Thomas Sowell put it, "I have never understood why it is 'greed' to want to keep the money you have earned but not greed to want to take somebody else's money." That goes back to bad branding.

Furthermore, when someone brings up greed, where is the line? Is it only greedy for me to want to keep what I have earned? What about other stuff? Why is it always just currency and investments? Is it greedy for me to want to keep a painting on my wall? The painting is my money turned into a good. If it is okay for me to keep a good, why is it different to keep the currency before it is turned into a good? What if the painting is a Picasso worth tens of millions of dollars? Do I need to sell my Picasso because I don't need it? What if I have three? When you start making arbitrary lines of what is greedy and what property you should be allowed to keep, you kill the principle of individual rights, including property rights.

Keep asking questions: Are politicians greedy? Is the government greedy? Why do we have financial and related responsibilities to people occupying the same landmass, and where do they end? How much more do you have than the average person in Venezuela? (As noted earlier in this chapter, the median net worth in Venezuela at the time of this writing was $0.) When you get away from a moral code and you start playing the greed game, even if you are among the most impoverished persons in America, you are going to be considered greedy in a worldwide assessment.

These arguments are discussions of emotion, not logic or reason. They are also not of principle. There is no mechanism to say what is enough nor a moral authority for one person to dictate what another should be doing with their life, liberty, and pursuit of happiness. Therefore, we need to push back on these arguments and recapture the branding or risk it being used as a ruse to beget more government and the inferior outcomes that come with it.

But Isn't Acting in Your Own Self-Interest Bad?

There will still be people who argue against human nature and say that you should be concerned with others or the group and not yourself. They will say that acting in your self-interest is wrong or greedy. As mentioned above, it's human nature to prioritize your own needs and the needs of those with whom you have relationships. Is that bad? Under capitalism, no.

As Adam Smith wrote in *An Inquiry into the Nature and Causes of the Wealth of Nations*, "It is not from the benevolence of the butcher, the brewer, or the baker that we expect our dinner, but from their regard to their own interest."[25]

That's to say that you don't get all of the modern conveniences and luxuries, or even your basic needs filled, because you are waiting around for a bunch of Mother Teresas to take care of you. Your needs are filled because other people are serving their own interests. Butchers and bakers pursue their skill to take care of themselves both directly and indirectly, by trading their output to others who desire it for money, which they can then use to buy the things they want.

Self-interest fuels the markets. That's not to say that people aren't generous and do things for others, too. The United States has ranked as the most generous in the entire world for more than a decade and Americans gave approximately $450 billion to charity in 2019 alone, hardly consistent with the reputation of greedy capitalists. But in terms of doing for others, the difference is whether it should be done by free choice or by force and whether you should have a direct say in how you help.[26]

Contrast this to socialism or central planning. What happens when those who have unmitigated power use force and coercion to take away freedom of choice and instead make their own decisions for the masses? Greed, in that case, is bad. There is no counterbalancing market force. Sure, you can argue that you can vote some people out, but the structure is in place. Once it is in place, it becomes more difficult to tear down.

Think about the government in 2020. While others were struggling, jobs were lost, and businesses shut down, did politicians take a pay cut in solidarity? You can probably guess the answer—a resounding "no."

Greed is good in capitalism because it leverages it in a market "system." Greed is terrible in a socialist system because it leads to a small number of people making decisions on behalf of everyone else and cementing their power at someone else's expense, not their benefit.

To believe in socialism, you have to think that greed doesn't exist. You have to think that people don't seek out power and their own self-interests in benefits. If you believe that greed exists, you should want capitalism.

CHAPTER 11

Trading Capitalism for Cronyism

*Why the "Game Being Rigged" Is Coming from
Government, Not Capitalism*

By the end of April 2020, around one-third of the coronavirus deaths
in Indiana had been in nursing homes and long-term care facilities. Though many other states were reporting data on a facility-by-
facility basis, according to the *Indianapolis Star*, the state of Indiana
was withholding those data and relying on facilities to report statistics directly to families. Though Indiana governor Eric Holcomb
blamed it on private enterprise, when the *Indianapolis Star* had in-
vestigated Indiana's nursing homes the previous month, it had found
that 90 percent of the state's facilities "are owned by county hospitals, which are units of local government," and received billions of
dollars in public money, including Medicaid and Medicare payments.

The *Star*'s investigation also revealed that the hospitals had, over
the two previous decades, diverted north of $1 billion in federal pay-
ments for nursing homes to unrelated projects, many of which were
undisclosed by county hospitals.

The pressure caused by the discovery pushed Indiana government officials to agree to share aggregate facility data but not data
on a facility-by-facility level. The *Indianapolis Star* reported advocates as saying that the entire scenario "reeks of cronyism" and did
a disservice to the state's residents. A frustrated resident who had
been trying to get information on a facility his mother was in was
quoted as saying, "I'm guessing the nursing home association has a

very close relationship with the current administration, so they are trying to block it."[1]

It is not surprising that we would see cronyism playing a substantial role in the 2020 fallout because it has been an increasing factor in government creep, power, and, ultimately, failure. It's also a pillar of the war on small businesses.

To understand that and why it is the antithesis of capitalism and protection of individual rights and ultimately how it has created a government burden that has played a significant role in 2020, it is vital to understand what cronyism is and is not.

"Crony Capitalism" Is to Capitalism as Chinese Checkers Is to Checkers (i.e., Cronyism Is Not Capitalism)

To understand cronyism, we have to compare and contrast it to capitalism, with which it is often confused. We often hear as an objection to capitalism that "the game is rigged" and that "the few and powerful get special treatment." However, though the blame is misplaced on capitalism, what those decriers are objecting to is not free markets but government power.

Inexplicably, people who raise those issues typically think that more government power is the solution.

The concept of capitalism and its free market foundation means that companies must compete in the market for customers, talent, and capital based on innovations, risk, product differentiation, customer service, and other tools at their disposal. A free market allows any person or entity to enter the market at any time and try to compete on those factors. Furthermore, no entity receives any special advantages it hasn't earned.

However, government power—without exception—leads to

interference with the free markets under the label of cronyism. Cronyism is loosely defined as awarding special advantages to friends and connections, not based on merit, but based on relationships and favors, typically with the expectation of some type of returned favor or support in the future.

As my friend the bestselling author Bob Burg says, "crony capitalism" is to capitalism as Chinese checkers is to checkers: they have nothing in common except for part of their respective names. I agree and take it a step further—I do not even call cronyism by that unfortunate colloquial term "crony capitalism," and I ask you to differentiate between the two as well.

Cronyism happens when government moves away from its job of protecting individual and property rights that set the foundation for free market competition and toward picking winners and granting favors with their power. Big government and central planning enable cronyism because people seek out power and benefits—again, that's fundamental human nature. However, government planning doesn't have the smooth mechanisms the free market has to make that work to everyone's advantage (by creating lower prices, for example).

Via cronyism, the government doles out favors and benefits in several areas and industries to nonprofits, unions, other government entities, and corporations alike. As it relates to the economy, these may take the form of favorable legislation, subsidies, tax treatment, bailouts, or even government-mandated monopolies. None of these is a component of capitalism, and all are fundamentally opposed to the tenets of capitalism.

Cronyism is big business for politicians; it helps them get reelected and "get things done." Though lobbying isn't the only way cronyism presents itself, it is one good proxy to help illustrate its influence, particularly on the economy. It has been estimated that, as of 2019, total lobbying expense was a whopping $3.5 billion a year. One can surmise that the organizations spending those billions have to earn a return on that "investment" to make it worthwhile to spend, so the "payback" (in terms of beneficial impact to supporters) is many times that.[2]

As the lobbying expert Lee Drutman wrote in a piece for *The Atlantic*:

> business lobbying has built itself up over time, and the self-reinforcing quality of corporate lobbying has increasingly come to overwhelm every other potentially countervailing force. It has also fundamentally changed how corporations interact with government—rather than trying to keep government out of its business (as they did for a long time), companies are now increasingly bringing government in as a partner, looking to see what the country can do for them.[3]

This is the fundamental shift from embracing free markets and capitalism to allowing government to choose winners and losers or at least give some special rules to some players or teams.

Cronyism in Action

The government creep enabling more government power has been building over many decades. Back in the nineteenth century, most lobbying took place at the state level, as the federal government had a smaller purview at the time and was not involved in many economic matters.[4]

In the first half or so of the twentieth century, nonbusiness special interest groups and unions were the primary crony influence in politics. However, in the latter half of the century, changes in campaign laws and the rise of so-called soft money (as the Center for Responsive Politics defines it, funneling money through corporations and unions because those groups were not officially tied to a particular political campaign) shifted that. And of course, the Supreme Court ruling in the 2010 case *Citizens United v. Federal Election Commission* that corporations were, in effect, people, thus removing the expenditure limits for corporations and labor unions on "electioneering communications," quickly led to the birth of "Super-PACs" and, shortly thereafter, the most expensive election cycle in history.[5]

However, even back in the late 1800s and early 1900s, powerful business owners knew that only government intervention could beat the free markets. In *The Case Against the Fed*, Dr. Murray Rothbard recounted the story of how the Morgans (the noted and influential financiers and businessmen) tried to create cartels in the railroad industry to increase profits. However, the free markets kept winning; someone would always break the cartel pact for his own interest and lower prices to get more business. The Morgans could not dominate the free market.[6]

The only way they could dominate was with the help of the government. So they partnered with the federal government to regulate the industry and restrict competition. That resulted in the creation of the Interstate Commerce Commission to "enforce the cartel that they could not achieve on the free market."[7]

Cronyism and government creep have gone hand in hand, creating a vicious cycle that cements more power and money for the government, which they use to "feed" special interests, including businesses, which then drives more money and support into politics and continues the cycle. The outcome of the government side of this equation can be seen in a number of proxies, including the size of budgets, deficits, and overall debt.

In the early 1900s, governments at the state, local, and federal levels were spending only about 7.5 percent of GDP, a number that has ballooned well past 30 percent, even before 2020's "emergency" expenditures. Federal spending alone before the COVID pandemic had mushroomed past 20 percent of GDP.[8]

By the year just prior to 2020's insanity, which ended from a federal fiscal perspective on September 30, 2019, the federal government ran a budget deficit of nearly $1 trillion. Despite the booming economy and just more than 4 percent growth in "revenue" (mostly taxes collected), continued increases in government spending, including on interest, put the US budget gap back into a territory not seen since earlier in the decade (during the Great Recession).

Though the US population grew by around 15 percent between 2001 and the end of FY 2019, government spending increased by nearly 140 percent. And with around $23 trillion accumulated to that point (now many trillions in excess of that, due in part to general overspending and in part to "emergency" COVID spending), every dollar of the deficit adds to the total outstanding US debt, as debt financing is pretty much the only tool the government uses to finance that overspending.

More spending means more power and control for the government. More agencies, more regulations, and more centralized control ensued.

At the state level, in November 2019, The Center Square analyzed the State Expenditure Report by the National Association of State Budget Officers and found that state spending had been increasing, on average, for the previous thirty-three years, by about 5.6 percent per year (5.7 percent in FY 2019). And an analysis by the Pew Charitable Trusts found that the second largest source of income for the states is the federal government (again, you send your tax payment to the federal government, which then sends some of it back to your home state and some to other states, acting as a "clearinghouse" of sorts). In 2017, Pew found that federal revenue accounted for an average of 32.4 percent of total state revenue, demonstrating the close ties between federal and state spending.[9]

According to Pew, the states also reported nearly one trillion dollars in unfunded pension costs and more than $1 trillion combined in unfunded retiree health care liabilities and outstanding debt. However, reports of the actual unfunded liabilities at the state level are widely pegged in the $6 trillion to $7 trillion range.[10]

How does this tie back together? As a recent report by Clive S. Thomas, Ronald J. Hrebenar, and Anthony J. Nownes on lobbying noted, the increasing regulatory role of government has been a major impetus for many special interests to become politically active. As regulation increases, more money goes into lobbying, which begets increased regulation, becoming a cycle that has been a significant force in ballooning the size and scope of government at all levels.[11]

Power in All Forms, at All Levels

The ways that cronyism takes hold encompasses many forms. Below I go through a handful of them, so you can get a sense of the places where government power and special favors seep into the markets and how politics and cronyism create a vicious cycle of enablement and game rigging.

Subsidies and Special Tax Treatment

States and cities across the country have various ways they use tax treatment and other subsidies to incentivize businesses to relocate, expand, or set up shop in their states. There are formalized programs, such as New York's Excelsior Jobs Program and the One North Carolina Fund. As noted by the Good Jobs First organization in an analysis of several state programs, the majority of grants and dollars in these types of funds went to large companies, the ones that can afford lobbyists and have political influence.

There are all kinds of special deals that a large business can cut with government entities. Amazon fully exploited that fact when it held basically a cronyist beauty pageant to decide on the location for its second headquarters location (dubbed "HQ2") from 2017 to 2018. The company received 238 bids promising everything short of firstborn children in exchange for being chosen. From tax benefits to cash to city naming rights, states and cities begged Amazon to call them home. When do you think was the last time that a family restaurant, barber, or day care center could get a local politician to return a phone call, let alone throw benefits, perks, and more at them? Amazon's original choices, which included an operations outpost in Nashville, as well as a headquarters in media-central New York (rescinded by Amazon after a high-profile fight between Democratic politicians in New York) and Washington lobbyist central, northern Virginia, were mostly expected, and the "stunt" contest was used to see how many benefits it could extract. Though Amazon pitched what it could do for those states and cities, the important thing was what those cities and states and their respective governments could do for Amazon.[12]

At the federal level, even as President Trump promised to "drain the swamp," his administration's policies were fraught with crony undertones. Front and center was his trade war, which featured tariff exemptions for individual businesses, including those that lent him political support. As one of many examples, according to a ProPublica report, Brian Ballard, Trump's ally and the head of his inauguration committee, was paid, along with a colleague, $540,000 to lobby for exclusions from tariffs on behalf of Varian Medical Systems. "Four of Varian's five exclusion requests [were] approved—which, the company said in an SEC filing, boosted revenues by $23 million."[13]

ProPublica's research also showed that decisions had been arbitrary and often to the detriment of small business owners. For example, as it reported, at one point, "Non-electrical wall candelabras, of wood, each with 3 wrought iron candle holders" were exempted from import tariffs, but those with one or two candle holders were not.

During 2018 and 2019, lobbying specifically related to trade and tariffs was substantially higher than previous years, recording the highest total dollar years on record to that point.

Overall, many outdated policies have increased in scope to prop up different industries, with the government deciding who is worthy and at what cost. For example, the Foundation for Economic Education noted, per Pacific Standard's Emily Moon, that in 2019, subsidies to milk farmers exceeded demand for the product, but rather than reducing dairy subsidies and angering those constituents, "the USDA has been paying to have surplus milk made into cheese" and is sitting on a stockpile of more than 1.4 billion pounds of US-made cheese.[14] I like cheese, probably more than the average person does, but there is no justification for this type of government intervention.

Bailouts

In addition to cheese, we know that bailouts and congressional spending bills, in general, are stuffed with pork (the colloquial name for spending intended to benefit special interests so that those politicians can reap the support of such groups). The CARES Act, as discussed in chapter 4, clearly lays out many of those crony behaviors, prioritizing big interests over the most vulnerable small businesses.

The CARES Act is just one of the latest symptoms. The auto company bailouts that took place under Presidents George W. Bush and Barack Obama prolonged an eventual bankruptcy process for General Motors and Chrysler in order to benefit unions at the expense of other creditors and taxpayers, a crony transfer estimated at more than $26.5 billion.[15]

Of course, that was done under the guise of ensuring that the small businesses that served these big companies wouldn't go out of business. But the government didn't prioritize a plan to provide relief or even backstop the liabilities for those small businesses, the kind of effort it would have made if that—and not cronyism—had been its actual objective.

Favorable Legislation and Regulatory Capture

Legislation always comes about under the cloak of theoretically no-ble causes, such as protecting consumers or the public at large or promoting competition. But when legislators stray from the princi-ple of protecting individual rights, this legislation can and does go astray. As government gets bigger and less transparent and more money comes in from lobbyists and other crony interests, legislation can be a tool to provide favors to those special interests and busi-nesses and even be anticompetitive.

This can also come about in the form of regulatory capture. As PolicyEd explains, regulatory capture can occur when regulatory agencies become dominated by the very industries they were charged with regulating, sometimes sharing resources and information, and prompting regulators to advance those industries' goals and interests.

In *The Case Against the Fed*, Dr. Murray Rothbard described how in 1906 it was the large meatpacking companies that pushed for the legislation and the "costly federal inspection of meat . . . to place cripplingly high costs on competing small meat packers." As demonstrated throughout the text, the "Progressive Era" was basi-cally big businesses and their financial backers having the govern-ment enforce the cartel behavior that they themselves could not in the free market.[16]

A recent example is the Dodd-Frank Wall Street Reform and Consumer Protection Act, passed during the Great Recession, whose purpose was ostensibly to ensure that the banking system would re-main stable and sound. However, because of the massive costs of the legislation, its beneficiaries were the larger banks that had caused the crisis, the outcome being that smaller banks were put out of business. In fact, it killed off the ability of new banks to come into the market to compete.[17]

In March 2015, the Federal Reserve Bank of Richmond put out a report that showed that for the six years following the financial crisis, the number of independent commercial banks had shrunk by 14 percent (more than eight hundred institutions), mostly in the realm of community banks. The report said, "While some of this decline was caused by failure, most of it was driven by an unprecedented collapse in new bank entry. The rate of new-bank formation has fallen from an average of about 100 per year since 1990 to an average of about three per year since 2010."[18] The government's regulation had explicitly made it impossible for a small bank to enter the market.

Such regulation often has further unintended consequences. A June 2018 report by the National Bureau of Economic Research showed that the Dodd-Frank legislation also had the effect of making it harder for small businesses and new businesses to get financing. As small businesses are a critical economic engine and grow at a faster clip than big companies, that decrease in access to capital led to slower growth and a slower recovery from the financial crisis. After adjusting for economic conditions and other factors, the share of smaller loans had "fallen by 9 percentage points since 2010,"[19] at generally the same time that banks had seen their large-loan volume increase by 80 percent. In relation to the report, *Investor's Business Daily* published an editorial that noted, "Smaller banks, which mainly do only small business loans, saw their loan volumes decline by twice as much. This is why there has been a silent depression in the once-vibrant small-bank industry."[20]

So legislation meant to rein in the big banks in fact gave them more free rein.

All sorts of nonfavorable legislation is enveloped in cronyism. In March 2019, after testifying in front of Congress, Facebook CEO Mark Zuckerberg wrote a *Washington Post* op-ed on why the internet needs more regulation. This is something that happens more frequently than you may realize, and you may even think it is counterintuitive. Whether quietly or overtly, big businesses often call on Congress to enact rules and regulations in their industry. Zuckerberg and his counterparts in the tech industry are more than capable of forming a council and deciding on appropriate standards. They have boatloads of knowledge in excess of what government officials possess. However, they want to force regulation. The reason: regulations are anticompetitive and make it harder for small businesses to compete and for new competition in the form of startups to enter the industry.

Whereas big companies have substantial human and monetary resources to comply with complex and costly regulation, small companies do not. Such regulations create a disproportionate burden for small and new entrants that end up limiting competition for the bigger companies.

This is a tricky way for cronyism to take effect without significant political fallout. It may look as though government is being responsible and "helping," but in fact it is creating barriers to entry, removing competition, and indirectly influencing who will be winners and who losers.

This also happened recently with minimum wage laws. Companies such as Amazon, which has the scale to absorb increased costs, and even McDonald's, which has many small business franchise operators but can leverage its systemwide resources to replace labor with technology (think kiosk instead of cashier), abandoned opposition and in some cases began to favor higher minimum wage legislation, knowing that it would put many smaller competitors out of business and make it much harder for new entrants to come into the market. This ends up being bad not just for small businesses but for consumers, who have fewer options to choose from and may end up paying higher prices due to less competition and increasing operating costs.

Though you might be tempted to think of the minimum wage as a good thing, artificial price controls always limit opportunities. The minimum wage was passed as legislation precisely to exclude unskilled workers, particularly immigrants, minorities, and women, from the workforce. It has the same effect today.[21]

Whether it results from outcomes swayed due to lobbying, an attempt to move more people onto the government dole, or simply the government's being ill equipped to pick winners and losers, this trend toward cronyism and non–free market allocations of benefits and incentives disrupts market forces, creates unfair advantages on the playing field, and ultimately disrupts efficiency and productivity. This further results in lost opportunities, growth, and consumer choice. It begets fewer small businesses, stronger big businesses and unions, and more government power.

So Many Cronies, So Little Time

Why would politicians engage in cronyism? To understand, look at how they benefit from it. While they are in office, engaging in cronyism helps fill their coffers, particularly for reelection campaigns. During the 2015–2016 campaign cycle, the Federal Election Commission reported, presidential candidates raised and spent $1.5 billion, congressional candidates collected and disbursed $1.6 billion, political parties received and spent $1.6 billion, and political action committees (PACs) raised and spent $4 billion.

After they leave office, politicians may be rewarded with large speaking fees or high-paying jobs that they are otherwise unqualified for or, in many cases, are for the same types of companies they once regulated or otherwise saw lobbying efforts by. There are myriad examples; just think of the former Securities and Exchange Commission (SEC) chair Mary Schapiro joining the board of Morgan Stanley, former director of homeland security Jeh Johnson joining the board of Lockheed Martin, or former Texas governor and secretary of energy Rick Perry's board and consulting positions, including at Energy Transfer, which is controlled by major political donors and lobbied the Department of Energy while Perry was in office.[22]

Or perhaps a job or contract is directed toward a friend or relative. Unfortunately, as government gets bigger, as it has in the United States, there are more of these bastardizations of free enterprise sprouting up and few rules to keep them in check.

Do you believe that entrepreneurs and business management should be seeking to curry favor with more politicians or more of their stakeholders, including investors, customers, and employees? Should companies be investing in innovation or making friends in Washington, DC? They need to do the latter only when the economy and policy making are moving away from capitalism toward more central planning. It's why Tim Cook, the CEO of Apple, invested in spending time with President Trump and why Wall Street firms' management and key employees often give money to members of both major political parties to have their bases covered.

Furthermore, do you believe that government officials should be representing the interests of their constituents or working for their personal benefit?

Hopefully, it is clear that crony behavior is something that isn't good for everyone.

If you object to cronyism, which is government playing favorites and rigging the game, why on earth would you believe that the solution would be more government?

When government officials gain more control over economic decisions via more central planning, it enables those in power to give preferences, pick winners and losers, and grant special treatment, all behaviors against the nature of free markets.

If government power is limited, then no matter how rich or influential an individual or a business is, they will also be limited in influencing said government.

In regard to cronyism, the Atlas Society says:

> Those who insist that the rich and powerful *always* will exert their influence to extract favors and advantage from

politicians and bureaucrats may welcome this advice: Devise a government strictly limited by its constitution (as did the founding fathers) so that politicians and bureaucrats simply don't have the power to help or hinder business. Then there will be no use lobbying, bribing, or putting friends into office. Do not say that capitalism is impossible without cronyism until you separate government and the economy in the same absolute way that the U.S. Constitution separates government and religion.[23]

You may argue that cronyism happens in the free market, too. Perhaps someone gets a job because of a connection instead of merit or a company chooses a vendor based on a cozy relationship. Though this can happen, it can't happen for extended periods without impacting how the company competes in the market. Whether it is via subpar returns to shareholders, inferior value to customers, or a toxic work culture created when something happens in business based on anything other than merit, such behavior creates a vulnerability that the company brings into the market that other companies can exploit. That leads to the company either correcting itself or operating at a handicap.

Moreover, given the economic freedom that everyone is granted under capitalism, no individual has to deal with any given company—unless, of course, it is a government-granted monopoly that precludes them from exercising their capitalistic choice. As a consumer, you have the freedom to deal with your preferred provider of goods or services—a luxury you never have with the government.

People are worried about billionaires buying and controlling elections, but what about the unions? Two of the largest national unions, the National Education Association (NEA) and the American Federation of Teachers (AFT), have around 3 million and 1.7 million members, respectively. The NEA is the largest labor union and professional interest group in the United States, wielding a budget north of $300 million. During the 2020 election cycle the NEA and AFT spent more than $52 million, via individuals, PACs, and "soft money," on political campaigns. Despite saying they are nonpartisan, analysis by Influence Watch shows they have given nearly all of their money (97 percent) in recent years to support big government Democrat politicians and have significant power when it comes to lending their endorsements to candidates. They also spend millions on lobbying efforts.[24]

With the millions of members that the unions represent, they have strength and power that no group should be able to wield in the political arena. Because schools are funded at the federal, state, and local levels, these unions influence politics at all three levels. Their stranglehold, which includes promoting forceful, coercive, non–free market policies such as opposing merit pay for teachers, school choice, and competition from charter schools, has become a scourge on the education system.

I want to be clear that not all cronyism is outright corruption or even subtle favor granting for gain. Sometimes, it is just the government thinking it knows better and making decisions without the benefit of free market forces or merely covering its incompetence. Without elements of free markets such as transparency, accountability, ongoing competition, and so on, government outcomes are never the best ones. Their interference just creates more government inefficiency. It may seem like a small thing individually; however, when replicated throughout the behemoth that is the US government system, it is costly in many ways.

If you want to unrig the game and make the field more equal for everyone, understand that happens with more capitalism, not less. More government power and movement away from free markets will favor the big, powerful, well-connected guys, no matter how many times they pretend they will be the guardians of the vulnerable. More government power and control are not solutions to any objection.

Cronyism and Small Business

Whether at the federal, state, or local level, the impact of cronyism shows up on a nonlevel playing field that is always slanted against the "little guy." In the realm of businesses, that means it is tilted toward big businesses and against small businesses.

A 2015 study by the government watchdog group discussed earlier, Good Jobs First, analyzed more than 4,200 government business stimulus initiatives in fourteen different states, worth more than $3.2 billion. This is the state government deciding who gets stimulus and who doesn't. Perhaps not surprisingly, despite small businesses' accounting for more than 99 percent of all businesses, 90 percent of the dollars awarded were given to large companies.[25]

That is just a small drop in the bucket. The same group wrote in its report "Subsidizing the Corporate One Percent" that 75 percent of the dollar value of state and local incentive deals they analyzed, accounting for $110 billion in overall deals, had been given to just 965 global parent companies. And in its "Uncle Sam's Favorite Corporations" report, it noted that over a fifteen-year period, the federal government had given $68 billion in grants and special tax credits to business, with two-thirds of that going to large businesses, which account for less than a fraction of a percent of all businesses and certainly are not the most vulnerable or "needy."[26]

At all levels of government, the backbone of America, small business, has not been afforded the same assistance, tax breaks, or other incentives to spur its economic activity. Small businesses have faced more regulation, much of it, as discussed above, spurred by crony efforts of big business to limit competition. By big companies' seeking benefits, regulation, or other roadblocks that make it more difficult for small companies to start and compete in the market, the little guys have had their lunch eaten by the bigger companies, capping industry growth and competition.

Even if your heart is in the right place and you believe that government intervention is necessary to "level the playing field" and "take care of the little guy," you can see that that has not been the outcome. With their immense lobbying power, money, and sway, big businesses have been receiving benefits to the exclusion or detriment of small business.

As noted above, it's not as though Joe's Pizza Parlor can hold a contest like Amazon's to get local leaders' attention. More likely, Joe is going to face all kinds of licenses, permits, and other hurdles that will make it more difficult for him to set up shop.

The language in a piece of California state legislation called AB5 (discussed in detail in chapter 13) has made its way into legislation passed by the House of Representatives for the second time at the time of this writing called the Protecting the Right to Organize (PRO) Act. It is sponsored by unions in an attempt to kill independent contractor and gig jobs, not only providing less choice for individual workers but again making it more difficult for smaller companies to compete. This is cronyism to prop up the power of the government and unions at the expense of small business owners, contractors, freedom, and choice.

There is also little, if any, effort on the part of governments to ensure that they bring smaller guys along for the ride when they cut big deals. When negotiations take place for a large company to move into prime real estate in a city, rarely do you see the inclusion of underserved areas as part of such a deal. Why not ensure that those areas also get investment? Because doing so would create a threat to big government. In theory, moving people from government dependence and economic expenditures to self-sufficiency and generating revenue is a double win. In practice, big-government proponents do everything they can to make the poor dependent on the system in an arm's-length effort to buy votes, which creates the cycle that makes them remain dependent upon—but not truly benefited by—the government.

The 2020 Crony Table

The increase in cronyism set the stage in many ways for the debacle of 2020. Cronyism helped balloon the government, create more central planning and fewer free market solutions, waste resources, run up debt, and distort financial markets and the dollar, all of which made the too-big-to-succeed government a ticking time bomb.

In 2020, this setup rewarded politicians for favoring big businesses and other special interests over small businesses. It punished savers and favored spenders and it forced people to take financial risks that they would not have otherwise.

Cronyism permeated the CARES Act, discussed in chapter 4, from the Kennedy Center and National Endowments for the Arts and Humanities getting a combined $175 million in handouts while small businesses had to jump through hoops to get a small amount of relief (after they were shut down). The structure and execution of the Paycheck Protection Program led to banks taking care of big customers before most small businesses. However, that wasn't the start of cronyism; it was its outgrowth and isn't that far from simply paying for votes. The repercussions are trillions of dollars spent, with a poor return on investment, to many entities that didn't need them, with not enough to those that did, that didn't turn around the vulnerable parts of the economy, and that saddled the United States with even more debt.

The stimulus was structured with a $600-per-week unemployment boost that made it hard for small businesses to get their workers back to work but made it appear as though the politicians were "looking out for the little guys," when in actuality, they were killing their jobs in the long term.

The economic advisory staff of the White House, including the Treasury secretary, helped their Wall Street buddies. Actions such as engaging BlackRock to buy non-government-backed securities meant fees galore to the financial sector.

That's not to mention the Fed's intervention, which, it could be argued, in its effort to prop up the markets artificially through their interest rate and money supply policies, was also driven by crony relationships for years, and continued at record levels in 2020. That meant that the big companies didn't share in the pain of the global pandemic, "zombie" companies were again propped up, and larger companies' benefits were financed on the backs of average taxpayers and small business.

On the PPE front, the federal government awarded many large contracts to help secure supplies. The *Washington Post* reported that in late March and April 2020, the government entered into N95 mask contracts at prices nearly eight times what they would have cost in January and February. Contracts were awarded to several large companies, including Honeywell, whose CEO was appointed to one of Trump's business advisory groups.[27]

You may believe that it made sense for larger companies to be favored in this instance. However, the *Washington Post* reported that, via FEMA, the federal government had awarded a $55 million contract, without a competitive bidding process, to a company called Panthera Worldwide LLC. Panthera Worldwide had some previous government connections but no history of making or procuring medical equipment. Its parent company had filed for bankruptcy in 2019 and had said that it had no employees since May 2018.[28]

In July, the Trump administration invoked the Defense Production Act to give a $765 million loan to support the launch of Kodak Pharmaceuticals, ostensibly to help the longtime photography titan shift to producing generic pharmaceutical ingredients. Though you may agree with the strategy of lessening the United States' dependence on China or other foreign countries for critical supplies, the government's playing banker does not create the right free market incentives.[29]

The move drew a lot of scrutiny from various entities. Scott

Lincicome of the Cato Institute said that the decision had been made with no congressional input or oversight—or transparency. He questioned its urgency, saying:

> According to the Food and Drug Administration, of the roughly 2,000 global manufacturing facilities that produce active pharmaceutical ingredients (APIs), 13 percent are in China; 28 percent are in the USA, 26 percent in the EU, and 18 percent in India. For the APIs of World Health Organization "essential medicines" on the U.S. market, 21 percent of manufacturing facilities are located in the United States, 15 percent in China; and the rest in the EU, India, and Canada.[30]

Lincicome further questioned—as others had—"Why pick Kodak?," which was on the brink of extinction prior to the move, saying, "Even assuming for the sake of argument that sagging domestic API production qualifies as a national emergency, why did Kodak, which has no API or other pharmaceutical experience (though it does make chemicals), receive this government loan, instead of it going to one or more of the *hundreds* of API facilities already operating in the United States?"

It also posed the question that if there was such a dire need, why wouldn't the "greedy" pharmaceutical companies step in and fill it? Did the government need to be giving out a $765 million loan and picking a company, seemingly out of thin air, to fill whatever the need might supposedly be?

Moreover, the effort was supposed to help create hundreds of jobs; imagine the number of jobs that would be supported if $765 million had gone to small businesses instead.

Additional scrutiny was on Kodak's executive chairman, who received, through an arrangement with the board that wasn't disclosed, significant stock options the day before the loan was announced. The SEC announced an investigation on August 4. The loan remained on hold at the time of the 2020 presidential election.[31]

Though Kodak had no known ties to the Trump administration that anyone has uncovered at the time of this writing, it is a strong illustration of the shift from capitalism to cronyism.

At the state level, cronyism's effects were even more palpable and had a more direct economic impact than what happened federally. As state governors decided who and what was deemed essential—that you could get your pet groomed but not yourself, that the big box stores could stay open while smaller entities had to close or limit services—the picking of winners and losers was omnipresent all across the country.

By and large—pun not intended—bigger businesses were allowed to stay open while smaller ones were made to shut down, despite the smaller businesses being less equipped to handle the consequences and with no compensation or assistance for that order. One can only imagine that the mayors and governors did not want to get a call from the CEOs of companies such as Target or PetSmart or their lobbyists but were not bothered by disappointing or even putting out of business those without power: small entrepreneurs.

Many actions involved funneling cash to special interests. In Chicago, McCormick Place convention center was turned into a possible alternate care facility. The facility, which reportedly treated less than a few dozen patients, looked a lot like a means to funnel emergency money to union labor. According to a report, "The Illinois National Guard, U.S. Army Corps of Engineers and 600 Chicago labor union workers put in more than 60,000 man hours in two weeks." A similar situation occurred in New York City, which opened a makeshift hospital in the Javits Center and then closed it about a month later. Using labor union members who were out of work due to the lack of shows that would normally have been held at the center, in conjunction with military personnel, the center said it expected to be reimbursed for its costs by FEMA.[32]

Say "No" to Cronyism

The bottom line is that cronyism hurts productivity, creates more centralized power, and makes innovation more difficult. It takes away the power of freedom and choice of individuals to pick winners and losers and concentrates that power in government officials who do so for their own benefit.

We have also seen the politicization of everything spill over into our everyday lives, primarily, in my belief, due to cronyism and its effects on increasing the size of the government. Every facet of our lives, from sports to how we spend money to whether we wear a mask—a health issue, not a political one—has become political. As one of my Twitter followers, Matt Rentschler, responded to my discussion about this, "We've let politics shape our everyday lives and coversations [sic], instead of having our everyday lives and conversations shape our politics."[33]

So how do we proceed? If we are going to solve cronyism, we won't do it by giving government more control. The government is the one offering the handouts and picking the winners and losers. Without the government being able to do that, there will be no cronyism. You can blame the companies for lining up for special treatment. However, if you want to stop crony behavior, you need to stop it at its root, and that will happen by insisting on the limits of government powers and abilities at all levels.

CHAPTER 12

Trading Places

*China's and the United States' Respective Shifts
to and from Capitalism*

As China is one of the United States' major trading partners ($660 billion in two-way import and export trade in 2018), one of the largest holders of its public debt (it was number one until May 2019, and as of the end of December 2020, still held north of $1 trillion in US debt securities), and an important manufacturing source for large and small US companies alike, you might think that the United States has had a long, healthy relationship with China. However, the relationship is much more recent and highly fraught.[1]

After Chairman Mao's death in 1976, his appointed successor, Hua Guofeng, took over. Then, within a couple of years' time, in 1978, Hua was ousted for a new leader, Deng Xiaoping, who led the transformation of modern China as we know it, from primarily a revolutionary way of thinking to incorporate more economic ideas.[2]

Though China was still a communist regime, the push along the spectrum toward embracing more capitalism was transformational for both the country and its people.

A significant shift occurred in the 1980s, with the lure of China as an opportunity for the United States to spread capitalistic principles, capture market share, and potentially share democratic ideals.

It was a bet by US government planners that China, a country with a communist history, that was run by a communist party, and that did not believe in individual rights, would somehow be able to be transformed. Much of the West believed that once a rogue nation tasted capitalism, it would develop a hunger for Western values.

What downside could there be? From a US government perspective, China and its massive population presented an opportunity to grow the US GDP, to gain favor with cronies at large US companies, and to build up another country, which could then be able to help support the United States—diplomatically, militarily, currencywise, or otherwise.

However, it was a risky bet to make on a country with such a different ideology and system of values, beliefs, and most importantly, rights—not to mention at that time, China was a poor country, with mainly an interest in agricultural products. Could it somehow be transformed by more consumerism?

Though doing so was sold as a broad opportunity for everyone, it was just another example of government picking winners and losers.

In 1979, the US government went against its thinking of just over a half decade earlier and granted China most-favored-nation (MFN) status under President Jimmy Carter. The term, which is used widely and colloquially in dealmaking, means in the political realm that the country with this status must be treated as well as others with the same status in terms of tariffs, quotas, and other deal mechanics. In layman's terms, China received top-tier treatment in terms of economic dealings.[3]

That status did come with the stipulation of a conditional, annual review by Congress, whose members continually and arrogantly bet that this was the best way to spread some type of democracy in China.

At the time, according to the World Bank, more than 800 million people, almost 90 percent of China's population, were living in extreme poverty. They were about to see a huge transformation, thanks to the United States' change in stance toward the country and its export of capitalism.[4]

The Reagan Years

When he took over from President Carter, President Ronald Reagan was very outspoken about supporting Taiwan. But according to the *New York Times*, his team encouraged him to keep China as a cooperative partner, particularly as the United States was focused on the USSR as a political foe. In the first year of his first term, he decided to allow US manufacturers to sell arms to China on an ad hoc basis.[5]

A combination of Congress's willingness to overlook the objections to diplomacy with China by individuals and groups concerned about the country's human rights violations and other issues and its desire to open up more market practices on the ground in China ultimately transformed the Chinese economy.

Reforms allowed for a more expansive production and distribution of goods. As reported by the Library of Congress Country Studies, that set off an entrepreneurial expansion of individuals engaged in businesses in China rising more than forty-fold between 1976 and 1985 to 12.2 million, and "as state-owned businesses either were leased or turned over to collective ownership or were leased to individuals, the share of state-owned commerce in total retail sales dropped from 90.3 percent in 1976 to 40.5 percent in 1985."[6]

Back in the United States, as the Cold War ended, China became less politically important, as policy shifted to focus on trade with Japan. Though the renewal of China's MFN status by Congress was always a nonconsensus issue and legislation was introduced to terminate China's special trade status and to impose additional conditions relating to improvements in China's actions on various trade and nontrade issues, no formal legal action was taken by Congress.

However, large companies were excited. As Scott Seligman, the US-China Business Council's Beijing representative from 1980 to 1982, said in *China Business Review*, "Everybody was interested in doing business in China." Because the United States was exporting more to China than importing from it, he said, "The Chinese would constantly lecture us that if we didn't buy more from China, then they weren't going to be able to buy from us."[7] However, in a very non–free market maneuver, China began the model of requiring a local Chinese partner if a company was a US (or other foreign) entity doing business in the country.

As the decade went on, China relaxed certain economic restrictions, such as those related to foreign investment.

Despite continued concerns about Chinese human rights violations, including Tiananmen Square, trade practices, and other matters, economic and political relations moved forward. Congress and various administrations (including under presidents George H. W. Bush and Bill Clinton) felt that the best way to improve things for the Chinese people—and ostensibly for Americans—was to encourage more trade between the countries.

Jobs and the Trade Deficit

When then candidate for president Bill Clinton campaigned against President George H. W. Bush in 1992, a significant campaign issue was Bush's treatment of China. Clinton pushed hard against Bush's relationship with dictators and said that Bush had sent "secret emissaries to raise a toast with those who crushed democracy."[8]

However, once Clinton won the presidency, those tough words were abandoned. The Clinton administration embraced China, again parroting what others before him had said about a partnership benefiting the Chinese people (a prediction that he was ultimately correct about in some ways, but wildly wrong about in others).

In June 2019, FTR's Don Ake wrote about how the Clinton administration had worked to grow the US economy without inflation via importing cheaper products from China. As he said, "Usually, economic growth spurs inflation, which the Fed tries to control with higher interest rates. This can eventually lead to recession." But as he noted, by having access to lower-cost goods manufactured abroad, the individual's dollar could now buy more goods as prices were held down, suppressing inflationary forces.

The downside, as we well know, was that the jobs associated with making those higher-cost goods were being held down as well. Ake noted:

> This began the transition of the U.S. from a low-tech work-force to a new, high-tech workforce, a problem we still struggle with today.
>
> You may consider "grow the economy and import deflation" a short-term strategy with long-term difficulties. However, in U.S. political cycles, you leave after eight years. So, whatever consequences are created become someone else's problem.[9]

The timing of the 1990s dot-com boom provided cover for the economic shift on the US side. On the Chinese side, as the country moved more toward capitalism, poverty decreased, and by 1996, the percentage of Chinese living in extreme poverty had been halved to 42 percent.

However, in the United States, capitalism wasn't benefiting because the country's major trade partner wasn't playing by the same rules. That led to losses of manufacturing jobs (around 5 million between 1997 and 2017, although likely some portion of those would have been lost to new technology or other trade partners). Innovation opportunities for small businesses were quashed, as small and new businesses could not compete with this new partner playing by a different playbook. Central planning strengthened in the United States, as it continued to open up trade channels despite the glaring losses.[10]

During the second term of the Clinton administration, as US-

China trade continued to rise, Congress began discussions about granting the country permanent normal trade relations (PNTR) status. Doing so would substantially elevate China's status on the world stage, and President Clinton signed it into law in 2000.[11]

The PNTR recognition by the United States paved the way and frankly shepherded China right into the World Trade Organization (WTO) in 2001, which provided rocket fuel for China's continued explosive growth.

From there, China has never looked back.

According to the Council on Foreign Relations, between 1980 and 2004, US-China trade grew from $5 billion to $231 billion. In 2006, China surpassed Mexico as the United States' second biggest trade partner after Canada.[12]

In 2008, China surpassed Japan to become the largest holder of US debt (in the form of Treasurys; around $600 billion at the time), and by 2010, it had leapfrogged Japan to become the world's second largest economy.

By 2015, the number of Chinese living in extreme poverty had fallen below 1 percent, an incredible turnaround from the nearly 90 percent rate half a century earlier. It's an incredible story of the dependence of this communist state upon capitalism and, in the case of the United States, a capitalistic country inching away from it.[13]

Trump and China

Even before becoming president, Donald Trump had China in his crosshairs. Being tough on China dovetailed nicely with his promise to fight for US manufacturing jobs and the "everyman," and became almost an obsession. Over the next several months and throughout the first year of his presidency, he mentioned China everywhere from rallies to Twitter. He lamented a potpourri of issues with China, including the trade deficit, intellectual property (IP) theft, and unfair trade practices, including subsidies that impaired price competition. Some of it, such as the trade deficit, is of questionable concern, whereas some of it, such as IP theft and trade practices, is of valid and substantial concern.

Trump's predecessors had avoided dealing with the issues related to China. President George W. Bush had had to deal with the dotcom bubble and September 11 in the early part of his term and the financial crisis at the end. President Obama had inherited the financial crisis, and with his own policies leading to the slowest economic recovery on record, there was no economic opening for a crackdown on China. However, with President Trump being able to extend the economic recovery past what had been predicted and refuel the stock market, and with his no-rules style, he decided to try to undo what his predecessors had in large part created.

Intellectual Property

As Trump's focus on China's non–free market practices highlights what has caused much concern about China for decades, intellectual property comes to the forefront. And a key facet of intellectual property is property rights. True capitalism cannot exist without property rights.

When a country does not value property rights, it is impossible to value any facet of property rights, including intellectual property. A critical miscalculation made by the oh-so-smart-and-all-knowing government leaders was building up a partner that doesn't value the ownership of property. The issues that have arisen because of this are large in both size and scope.

Though the United States, which enforces property rights (some of the time, anyway), has been an innovation leader, the Chinese have been knockoff leaders. They know how to take someone else's innovation and produce it more cheaply and quickly, sometimes sacrificing quality. This intense focus on replication versus innovation means that intellectual property protection isn't in the Chinese vocabulary or business DNA. It can't be because it isn't a value of communism, which underpinned China's move toward capitalism, but never embracing full free market capitalism.

As the Chinese grew their manufacturing prowess to become the go-to manufacturers of consumer goods for companies worldwide, they have also never bothered to protect brands or other intellectual property.

Whether the product be clothing, beauty goods, accessories, light bulbs, home appliances, electronics, or, before digitalization, copies of movies and music discs, it is estimated that more than 86 percent of the counterfeit merchandise finding its way around the globe is produced in China and Hong Kong.[14]

That accounted for more than $400 billion worth of fake products produced in China and sold worldwide, which, in aggregate, is estimated to cost companies that own the intellectual property tens of billions of dollars a year in lost profits, many of which are US-based brands and companies.[15]

Though you may be tempted to think of this as only a luxury or big-brand issue, as a recent CNBC headline pointed out, "Counterfeit Goods from China Are Crushing American Small Businesses." Whether by way of knockoffs of small business products sold on Amazon or Alibaba-owned outlets, small businesses are widely seeing their intellectual property misappropriated. In 2017, one small business owner, Tannia Ospina of Belle Threads in Hasbrouck Heights, New Jersey, told BuzzFeed News that she had found a photo of her daughter modeling one of her designs being sold as a knockoff on AliExpress—for a fraction of the price, of course. Chinese manufacturers have been using the internet to find and then copy all kinds of products from small business owners and resell them—sometimes even using the original photographs, as in Ospina's case—on major sales platforms worldwide.[16]

The Rise of Shanzhai

The issue of property rights violations by Chinese manufacturers is not just for goods leaving the country but is part of what happens in and throughout China.

Replication of products and subversion of property rights are so ingrained in China that they have become part of its culture, and there is a term for it: *shanzhai*, which colloquially means "fake" or "knockoff." But whereas "knockoff" is a pejorative term in the Western world, in China, it's more than accepted. In the summary for the book *Shanzhai: Deconstruction in Chinese*, by Byung-Chul Han, a Korean professor of philosophy and cultural studies at the Universität der Künste Berlin, it says:

> *Shanzhai* is a Chinese neologism that means "fake," originally coined to describe knock-off cell phones marketed under such names as Nokir and Samsing. These cell phones were not crude forgeries but multifunctional, stylish, and as good as or better than the originals. Shanzhai has since spread into other parts of Chinese life, with shanzhai books, shanzhai politicians, shanzhai stars. There is a shanzhai Harry Potter: *Harry Potter and the Porcelain Doll*, in which Harry takes on his nemesis Yandomort. In the West, this would be seen as piracy, or even desecration, but in Chinese culture, originals are continually transformed—deconstructed.[17]

This is perhaps not surprising, because without enforceable property rights, it is too risky to create anything of your own from scratch. Why take the risk associated with innovation and development when you have no protection or ownership of what you create? It is less risky to build (or rebuild) off someone else's proven work. So, this *shanzhai* has overtaken China, much to the chagrin of those who have invested in building up valuable properties.

The examples are numerous and broad.

At the launch of a Dalian Wanda Group theme park owned by one of the wealthiest men in China, clearly fake *shanzhai* "Mickey Mouse," "Minnie Mouse," and "Stormtroopers," among other characters, were found wandering around and interacting with customers, prompting The Walt Disney Company (which owns such characters and their underlying intellectual property) to say it would take action.[18]

If you take a trip to China, you may reserve a room at a Hai-yatt Hotel, which is not owned by Hyatt, or one of many "Peninsula" hotels, which, except for the few locations that the well-known Peninsula luxury chain owns in the country, is not affiliated with them—or, per reports, particularly luxurious.[19]

In 2006, Starbucks, which has a host of imitators throughout China, as well as its own growing business, won a multiple-year legal battle against "Xingbake," which sounds like "Starbucks" in Chinese and used a knockoff of the Starbucks logo.[20]

On the tech side, the transgressions by Chinese businesses include misappropriating trade secrets and other IP of the companies that they manufacture products for, often by requiring tech companies to share their technology with local business partners as a way for these foreign companies to gain access to local Chinese markets. Sometimes, Chinese-led tech IP theft is enacted via cyberattacks or espionage.[21]

So as Treasury Secretary Steven Mnuchin, US Trade Representative Robert Lighthizer, and Chinese officials worked to finalize a deal regarding IP, from straight-out theft to cybersecurity issues and technology transfers, the unspoken question that loomed large was "How will China be able to change its culture?"

Imagine President Xi Jinping telling the manufacturers of hundreds of billions of dollars' worth of fake merchandise, skimmers who take authentic goods (or their rejects) and resell them in Chinese marketplaces, and technology thieves that their business models are dead and they need to find something else to do, which he has started to do. Now imagine the Chinese government actually enforcing and taking action on IP theft. Even if you understand that IP theft is wrong, you have to appreciate the difficulty of a nation telling its citizens that their valuable businesses are now basically worthless and fundamentally changing the *shanzhai* culture that has been developed over decades.[22]

Starting the Trade War

Though there is no doubt that intervention with China was necessary, the Trump administration's tactics were strangely big government, central planning oriented. From targeting various industries for tariffs but not others and having counter-tariffs ensue, both individual US consumers and businesses in targeted US industries bore the burden of the tactics.

Instead of initially going after Chinese IP registrations abroad, the ultimate irony in a country where *shanzhai* has become part of the culture, or going after foreign investments, the US government went back to picking winners and losers. That was right in its comfort zone but not exactly emblematic of "draining the swamp."

In January 2018, President Trump approved something called "global safeguard tariffs" on $8.5 billion worth of imports of solar panels and $1.8 billion worth of washing machines. The Peterson Institute for International Economics (PIIE) called the move "a relatively rare move historically even when the president is granted the authority to do so."[23]

That led to almost two full years of starts and stops on trade talks, economic wars, retaliatory measures, and related ups and downs in the stock markets. Overall, sophisticated investors never really believed much would come from a trade deal. They expected that although something would eventually come on paper, it wouldn't truly deal with the critical issues related to US-China economic relations.

On the last day of 2019, President Trump announced that he would be signing Phase One of a trade deal with China on January 15, 2020, which was when the deal was, in fact, signed. The timing, in critical ways, couldn't have been any worse. After finally attempting to bring a heavy hand to dealings with China after decades, the final negotiations aligned with news of a new virus coming out of China—information that the Chinese were desperately attempting to downplay and conceal.

After finally starting to move the needle with China and with a long way to go, was the administration going to go against the Chinese culture of respect and saving face? Had the deal not been made, it is likely, although still conjecture, that the administration would have been more eager to be diligent with the intelligence information linking China and the virus.

Crackdown on Listings

Back in 2018, there was a lot of buzz around a startup coffee company in China called Luckin Coffee. Starbucks had dominated the market in China, which was traditionally one of tea drinkers, not coffee drinkers, and China had become Starbucks' second largest market. Success begets competition, and backed by venture capital firms and Singapore's sovereign wealth fund, Luckin Coffee, according to an article in Quartz, had opened more than five hundred tech-enabled small-footprint coffee outlets in China in less than a year from its founding.[24]

By the second quarter of 2019, Luckin Coffee was already tapping US equity investors for capital. Its investors included BlackRock (the same company that was advising the Fed on its unprecedented market purchases, as discussed in chapter 5), just a month before going public on the US-based Nasdaq stock exchange in a wildly successful IPO. The financial media touted Luckin Coffee as the next big thing and Starbucks' biggest rival. By the end of that year, Luckin Coffee reported that it had surpassed Starbucks in terms of the number of units in China, with more than 4,500, compared to Starbucks' 4,100 units.[25]

By January 2020, Muddy Waters Research—described on its website as "Muddy Waters produces three types of research product: Business fraud, accounting fraud, and fundamental problems"—released an anonymous eighty-nine-page research report detailing the conclusion that Luckin Coffee was a "fundamentally broken business" that had engaged in fraud, detailing six red flags and five business model flaws. It also announced it was shorting Luckin Coffee stock.[26]

Though initially some other well-known investors didn't give the report credence, Luckin Coffee then announced that several employees had inflated revenue and fabricated sales transactions to the tune of more than $300 million, prompting the stock price to fall by more than 80 percent and wiping out $5 billion worth of stock value. Trading in the stock was halted. The CEO and COO were ultimately fired the following month. The company gave up its initial appeal and was eventually delisted from the Nasdaq near the end of June 2020.[27]

Carson Block, the founder and CEO of Muddy Waters Research, said on CNBC, "This is again a wake-up call for U.S. policymakers, regulators, and investors about the extreme fraud risk China-based companies pose to our markets," and asserted that all Chinese public companies are an "extreme fraud risk." "China is to stock fraud as Silicon Valley is to technology," said Block.[28]

That shouldn't have been news. Back in 2010, securities regulators had been probing massive fraud on the part of Chinese-listed companies. TheStreet had done an analysis and found that in particular, companies that had gone public via reverse mergers (meaning that they combined with a company, usually a shell entity, that was publicly trading rather than going through the traditional IPO process to list their shares) were more likely to be allegedly fraudulent. TheStreet's analysis showed that "Investors in the U.S. have suffered related losses in excess of $34 billion. . . . That total adds up all the market-cap losses for 150 stocks that appear to have been used to bring Chinese companies to U.S. exchanges." The 2010 report also discusses Peter Humphrey, a corporate investigator and due diligence expert based in Beijing. It said that, at the time, "Humphrey estimates that as many as a third of Chinese companies listed on major U.S. exchanges—the Nasdaq, Amex and New York Stock Exchange—are likely reporting fictional profits."[29]

As noted by Reuters, "The SEC has been locked in a decade-long struggle with the Chinese government to inspect audits of U.S.-listed Chinese companies, and its accounting arm is still unable to access those critical records."[30]

But as of October 2, 2020, 217 Chinese companies were listed on US exchanges, with a total market capitalization of $2.2 trillion. Thirteen of those companies were considered "national-level Chinese state-owned enterprises" by the US-China Economic and Security Review Commission.[31]

A bipartisan bill sponsored by Louisiana Republican senator John Kennedy and Maryland Democratic senator Chris Van Hollen sought to crack down on the fraud, an outgrowth of a recommendation made by the President's Working Group on Financial Markets, and, as reported by the *Wall Street Journal*, was "intended to protect American investors from what the administration has described as risks posed by Chinese companies." The bill included a provision that Chinese-listed companies would be forced to delist if they didn't comply with specific measures, such as having audit work papers inspected for three years by US regulators and having companies certify that they are not controlled by the Chinese government. Companies not yet listed would need to comply with the measures up front.[32]

The bill passed unanimously in the Senate, and a companion bill was introduced in the House by California Democratic representative Brad Sherman, who served on the House Financial Services Committee. The Holding Foreign Companies Accountable Act passed the House on December 2, 2020.[33]

Central Planning and the Bogeyman

While Congress was dealing with the financial markets, the executive branch was looking into other issues. The Trump team declared a "national emergency" on the Chinese-owned and highly popular social apps TikTok and WeChat. Though there were clear demonstrations that TikTok could be used for spying, the move did seem more like the kind of thing China would do than the United States. The American Civil Liberties Union (ACLU) pushed back, saying that it was a violation of speech and stating, "This is another abuse of emergency powers under the broad guise of national security."[34]

Under pressure from the Trump administration, which was going to block downloads of the app in the United States and which also said at one point it wanted a transaction finder's fee, an unprecedented meddling of government into dealmaking, in September 2020, TikTok reached a partnership agreement with Oracle and Walmart to assuage the administration's concerns. However, a US district court judge granted a preliminary injunction against the block and, as of the date of the election, was waiting to hear arguments. That made the outcome of the initially negotiated deal unclear.[35]

Though there are some concerns about Chinese-domiciled apps and technology, the Trump administration's policies remain consistent with big government creating a "bogeyman" of sorts to infringe on rights in the name of safety.

In fact, around the same time the TikTok drama was unfolding, the *Wall Street Journal* reported that Anomaly Six, a US defense contractor with military ties and a background in intelligence, had "embedded its software in numerous mobile apps, allowing it to track the movements of hundreds of millions of mobile phones worldwide, according to interviews and documents reviewed by The Wall Street Journal." Per the report, the company had software development kits (SDKs) that harvest data embedded in apps, which weren't disclosed in privacy policies. The report further said that "Anomaly Six is a federal contractor that provides global-location-data products to branches of the U.S. government and private-sector clients. The company told The Wall Street Journal it restricts the sale of U.S. mobile phone movement data only to nongovernmental, private-sector clients."[36]

I guess, then, that privacy violations and "spying" are okay with the US government—if you are a US company and specifically a US defense contractor. That sounds more like a policy that would come out of China, but here we are.

The Conscious Uncoupling
of the Supply Chain

As China tried to build up its market heft, it had another problem to worry about: its manufacturing prowess. The several-years-long "trade war" was a catalyst for many companies to look at their sourcing from China. The reality is that China isn't an emerging market anymore; it has emerged. With its rising prices, intellectual property and cybersecurity issues, and a poor human rights record, it was the right time for US companies to diversify their supply chain. The trade war gave US companies an excuse—and a kick in the butt—to explore supply chain diversification.

Southeast Asia and India seemed to be big recipients of the fallout, with Vietnam, Malaysia, and others making strides as potential new manufacturing hubs. Apple is one major manufacturer that was reportedly moving potentially billions of iPhone production business to India in conjunction with its vendors.[37]

Of course, the administration also tried to recapture some business back to the United States, but that was not without issues.

When Government Goes Away, Capitalism Will Play

Rewind to the early days of the pandemic, and there were runs on toilet paper, hand sanitizer, and disinfecting wipes. Senator Marco Rubio took to the *New York Times* opinion pages to lament the breakdown of US supply chains and US consumers' overdependence on the Chinese for everything. On social media, people showed memes of empty shelves in grocery stores and big box retailers, comparing capitalism to socialism. The truth is that under socialism, store shelves always look like that. But within a few months, toilet paper and cleaning products weren't that hard to find in the United States.[38]

Was it some kind, benevolent, all-knowing government force that produced this miracle and shift in toilet paper availability fortunes? Did the US government's obsession with China create excellent policy? No—it was capitalism. As there was more demand for a product, the market stepped up to fill that demand. Go figure.

On the toilet paper side, within a short time in March, toilet paper was sold out at 70 percent of "U.S. grocery stores (including online sellers)." Americans were very concerned about their backsides' fate during the pandemic, which seemed odd but nonetheless happened. However, within a few months, as producers and retailers alike realized the demand, toilet paper was back in stock and available. The temporary blip in supply also led Americans to be problem solvers themselves and look to alternatives. US bidet sales (my personal recommendation, as an aside) also spiked in response to the toilet paper grab.[39]

For the sanitizing products, several smaller players entered the fray when the big companies failed to meet demand. So although some companies may have depended on China, the EPA identified hundreds of disinfectant products that work to kill SARS-CoV-2, and a quick internet search showed that you could use easily found ingredients to make your own as well, as detailed by several articles, including one on Quartz.[40]

What helped was that the government got out of the way. CNN noted that the massive demand increase led the FDA to "temporarily ease restrictions on manufacturers looking to make sanitizer, outlining that 'the agency does not intend to take action against manufacturing firms that prepare alcohol-based hand sanitizers for consumer use.'"[41] It is hardly magic that making it easier for the market to be free, not some government policy, helped it stabilize.

It wasn't China holding back small business opportunities; it was government regulation.

The 2020 Relationship: Holding Up a Mirror

As 2020 began, the US government's history with China was a perfect example of a long history of central planning officials thinking they know what is best and, when they don't, not having to bear the consequences.

The US government had courted China for a very long time, thinking it was to its own benefit when in fact it was far and away to China's advantage. The consequences were numerous, severe, and consistently in need of addressing.

The US government sold out capitalism and small business to a partner that was moving toward capitalism but didn't value its core tenets.

By the time the US government finally got around to addressing the problem, it had already expended so much political capital that it created a blind spot on intelligence and had the United States trying to play good cop, coordinating and ultimately sending nearly eighteen tons of PPE that could have been used in the United States to China.

Who has benefited the most from the United States' move away from capitalism to court a partner that couldn't be worthy because they foundationally held different values from those that are the backbone of capitalism? Ironically, the Chinese people did. The United States' willingness to open up relations and trade with China, including legitimizing them vis-à-vis the World Trade Organization, has helped almost eradicate extreme poverty in China over the course of a few decades—from nearly 90 percent in 1976 to less than 1 percent.

The February 2020 Hurun Global Rich List revealed that Greater China, including Hong Kong and Taiwan, had surpassed the United States in the number of billionaires minted in the previous year, with the Chinese generating them recently at a rate of three to one versus the United States.[42]

Through its policies and actions, the US government didn't help capitalism here as much. People lost jobs and companies lost business to competitors that weren't playing fairly in the market, and many companies were blocked from the Chinese market entirely. The same thing goes for lost profits and other value due to Chinese IP theft. Following the US government's lead, US companies overvalued supply chains and depended upon a market that, at its foundation, wasn't dependable.

Yes, the United States saw growth. But growth needs to be evaluated based on its costs and overall return on investment. So, at what cost was this relationship? Cheap goods and low inflation were swapped for subversion of capitalism, loss of jobs, holding down wages, suppressing innovation, reducing opportunities for small business in a fair playing field, intellectual property theft, and a government that moved away from free markets toward central planning. It strengthened the government and weakened free markets.

Adding to the costs, as a buyer of US debt, China's growth allowed the US government to undertake another trillion dollars' worth of sloppy, unaccountable spending.

Plus, today China gives the US government cover as the bogeyman or enemy to justify the taking of more individual rights.

Over and over again, China has exposed, albeit unintentionally, the weaknesses of US politicians who think they know what is best. It has been an ally in the creation of the too-big-to-succeed status of the US government.

Ultimately, there is a bit of trading places going on. As China has become more like the United States, the United States has become more like China. The United States has moved away from free markets, while the world's most powerful communist state has become critically dependent upon moving closer to capitalism globally.

The Chinese Dream Versus
the American Dream

As a side note, the "Chinese Dream" won't be fully realized, either. Even though China has moved toward capitalism, its inherent unwillingness to go far enough along the spectrum to protect the individual and his rights will be its downfall.

Unless China enacts significant reforms to individual rights and their underlying culture, China will likely never be the world's reserve currency, as many fear. When a fiat monetary system exists (one backed by faith in a government system), who will trust a country that flouts fundamental rights (whether it is the Uyghurs or intellectual property rights), doesn't allow free speech, knowingly engages in fraudulent financial reporting, and carries out other nefarious endeavors? Not to mention the country's unleashing a virus on the world along with a cover-up that caused critical time to be wasted in containing it and brought financial ruin in its wake.

Whether it is the Uyghur situation or the Hong Kong conflict, continued rights violations, which are consistent with and emanate from China's centralized, collectivist system, will continue to create separations between the country and its partners, including the United States.

China will likely reap its own central planning failure, as its one-child policy leaves behind a cadre of young men with no marriage prospects, among other issues, including, per a report from the Chinese Academy of Social Sciences, a declining population. In fact, not only will it be going from one of the highest birthrates in the world to one of the lowest, but as soon as ten years from now, the demographics will shift to a point where the number of pensioners will be double that of the taxpayer base. Projections show that by 2050, around a third of the Chinese population will be over the age of sixty-five.[43]

In the meantime, the United States needs to recapture its focus on capitalism and individual rights, but it won't be easy. The cracks in the United States' economic foundation may be covered with paint, but they are there.

To do that, the government needs to get out of the way and stop trying to act like China. The result of President Trump's trade wars? In July 2020, the United States' trade deficit rose to its highest level in twelve years.[44]

CHAPTER 13

Decentralization Versus Centralization

How to Prevent Further Central Planning
Attacks on Small Business

The government war on small business is a series of battles that are part of a greater war of decentralization versus centralization. The government and its allies, special interests and big businesses, want to concentrate power and seek to destroy anything that stands in their way.

These attempts at centralizing power have been inhibited mostly where individuals have stood firm on their individual rights, not just with words but with actions. There has been a movement toward individualism and decentralization that has been supported and accelerated by access to robust technologies.

The second amendment is a strong example of where individuals have pushed back against central powers. The more the government has threatened to take away second amendment rights, the more individuals have purchased guns and ammunition. Individuals have stood firm on decentralizing power and addressing the concerns that they cannot trust centralized local and national institutions with their protection—and that they may need protection from those powers as well.

There are other examples of individual pushback against those with centralized powers. There has been a repudiation of central banking and Wall Street via cryptocurrencies and other decentralized finance initiatives. There has been a rejection of the traditional structure of the corporate job via the gig economy, enabling flexible, self-driven work for 59 million people in the United States alone. Small business and capitalism also embody decentralization.

In 2020, the decisions made by centrally planned primary and secondary schools accelerated families opting out of them, pursuing education options from the flourishing private schools we discussed in chapter 10 to pod learning and homeschooling.

The embracing of decentralization is a threat to centralized power, and the government and their crony beneficiaries do not want to see this happen. They will do whatever they can to try to damage, stop, and reverse these trends and actions.

Centralizing economic power is a priority for central planners, for obvious reasons. With half the economy in the hands of decentralized small businesses—an even larger percentage when you include the gig economy—destabilizing and rolling up those independent economic entities is a priority for central planning. The playbook, as laid out by current democratic policies at all levels of government, has unfortunately been effective: Kill a bunch of small businesses via prolonged shutdowns. Get their employees moved to big business or reliant upon a government handout. Hit the small businesses that survive with restrictive legislation from raising the minimum wage to reclassifying gig and independent workers as employees. This will put even more decentralized businesses and gig workers out of business, forcing those workers again into big businesses, where unions can become more powerful, or back onto the government dole. Propose UBI as "compensation" for all of these tremendous losses—which will undoubtedly be blamed on technology but will really be the function of central planners using slimy tactics to subvert rights and do whatever they can to stop decentralization from thriving.

There are all kinds of arenas in which we need to stop the further centralization of power, from reining in the Fed to rejecting more government involvement and supporting more capitalism and decentralization in areas such as health care and education. Social Security needs to be restructured so individuals can regain full control over their retirement planning. We need to decentralize politics and break apart the duopoly of the two-party system in the United States, enact spending reform, and more.

However, as the discussions of these endeavors could be another volume in and of itself, I will stay focused below on a few issues that are front and center as the big issues the Democrats, their allies, and other beneficiaries of central planning are pushing currently that directly impact small businesses and capitalism.

Minimum Wage Laws

One economic ruse that progressives in particular have long been in favor of has been the minimum wage. Many states and localities, particularly blue cities and states, have been rolling out higher minimum wages in recent years.

The Biden administration, in concert with many progressive allies, came out of the gates proposing to increase the federal minimum wage to $15 per hour, more than double the current level on the books. While it is easy to fall into the trap of believing that this is a good thing for workers, it is not, nor is it a good one for small businesses. It is a diversionary war tactic in the quest to roll up and centralize economic power.

Thomas Sowell, in *Basic Economics*, talked about the reality of minimum wages and related laws, saying:

Making it illegal to pay less than a given amount does not make a worker's productivity worth that amount—and, if it is not, that worker is unlikely to be employed. Yet minimum wage laws are almost always discussed politically in terms of the benefits they confer on workers. Unfortunately, the real minimum wage is always zero, regardless of the laws, and that is the wage that many workers receive in the wake of the creation or escalation of a government-mandated minimum wage, because they lose their jobs or fail to find jobs when they enter the labor force.[1]

I believe that minimum wage laws are a violation of the Constitution. Not dissimilar to the issues around the gig economy, discussed below, employees and employers should be able to make an agreement on wages and other employment issues without government intervention.

Most people who believe in a minimum wage or raising the minimum wage come from a good place. But as I have said many times in this book, good intentions don't produce good outcomes. When your good intentions don't take unintended consequences into account, they usually end up adversely impacting the exact people they're purporting to help. That's a key problem with artificially mandated wage increases; they lead to no greater spending power and fewer jobs for those with the fewest skills. It's also a violation of individual rights.

Minimum wage laws were introduced in the United States by progressives in the early 1900s specifically to keep low-skilled and immigrant labor out of the workforce. The laws have the same effect today. Whether they are replaced by technology, more skilled labor, or a combination of both, the higher the minimum wage, the bigger the barrier it is for those with few skills to enter the workforce. Being kept out of that first job has a cascading effect on not being able to learn on-the-job skills and progress to higher-paying jobs. It keeps both young and vulnerable people out of the workforce altogether for long periods of time—perhaps forever.

Additionally, always left out of the discussion around minimum wage is the effect on entrepreneurs and small businesses. Nobody guarantees the wage of small business entrepreneurs. They risk their capital, time, and money, without any guarantee of pay or outcome. Many small business owners work exceptionally long hours and endure enormous amounts of stress, and that was before layering on having to deal with mandated government shutdowns.

Why should small business owners risk their money and be forced to pay someone else more than they are able to earn themselves? That concept is nonsensical and against the basic tenets of free market capitalism and American opportunity.

I have heard people say, "Well, if you can't afford to pay a living wage, you shouldn't have a business." I throw that right back: if you don't think that a business compensates you enough to live on, you shouldn't take the job. Nobody owes you a job. It should not be a business's responsibility to figure out how much individuals require to live on and meet their needs; that's a Marxist nightmare. Both employers and employees present an opportunity, and, if there's a match, a job and payment are traded for experience and time. There's no need for you, me, or government to be involved.

I will also suggest that most of the calculations of "need" rely on a forty-hour workweek, and I can tell you that most people starting out as entrepreneurs work at least 50 to 100 percent more than that. If you are struggling, you should not be expecting to work forty hours a week. Here's an inconvenient truth: if you seek to support yourself or others on a minimum wage job, you will have to work more than forty hours per week and/or take a second job, live with a roommate or family member, make sacrifices, and so on.

Though nobody "deserves" a job (the petulant cry of people who are too spoiled to know what real hardship is), what people not only deserve but have the right to is the opportunity to negotiate and accept what works for them without government force; you know, that whole individual rights thing.

The media feeds this problem because they tend to focus on the biggest fraction of a percent of businesses instead of the 99 percent–plus of small businesses and entrepreneurs. We hear about Walmart when around half of the working population is employed by small businesses. So although I disagree with the premise of minimum wage increases, I challenge those who want to penalize a handful of big companies with a change that will affect millions of small businesses that would also have to abide by the same legislation. As discussed in the cronyism chapter, big businesses actually love these laws, because they end up hurting or eliminating their competition. Walmart can afford pay increases, whereas a startup retailer trying to bring goods and jobs to a struggling area of a city cannot.

I will also remind you that you can actively support the idea of businesses paying better without having the concept stringently codified into law, let alone federal law, which means that the same rules apply in New York City as in Lafayette County, Arkansas—no exceptions.

Having to pay a higher minimum wage creates many challenges for small businesses. It may mean that a company has to wait longer to hire a new employee, making it more challenging to grow the business and riskier to start one. It can also lead to a small business owner hiring fewer employees overall. Raising the minimum wage typically means that those earning above the minimum wage want a bump, too, noting the value of their skills above those of the minimum wage earner. As the costs accumulate, the small business owner will bear the cost differential and take home less pay. Ironically, after adding up his or her time, it may mean that for years an entrepreneur will take home an amount less than the minimum wage on an hourly basis.

Though raising the minimum wage may not stop a large company from opening a business, it creates a pause and a bigger challenge for a food truck operator, small retailer, or other entrepreneurial startup with limited capital or a smaller-revenue business model. The minimum wage creates a barrier for those without access to capital to take advantage of capitalism and decentralized opportunities to lift themselves up, create their own destiny, and generate equity, a critical component of generating wealth.

Are those who are concerned about minimum pay also planning to guarantee all small business owners' incomes? We certainly shouldn't, just as we shouldn't for anyone who works for a small business—or any business, for that matter. Appropriate compensation is what the market sorts out if allowed to operate freely.

The minimum wage hurts those most in need of getting into the workforce by keeping them out of the workforce. Thomas Sowell said in a video about his book *Knowledge and Decisions*:

> There is no inherent reason why low-skilled or high-risk employees are any less employable than high-skilled, low-risk employees. Someone who is five times as valuable to an employer is no more or less employable than someone who is one-fifth as valuable, when the pay differences reflect their differences in benefits to the employer.
>
> This is more than a theoretical point. Historically, lower skill levels did not prevent black males from having labor force participation rates higher than that of white males for every US Census from 1890 through 1930. Since then, the general growth of wage-fixing arrangements: minimum wage laws, labor unions, civil service pay scales, etc. has reversed that and made more and more blacks unemployable despite their rising levels of education and skills: absolutely and relative to whites.[2]

"In short," he continued, "no one is employable or unemployable absolutely, but only relative to a given pay scale." Once again, the progressive social justice, centrally planned outcome has fared worse than what a free market could otherwise provide.

To that end, we have also predictably seen technology take over jobs. From ordering kiosks to robots that flip hamburgers to entire self-serve concepts, many businesses will find a way to substitute technology for jobs because they aren't in business to provide jobs. Companies offer a job opportunity only when the person they hire can provide value, and as with any other investment, there is a cap on the cost of that. For example, Flippy, a robot burger flipper being implemented at Dodger Stadium as well as other locations, costs approximately $3 an hour, has no associated taxes or benefits, and isn't unionized (at least not yet!).[3]

In addition to technology, we have seen the effects of outsourcing jobs overseas. However, that didn't happen in a vacuum; it happened in part because of mandates on wages and expenses.

In areas where wage hikes have been mandated, the effects have led to closures. *Restaurant Business* conducted a survey in 2019 (a year before the impact of COVID on the industry) that found that "Nearly 1 in 10 restaurateurs in areas with a recently increased minimum wage have closed an operation since the cost hike . . . 43% of establishments in areas where the minimum was raised have eliminated positions, and 64% have reduced employees' hours."[4]

A higher minimum wage does not create more jobs, more opportunities, and more growth. Opposing legislation like this helps to quell government interference in individual rights and is an important way to ensure that they don't price jobs, particularly entry-level jobs that put people on the path to job growth, out of the market with legislation.

Allowing minimum wage increases to continue will keep people out of the workforce. Even the CBO estimated that the Biden federal minimum wage increase proposal could cost 1.3 million American jobs. Where will those workers go, and what will they do for work? They will first go on the government dole, followed by a cry for more UBI, as discussed below.

Protection of Gig Workers, Independent Contractors, and Entrepreneurial Flexibility

As technology, work, and opportunities have changed, the ability for people to pursue a livelihood in new, flexible, and decentralized ways has emerged. A big piece of this is via gig and independent contractor work structures.

In the United States, which is supposed to be the land of freedom and opportunity and by extension freedom to pursue opportunities, an estimated 59 million entrepreneurs have taken up work as free-lancers and independent contractors in the gig economy or as part of the way they run their independent small businesses. While independent contractors have existed for decades, in capacities ranging from staffing on movie and TV sets to those who support a variety of small business clients, technology has created new gig workers who provide services ranging from transportation to grocery pickup to dinner delivery and more.[5]

Why would anyone want to be this kind of an entrepreneur and not a full-time employee? Gig work can provide flexible ways to earn money on your own time and terms—you know, freedom and choice! Across myriad industries, everyone from moms with kids to students to partially retired individuals to artists and entrepreneurs funding other projects enjoys setting their own hours, working as often as they want, providing a customized experience, and being their own boss. In other industries, project-based work is the norm.

With all of the benefit to the economy, all of the willing partic-ipants, and all of the good outcomes for consumers, who get more choice and new products and services, you would think that the gov-ernment would want to make it as easy as possible to do this kind of work and do everything it could to help these folks succeed, right?

Wrong.

This freedom and decentralization are threats to central planning. So predictably, those freedoms came under attack by government.

Through a slew of centrally planned laws, regulations, and requirements, the government actively makes it more difficult and expensive for people to get into business, even the simplest of businesses. Plus, ongoing requirements and shifting laws make it harder to compete in the market once they are in business.

The attack on gig work began in California, the test ground in recent times for central planning rule, with a state law called AB5. AB5 was sponsored heavily by unions and shepherded by Assemblywoman Lorena Gonzalez. It was sold as imposing better regulation on big companies such as Uber and Lyft to help drivers. This is the oldest trick in the progressive government and central planning book. As Ronald Reagan famously said, "The nine most terrifying words in the English language are: I'm from the government, and I'm here to help." By saying it is trying to help workers get more benefits or regulating big and bad companies, government wins the hearts of people who think that politicians always have good intentions—or worse, that good intentions lead to good outcomes. However, the central planners aren't trying to help you; they are trying to help themselves and their cronies.

Via AB5—and interfering with the Constitution—government created roadblocks to work. Even if you want to work for a company independently, you cannot. Because laws and regulations create more costs around employees in terms of taxes, insurance benefits, compliance, and other issues, it makes the cost of taking on workers prohibitive for many employers, particularly small ones. These businesses are not financially able to hire people at all, and thus, such regulation kills jobs. It also takes away your freedom as an individual to work how you want.

This started because the unions lose out when so many workers can work freely and aren't forced to pay union dues. Specifically for AB5, the taxi unions were angry that they were subject to all kinds of government rules and regulations, and accordingly costs, that Uber and Lyft were not. Instead of undoing the free market–interfering rules that were causing the issues, the route was taken to punish more businesses with more rules. Not only Uber and Lyft were punished, but also every single independent worker in the state, along with the businesses with which they worked.

Though unionizing can serve a purpose, unions tend to run into the same issues as other centrally planned groups. If unions existed without force and control and allowed for freedom and choice of others, they would be more tenable. But they fall victim to the pitfalls of human nature, looking to enrich their power and strength under the guise of helping others and standing in the way of freedom and choice. If something is the right thing to do, to participate in or be a part of, you don't need to be forced to do it.

Though I am incredibly sympathetic to the frustration of taxi drivers toward Uber, the reason they are frustrated is that they have too much regulation themselves. They have had to pay insane medallion and licensing fees and higher insurance and jump through hoops. All of that hurts their economics when other companies and decentralized workers that aren't subject to the same regulations— and the costs that come with them—enter the market. However, the way to level the playing field isn't to inflict more restrictions and regulations on everyone but to lower them for everyone! This isn't suggesting eliminating all regulation (most people would likely agree that a background check is a good thing for drivers), but the further away from the free market things get, the worse they become.

Others will argue that the companies aren't providing medical insurance to contractors. Well, I would first ask, why is health care even tied to your job? Solve the problem (in this case, reduce regulation to allow for more free market medical insurance options), not the symptom. Additionally, many people don't need medical insurance from their job. They may receive it from a spouse or a parent.

They may receive it through another job or an independent marketplace. Whether or not you think companies should offer medical insurance, why are you advocating for forcing people who don't want or need it to have it based on your thoughts about what they should have? If they want to take the gig without it, butt out.

Back to AB5. As noted, though that legislation wouldn't have been okay if it had focused only on Uber and Lyft, it turns out, unsurprisingly, that it didn't stop there. Under AB5, independent writers, caterers, cleaning crews, stylists, photographers, and myriad other professionals in a slew of industries who work heavily as independent contractors instead of employees found themselves out of work entirely.

Note also that the AB5 law standard for being an independent contractor is different, and far more stringent, than the IRS's standard on the same issue.

Independent contractors and freelancers are purely entrepreneurs who want the freedom to work when and how it aligns with their lives, goals, and objectives. Whether it is a mother who has only a small number of hours per month when she can work, a student pursuing a side hustle while studying, or a creative who just likes the choice and flexibility of freelancing, they are a large and essential part of the economy. No politician should be able to say, "No, you can't work." It is an unconstitutional abuse of government power and individual rights, the same type of unreasonable control that so-called democratic socialists want to enact. My work, my choice.

AB5 is the ultimate example of the government getting away from protecting individual rights to pick winners and losers. And although it is always sold as helping the little guy, the real benefit goes to the big guys. It goes to the big companies that can afford to pay for more benefits, insurance, licensing—whatever. It goes to the unions. And the unions ultimately flex it to cement the power of the politicians. So pretty much everyone except the very littlest guys, including the littlest guy of them all—the individual—are helped.

Power is concentrated. Decentralization of work is disrupted—in a bad way.

Paved with Good Intentions

AB5 is the perfect example of people not understanding the unintended consequences of legislation. What is portrayed as "helping" usually limits freedom and choice. But as the saying goes, the road to hell is paved with good intentions. On Twitter, under the hashtags #AB5 and #RepealAB5, there are staggering stories about how the law quickly destroyed livelihoods.

Kevin Kiley, the California assemblyman who led a vote to try to repeal the law, shared some stories of the aftermath. One constituent wrote, "I survived cancer and had 36 surgeries while raising kids, and still live with a traumatic brain injury. I can't work a regular job. But with the support of my family, I was finally chasing my dreams as a writer, poet & Voice Over actor. Now #AB5 won't let me."

Another story he shared was "The total cost of daycare would be $3,000 a month for both my children if I have to give up my freelance career, as #AB5 mandates. More importantly, the thought of spending less time with my children during their most formative development breaks my heart."

The stories go on and on. Unfortunately, Assemblyman Kiley's call for a vote to repeal the law was struck down. Kira Davis, editor at large at RedState and one of the many individuals who worked tirelessly to try to get AB5 repealed, said:

It is grossly disappointing that the California assembly would not allow a repeal bill to be heard, and furthermore refuses to suspend the enforcement [of] AB5 while the state studies the massive problems surrounding the bill and how to fix it. . . .

Lorena Gonzalez and her cohorts in Sacramento have

willfully turned a blind eye to the suffering of independent contractors across the state. They have no care for the unprecedented pain and job loss their ill-conceived bill has caused for the average CA citizen.[6]

The law went into effect on January 1, 2020, a massive blow to many workers who thereby lost their jobs before the pandemic even came into play.

The blowback was fierce, but instead of scrapping the law, its creators tried to amend it via a list of which industries it was acceptable to work in as a contractor in the fall of 2020. It was yet another example of government picking winners and losers for its own purposes and benefit.

If you live outside California, you might not feel empathy for the plight of the freelancers in the state, but it has also become a national issue. The same language that was used in AB5 was, according to Kira Davis, sneaked into federal legislation that passed the House of Representatives called the Protecting the Right to Organize (PRO) Act.

This law, which is heavily pro-union and seeks to repeal right-to-work laws, also tries to do away with freelancing. This awful legislation threatened the entire backbone of the US economy even before the COVID government black swan hit. Davis said, "With the PROact looming on the horizon for the country at large, California artists and freelancers are not giving up this fight."[7]

Despite many companies' complying with the AB5 regulation, Uber and Lyft, among others, decided to fight back. In August 2020, the California attorney general obtained a court order requiring ride-share companies to hire drivers as employees immediately or suspend operations.

Uber and Lyft appealed the decision and received a temporary stay.

Representative Kevin McCarthy of California, at the time the

Republican minority leader of the House of Representatives, issued a press release against AB5 and California's efforts. Among other things, he said:

> AB 5 does not work, and it never has. Now, the two largest ridesharing companies in the United States, both of which were founded and are currently headquartered in California, are prepared to leave the state because Democrats refuse to fix their terrible error, even though it is crushing gig economy workers and the people who use these services.
>
> For months, gig workers have vocally expressed their utter opposition for AB 5, but sadly, their cries of frustration have fallen on the deaf ears of Sacramento Democrats who have been unwilling to reverse course. AB 5 is not only hurting these drivers—nearly 90 percent of whom are expected to lose their jobs—but countless Californians with limited transportation options who rely on these services to manage traveling to work, school, and doctor's appointments in the midst of a pandemic.
>
> California is known as the land of innovation, technology, and creativity—our movie industry is based here, as is Silicon Valley. Yet, day after day, companies are choosing to take their business elsewhere because Sacramento's liberal policies, like the failed high-speed rail; the inability to get residents the water they need and deserve; rolling blackouts or brownouts; the worst homelessness problem in the country; and now AB 5, have changed the very foundation that draws people to the Golden State.[8]

His statement also included some statistics and information that a poll conducted by Global Strategy Group had found that drivers had consistently said they wanted to remain independent contractors as opposed to becoming employees by a four-to-one margin, AB5 staying in effect would mean that 90 percent of drivers would lose the ability to earn from their platforms entirely, and that 38 percent of Lyft rides start or end in low-income neighborhoods with limited travel options, which would impact lower-income riders vis-à-vis affordable transportation options. So who is being helped?

Think about the concept that someone who decides to drive for Uber one day because he or she has some free time and wants to earn cash has to be an employee by law in America. Is your babysitter going to be your employee? Do you become an employee of a flea market when you set up a table to sell your old clothes there? The entire concept is a centrally planned nightmare in direct opposition to the American Dream.

Importantly, this is not a red or blue choice; it's a green (money/financial) choice. It's freedom of choice, and it's why the backlash against AB5 was from a bipartisan group of individuals.

Uber and Lyft saw a big victory on Election Day 2020 when Proposition 22 passed, with the people of California voting not to make delivery and ride-share drivers employees, thus preserving their independent contractor status. However, the big guys took care of their own and didn't bring some of the smaller contractors in other industries along for the ride. It still left many gig workers in limbo due to AB5 and the PRO Act a concern nationally as 2020 closed out.[9]

Unfortunately, although the PRO Act technically died when Congress changed over, it would be brought back from the dead. The law was billed as "pro-worker," despite suppressing worker freedoms and likely killing seven to eight figures' worth of jobs. Still, President Biden had been partnering with unions since before his inauguration with the intention of trying to get the legislation passed within the first hundred days of his administration.

This is central planning again saying that they know what is right for you and they want to limit your freedoms by codifying it into law. Of course, this is only lip service, and the real beneficiaries will be those with power. If they succeed, it will be a huge blow to decentralization and capitalism, to small businesses that rely on gig workers, and to gig workers who want to remain flexible.

What will happen to the economy if the PRO Act passes into law? Just as the playbook has laid out, small businesses will go under. Their market share will be taken by big companies, which will become more powerful. Some of those will have unionization. The unions will become stronger, and they will all support their crony politicians who enabled this outcome.

The UBI Shell Game

In January 2021, Andrew Yang, the former technology entrepreneur and 2020 Democratic presidential candidate, declared his intention to run for mayor of New York. His mayoral platform was ported over from his national platform, which includes "giving" people their own—or someone else's—money through UBI.

Universal basic income, or UBI, was de facto pilot tested during COVID, as the COVID relief bills mandated sending non-means-tested checks out on multiple occasions. It was a way to give people a taste of what it was like to receive a check, with the very inaccurate perception of no strings attached.

UBI is ultimately a shell game that makes no sense. It "guarantees" income from a government that produces basically nothing. Sure, the government could print more money out of thin air, but then it just makes every dollar less valuable and goods and services more expensive in real terms. If we have learned one thing from underfunded liabilities, such as those plaguing Social Security and many state pension systems, it's that a program should never, ever guarantee a benefit. Never. It's guesswork and always ends up a losing proposition. Anytime benefits are guaranteed, the money eventually runs out, so why double down on an unsound practice?

UBI is a fundamentally flawed concept. It is not needs-based or means-tested; it is universal, meaning, for everyone. For those who have jobs or other means of deriving income, UBI is a costly way to return your own money back to you. Why would you need the government to reissue back to you the money you have paid it? It's nonsensical, it's inefficient, and it's expensive. You pay x dollars to the government, it collects a toll, and then it gives you some of your money back? Why is that something for which anyone would ever advocate?

It's the same misunderstanding made by those who think that their tax refund is a government benefit they get, rather than an interest-free loan that they have given the government all year. Giving a dollar to the government and having it hand it back to you several months later isn't a benefit.

If government believes, as I do, that people should keep more of their own money, it does not need to be an intermediary in the process—government can just lower taxes on individuals to begin with.

For those who are struggling financially, too many ineffective and inefficient programs (which, by the way, need to be streamlined) already exist. There need to be fewer, more effective programs, not more programs.

Looking at the specifics of UBI requires examining its funding mechanism. Some UBI proposals would be paid for via a value-added tax (VAT), which is a complex system where taxes are added on at every step of the supply chain, from raw materials to final consumption. This adds a lot of inefficient administration into the market, dragging down productivity. As you have seen with other regulation, it would create an outsized burden for small businesses to add staff to comply with this additional administration, making them less competitive than their bigger competitors. As VATs reside under government purview, there's also the opportunity for the government to offer rebates and incentives under certain circumstances, and history shows us that it will always end up favoring big businesses.

Additionally, with around 70 percent of the US economy being consumer spending based, if everything becomes more expensive because of taxes, that means inflation; your dollar now buys less. Like every other "good idea," UBI ends up being a tax on those less fortunate; they will bear more of the burden of the costs of essential goods and services going up so the government can run its shell game of shuffling money around without creating any value. No, thank you.

In the *Wall Street Journal*, the economics professor David R. Henderson also warned that because you "don't see the tax itemized on your receipt, you may not be aware of how big the tax is," which, unsurprisingly, usually leads to higher VAT and more government. He added, "the sad truth is that VATs are not an engine of economic growth but rather an engine of government growth."[10] The same is true of UBI.

UBI is the bait to get people more comfortable with government-induced job losses due to bad policies such as higher mandated wages and the elimination of independent contractors and gig workers. It's not for your benefit, and it is not a "hand-up"; it is another deceptive tactic in central planners' quest for power.

Regulatory Reform

In addition to halting new legislation meant to disrupt decentralization, capitalism, and small businesses, there are a number of existing regulatory reforms to consider.

Along with all of the other headaches and challenges that small businesses have to contend with, a 2016 survey by the National Small Business Association confirmed what many other surveys and studies have also shown: that administration and regulation is consistently one of the biggest challenges to small businesses. Like their bigger counterparts, small businesses have to deal with labor and employment laws, including overtime, independent contractor tests, licensing, permits, advertising regulations, privacy, antitrust regulations, the tax code, and in certain industries, environmental laws, among others—the list goes on and on at the local, state, and federal levels.[11]

The 2008 World Bank Group Entrepreneurship Survey, which covered a hundred countries, "indicates a very strong (and statistically significant) relationship between entrepreneurship and a better business environment" and showed that countries with more business regulations create more barriers to entry for new business formation (and, as a result, have fewer new business starts than they otherwise would have had).[12]

This is a general problem but a larger one for small businesses. As reported by Small Business Trends:

> as Nicole and Mark Crain of Lafayette University explain, regulatory compliance exerts a disproportionately large burden on small companies because the fixed costs of adhering to rules can be spread out over more revenue in large firms than in small ones. Crain and Crain estimated the per employee cost of complying with Federal regulations at $10,585 for businesses with fewer than 20 employees but only $7,755 for businesses with more than 499 workers.[13]

Additionally, these regulations make small businesses less competitive against foreign competition and create uncertainty, which keeps small business owners from investing and hiring, and of course, creates other unintended consequences, which are rarely positive.

This is why many big businesses pursue regulation, knowing that it creates an undue burden on smaller and emerging competitors and will reduce their competition.

The piece also illustrated that the supposed land of the free and individual rights wasn't living up to its name, reporting, "The Organization for Economic Cooperation and Development (OECD) found that the U.S. had higher regulatory barriers to entrepreneurship, greater administrative burdens on small business owners, and higher barriers to competition than a number of other industrialized countries" and that those regulations are growing.[14]

Regulation needs to be addressed and reined in for small businesses to have a full opportunity to compete. Though basic regulation is necessary to enforce individual rights, including property rights, and as discussed is a cornerstone of capitalism, any regulation that steps over the necessary protection of rights is anticompetitive and anti–free markets.

Though the Trump administration worked to roll back some regulations, many of the regulations that most impact small businesses are mandated at the local and state levels.[15]

To grow the economy and support small businesses in doing so, reducing and rolling back regulation are a must, as are transparency, accountability, and simplicity in any regulations that persist.

Licensing Reform

Licensing reform for individual entrepreneurs, other professionals, and small businesses could go a long way to boosting the economy. The pandemic unwittingly proved that case.

For example, the American Association of Nurse Practitioners listed almost two dozen suspensions and waivers of requirements in the medical arena to deal with perceived and real shortages of professionals to deal with COVID. The *National Law Review* reported on various waivers in the industry, including state-specific licensing requirements, demonstrating that the laws were roadblocks to getting resources where they needed to be.[16]

A piece in the *Orange County Register* by Jeffrey A. Singer, an MD and senior fellow at the Cato Institute, pointed out:

> Governors who recently suspended state licensing laws to address the COVID-19 pandemic tacitly conceded through this action that these regulations limit the free flow of health care services and contribute to shortages. States should learn from this moment and . . . consider replacing licensing with certification to remove barriers that block qualified people from entering health professions and traveling to places where they are needed.[17]

This is true not just for the medical industry but for every industry. A 2018 article for The Hill by Jarrett Dieterle and Shoshana Weissmann cited the Institute for Justice as saying:

> one in four Americans must obtain a government license in order to practice their occupation, and the average license requires at least one year of education, passing an exam, and paying several hundred dollars in fees. The Brookings Institution has calculated that licensing has resulted in 2.85 million fewer jobs across the nation, with a cost of $203 billion to consumers annually.[18]

Some of the industries requiring licensing are head-scratchers. For example, many states require a license for hair braiding. Not cutting, not using chemical processes, just doing the same thing that mothers and fathers around the country do for their children's hair before sending them off to school.

In Illinois, specialist licensing specific to hair braiding must be obtained. The requirements, at the time of writing, include a three-hundred-hour training course at an approved school. According to the Beauty School Directory, "The training program should cover scalp care, braiding techniques, styling knowledge, and hands-on practice." Additionally, the state requires practitioners to take fourteen hours of continuing education every two-year period . . . to braid hair legally.[19]

That is an unnecessary cost and time expenditure that keeps those who want to braid hair from going into business for themselves, working in a salon, or expanding their service offerings.

While the guise of licensing is oversight and consumer protection, a study by the Cato Institute revealed that licensing is more about cronyism and control than about skills and protection. The institute said that in health care clinician licensing, which is similar to other areas,

> It allows incumbent clinicians to control the education and training requirements for entry into their professions and the ability of other health professionals to compete with them. Incumbent clinicians use these powers to block entrants into their professions, to block other categories of clinicians from entering the markets for certain services they are competent to provide, and to block innovative education and training programs that could reduce entry barriers into their professions and competing professions.

This translates into higher consumer prices yet doesn't guarantee safety or outcomes; but it certainly concentrates centralized power. The Cato Institute suggests certification as an alternative in areas that require some training, vetting, and skills.[20]

What can be done to change this? The Institute for Justice took on licensing reform for braiding. As it says on its website and in its reports, braiding is simple and safe and does not require government interference or regulation. It exposes that becoming licensed costs thousands of dollars, can take hundreds to thousands of hours, and "in many states this training does not even teach them to braid hair, but does require them to learn totally irrelevant things."[21]

Yep, that sounds like central planning.

The institute believes that it is a constitutional violation and in 2014 launched a national "Braiding Initiative" by "filing lawsuits challenging onerous and anti-competitive hair braiding regulations," noting:

> Research demonstrates that occupational licensing laws, such as those governing hair braiding, create artificial and unnecessary barriers to entry for entrepreneurs seeking to take their first step on the economic ladder. That's especially true for occupations that traditionally cater to individuals just beginning a professional career. The right to earn an honest living is an essential part of our nation's promise of opportunity.[22]

These efforts have started to bear fruit. In fact, in Florida in June 2020, Governor Ron DeSantis signed the Occupational Freedom and Opportunity Act, which provides an overhaul of occupational licensing in the state based on these initiatives.[23]

In Illinois, as mentioned above, a bill was introduced to eliminate licensing requirements for barbers and cosmetologists, including hair braiders.[24]

Dieterle and Weissmann also suggested:

> Another option would be to step up the Federal Trade Commission's antitrust enforcement efforts that target crony and collusive licensing boards around the country. These boards often face little oversight and are stocked with industry insiders who have an economic incentive to prevent new competitors from joining their trade. The Supreme Court found such arrangements to be unconstitutional in 2015, and the FTC

should use this precedent to bring additional enforcement actions against other state licensing boards. To do so, Congress should consider modestly increasing funding for FTC enforcement actions, or simply require the agency to dedicate more of its existing resources to these efforts.[25]

Business Licensing Reform

Can you imagine visiting a lemonade stand run by neighborhood kids, only to see the police show up and shut it down? It sounds like something that would happen in a dictatorship, but over the past few years, that has happened in states as diverse as New York, Illinois, and Texas because the lemonade stands didn't have the appropriate licenses and permits to do business. Widespread media attention has gotten some bills and laws put into place to try to get rid of this insanity. Still, it illustrates how completely out of control government has become in a supposedly free country regarding regulation and licensing.[26]

Government again unintentionally made the case for licensing reform during COVID, as well as reforming other regulations. It fast-tracked the products it needed and created waivers to allow, for example, more manufacturers to make hand sanitizer to deal with shortages. Though the waivers were only temporary, they should be made permanent, and the government should be looking for places to continue to peel back this type of legislation.[27]

The same thing was widespread with arcane local and state laws regarding alcohol delivery and carryout that have no sound or valid purpose today (or frankly, when they were enacted).

The Small Business Administration (SBA) has a tool that helps small businesses navigate federal permits and licenses. On the federal level, the government actively requires businesses to get permits related to industries such as alcoholic beverages, agriculture, fish and wildlife, and transportation and logistics, among other areas.

At the state level, the SBA also provides counselors (via SCORE, a resource for small businesses that is vastly underpromoted by the government) to help small companies with licenses and permits needed at the state, county, or city/township level. As the SBA's website notes, "States tend to regulate a broader range of activities than the federal government. For example, business activities that are commonly regulated locally include auctions, construction, and dry cleaning, farming, plumbing, restaurants, retail, and vending machines."[28] Not to mention hair braiding.

Permits and licenses often expire, and with their expiration comes additional time spent to reapply, hoops to jump through, and, of course, fees. They not only suck up a ton of time for compliance but often cost thousands to tens of thousands of dollars to comply with in full.

Rolling back the licensing (and the administration that comes with it) would give entrepreneurs more time and money to put to work growing their business instead of having to deal with government interference in it. It would be a big boon for small businesses in competing with large companies.

Insurance Grabs

Another example of regulations that create a drag for small business owners are insurance requirements that are burdensome and frankly out of date with the modern workforce. In my business, located in Illinois, I have to spend several thousands of dollars per year on workers' compensation insurance. Everyone who works for me works from their own home, on a computer, doing such "dangerous" tasks as responding to emails and writing and editing copy, among similar work.

Though you may understand why a factory might need workers' compensation insurance, why would my small business or many others like it need it? Around 70 percent of all businesses are service businesses, many of those doing very low- to no-risk work, which don't need the same types of "protections" as potentially dangerous worksites.

On the state of Illinois "Worker Compensation Committee" website, it says:

> Illinois law requires employers to provide workers' compensation insurance for almost everyone who is hired, injured, or whose employment is localized in Illinois. . . .
>
> An employer that knowingly and willfully fails to obtain insurance may be fined up to $500 for every day of non-compliance, with a minimum fine of $10,000. Corporate officers can be held personally liable if the company fails to pay the penalty. Since 2006, the Commission has collected over $7 million in fines. This provides workers the proper legal protection and other employers a more fair competitive arena.[29]

How does this create a fair and more competitive arena? Why do people working from home on a computer need workers' compensation insurance coverage? These requirements create extra costs for small employers, making it more expensive to add their first employee and subsequent employees. It is a yearly expense that could be used to grow businesses instead. That's hardly fair or competitive and is more of a drag on smaller enterprises than on larger ones.

The website also notes that "Illinois has more companies writing workers' compensation insurance than any other state." That sounds like a crony deal with the insurance companies, not something benefiting small businesses.

Though you may think, "Well, it's just a cost of doing business," it isn't. It's a cost of doing business only because the government has stuck its nose into the process to funnel money to its insurance company buddies and generate fines. That's no way to support small businesses and the economy. And frankly, it doesn't need to be mandated. If a company has enough risk to be concerned about an employee lawsuit, it will buy insurance in the free market.

Small Businesses and Capitalism Thrive with You

For capitalism to be appreciated and decentralization to kick central planning's behind, more individuals need to be aware of their own role in capitalism. As it allows for individual choice, the choice you as an individual make is critical. If you want to support small businesses, you may need to be more thoughtful about how you allocate your dollars, in your community and online. If you support Amazon over your local vendor, don't be upset when the local vendor goes away. If you do so because Amazon gives you superior service or enhances your life in another way, that's fine, too. Just don't complain when the business you never patronize ceases to exist. That's not capitalism being broken; that's capitalism working.

I will mention again, in the interest of fairness, that Amazon also supports many small businesses. While it competes with and has been a burden for some, it does feature the products of small business owners and give them access to a large customer base. More than 1 million small businesses sell products on the Amazon.com website. Its AWS web platform also hosts many small business websites. However, that also gives Amazon unprecedented power over those small businesses indirectly, a relevant downside to consider, particularly as we look at the ongoing rapid centralization of power.

How you decide to engage with businesses is up to you. Every individual plays a crucial role in the free markets, including wielding power in the market by "voting with their wallets."

The real wants and needs of consumers influence prices, incentives, efficiency, and which goods and services are ultimately produced and provided, as well as which small businesses survive and thrive.

We have seen everyone, including politicians, complain about certain businesses and then get caught patronizing them. Recently there has been outrage at Google for being too big and powerful, leading to calls for breaking it up. Yet how many people do you know who use DuckDuckGo or Bing for their web searches instead of Google? You could even use Goodshop's "goodsearch" feature and earn money for charitable causes. It takes the same amount of time to do an internet search using each platform, but Google ends up being the default consumer choice, despite the rampant complaints about its dominance.

We see the same behavior with regard to Facebook and its various privacy and other issues. Though some people have deleted their accounts, many did so only on Facebook and not on the Instagram platform (also owned by Facebook); those who took action were a tiny fraction of overall users. In fact, according to Facebook's second-quarter 2020 10-Q filing, as of June 30, 2020, its monthly active users averaged 2.7 billion, which was actually up 12 percent year over year. People complain that Facebook is a "monopoly," but really, do you need to use Facebook or any of its other brands? No. Are there other social platforms? Yes. Are there other ways to connect with people and entertain yourself? Many. So consumers whine but don't take action, as either an organized effort or an individual choice.

Despite its trust-violating actions of opening fake accounts and charging fees, Wells Fargo, according to its second-quarter 2020 10-Q filing, still had around $2 trillion in assets and serviced one in three households in the United States because its customers just don't care enough about the bank's past behavior to vote with their wallets and take their business elsewhere. People complain that the government didn't do enough to punish the bank, but what about its customers? There are plenty of financial services options out there if the problem is important enough.

If consumers' actions matched their words, they would be leveraging the essence of the free market. If they didn't spend their dollars or time with companies they don't value, those companies would be forced to change, if they are salvageable at all, or go out of business. Consumers' voting with their wallets would instead direct more dollars or time toward companies aligned with their most important values, whether it be privacy, worker conditions, or other values. The reality is that consumers don't care enough to shift their behavior because they are getting other things they value more.

Though they like to complain about Amazon, people consistently show that they value its convenience. They give up their privacy many times a day, and it's not really a priority. They may scream for government intervention only because they are too lazy or happy with their existing lives to make small changes themselves that are entirely within their control.

The best thing about freedom is that power and choice are in your hands. If you want small businesses to succeed, make an effort to support them. Doing so may be slightly less convenient than one-stop shopping on Amazon, but many small businesses are online and deliver, so it's not that much less convenient. Your best course of action to make sure that the small guys have their due is to give more business to them and less to the big guys. You can even tell your friends or your social media acquaintances about them. That is the power of capitalism and it is in your hands.

Or, if you find value in the big companies, appreciate the fact that you have access to conveniences that improve your life and want the person who took the risk and executed to make that happen to be rewarded and for others to see that success, so they are incentivized to do such things to improve your life. That is, as long as it is done fairly in a free market, without special government intervention and favors.

Capitalism Is Small Business

Small businesses enable free markets, and free markets enable small businesses.

Rejecting central planning means we are letting the invisible hand of a decentralized free market allow individuals to make choices that signal what is best, instead of a committee of politicians.

The transfer of wealth and power by a committee of a few whose job it is to protect the rights of individuals needs to be stopped.

If that happens, there will be more small businesses, which will allow for more decentralization of economic power.

Small businesses will have a better and more equal opportunity to compete and grow, which will foster more innovation, products, services, and choice—not to mention jobs and economic growth.

Anyone, regardless of his or her background, will have the opportunity to pursue his or her ideas and take ownership of the rewards for their risk.

Small business and entrepreneurship are hallmarks of the American Dream and the opportunity for any individual to make their life better and pursue their goals.

Resist central planning. Make government smaller and let the individual succeed.

Epilogue

Big government is a risk to the smallest and most vulnerable. It is a risk to the individual. It is a risk to those who are less fortunate, and it is a risk to small business, the backbone of the US economy.

We have explored how government central planners have never cared about "the little guy." Individuals and small businesses, by their nature, stand against everything that helps big government grab power. Small businesses are decentralized in every way—from industry to geography to size—and therefore, they make it hard to consolidate votes and power among them. Small businesses and independent workers embrace freedom of choice instead of union cronyism. They are either too small to matter or a roadblock to control—or both.

The central planning system is set up to enable moral hazard. As Thomas Sowell put it, "It is hard to imagine a more stupid or more dangerous way of making decisions than by putting those decisions in the hands of people who pay no price for being wrong."

The friction between central planning and the backbone of capitalism created a host of legacy issues for small businesses. Whether via licensing, permits, anticompetitive regulation, or otherwise, the government has always made it harder for those who are smaller, who lack the resources and the clout to influence politicians, to play on a level playing field.

You would think that government would want to foster opportunity, not to mention the economic wins and tax revenue that come with it, but instead, it has made it more difficult through its own interference. Politicians do not care about the best interests and power of anyone but themselves and their cronies (who, in turn, influence the politicians' power in a vicious cycle).

Jobs, manufacturing, and other opportunities were limited for small businesses by government getting into bed with China, exporting capitalism to the communist country while simultaneously moving the United States away from it.

The Fed has been used by the government to bail out big corporations and to sell out savers and retirees to Wall Street, using their opaque and heavy-handed policies.

So 2020 provided the perfect backdrop for the government to finish what it had started and crush the small guys all at once. Was it a concerted effort to try to make government more powerful and convince these individuals and businesses to depend on the government, or was it sheer incompetence?

The black swan government actions disproportionately affected small companies, without appropriate compensation for the subjugation of individual rights to "society." Small businesses saw local governments bail on doing their job of protecting property rights, either via shutdown orders or by not protecting their property against rioters and looters.

The Fed, which had been enabling policy that helped Wall Street more than Main Street, doubled down—or, rather, quadrupled down. Its historic policies propped up big companies, even failing ones, taking away opportunities for new competitors and adding risk to the markets. The biggest companies became more powerful juggernauts, while many of the smallest closed up shop forever.

This all reeks of intention. It is easier for the government to maintain its power and control alongside a handful of powerful cronies. If you were intending to attack decentralization and try to roll up more centralized power without it being blatantly obvious, you would not do much differently.

Central planners sought more ways to fight decentralization, and

2020 gave them access to enable a historic consolidation of power. Only more decentralization can counteract that.

Central planning has crushed small business because small business is both too small to matter and too difficult to control. It has done the same with individuals in order to make them dependent on government handouts.

Central planning has broken the backbone of America.

Individual rights, economic freedom, and decentralization are the only way to repair it and to fight back.

Acknowledgments

Acknowledgments are always difficult for me because there are so many people I want to thank and to whom I have gratitude, but I know I would inevitably miss some. To that end, I am keeping this short and sweet with an extra "thank you" to the following people directly connected to this work:

First, to my best friend and love, Kurt. Thank you for enthusiastically supporting all my endeavors. An extra thank-you for your additional research assistance and the reading of many of the hundreds of drafts that helped shape this book.

To Tracey, my sister and right hand, who makes all my work better, and to Mike, for being part of our inner circle.

To my phenomenal editor, Eric Nelson. Without Eric, this book would not exist. Thank you for approaching and entrusting me with this "big idea" and for your patience as we, in real time, navigated the economic implications of government during an unfolding pandemic. This was a Herculean task, and I appreciate your thoughtfulness through all three-ish iterations of the book (which was, by the way, twice as long at one point)! I am proud of the work we did and our collaboration and this book is better as a result of your input.

To Ben Howe, thank you for putting me on Eric Nelson's radar, and to Bridget Phetasy, for putting me on several other folks' radar, your invaluable help, and your overall support and friendship.

To the rest of the staff at Broadside and HarperCollins, including Hannah Long for all of your indispensable assistance, Kyle O'Brien and the production team, as well as Theresa Dooley on publicity and Tom Hopke on marketing, thank you for all your efforts.

To Alan Roby, who has guided my professional journey and kept me sane along the way.

To Sophia LaDouceur, for your fantastic research insights that helped to track this pandemic in real time, and to Mark Hoekenga, for your research assistance on the topic of cronyism.

To Lynn Anderson and Chloe Bollentin, for your thorough and helpful copyediting, which truly strengthened my manuscript.

To Neil Cavuto, Ben Shapiro, Jon Najarian, Sharyl Attkisson, Kira Davis, and Andrew Gruel, thank you for lending to the book and me your endorsements and your powerful words.

To Britt Raybould and Ryan Hoover, thank you for your inclusions in the book, as well as everyone else whose work was cited.

To all my collaborators and colleagues, I appreciate every single one of you.

To my extended family, you know who you all are. Thank you for your love. I am proud to be part of such a special and loving group.

To all the many thinkers and economists, past and present, who have shaped the discourse around capitalism, free markets, and individual rights, I am humbled by the opportunity to build upon your work.

To the small business owners of America and the world—you did build that. Thank you for taking risks that have driven great economic growth for an innumerable amount of people worldwide.

To my parents, who are no longer with us, thank you for the foundation of self-confidence, work ethic, straightforwardness, and gratitude. I love and miss you every day.

Notes

INTRODUCTION

1. Santino DeRose and Pamela Mendelsohn, "Storefront & Center," San Francisco Apartment Association, 2019, https://www.sfaa.org//Public/Magazine /07_2019/Storefront___Center_July_2019.aspx.

2. Ari Levy, "Tech's Top Seven Companies Added $3.4 Trillion in Value in 2020," CNBC, December 31, 2020, https://www.cnbc.com/2020/12/31/techs-top-seven -companies-added-3point4-trillion-in-value-in-2020.html.

3. Roisin McCord, Edward S. Prescott, and Tim Sablik, "Explaining the Decline in the Number of Banks Since the Great Recession," Federal Reserve Bank of Richmond, Economic Brief no. 15–03, March 2015, https://www.richmondfed .org/publications/research/economic_brief/2015/eb_15–03; Steve Maas, "Small Business Lending Declined After Dodd-Frank Passed," *NBER Digest*, June 2018, https://www.nber.org/digest/jun18/jun18.pdf, 2.

4. Francesca Mari, "What My Dad Gave His Shop," *The Atlantic*, December 2020, https://www.theatlantic.com/magazine/archive/2020/12/harmony-audio -pandemic-small-business/616926/.

CHAPTER 1: The Government Black Swan

1. Bernard Avishai, "The Pandemic Isn't a Black Swan but a Portent of a More Fragile Global System," *New Yorker*, April 21, 2020, https://www.newyorker .com/news/daily-comment/the-pandemic-isnt-a-black-swan-but-a-portent-of-a -more-fragile-global-system.

2. Ally Marotti, "An Estimated 4,400 Chicago-Area Businesses Have Closed During the Pandemic. 2,400 Say They'll Never Reopen," *Chicago Tribune*, July 22, 2020, https://www.chicagotribune.com/coronavirus/ct-coronavirus -chicago-business-closures-yelp-20200722-nmhvpmv72fdyzdjgvzoun7rima -story.html; Sasha Lekach, "Yelp Says More Than Half of Restaurants Temporarily Closed Are Now Permanently Shuttered," Mashable, July 22, 2020, https://mashable.com/article/yelp-restaurants-temporary-permanent-closures/.

3. Lekach, "Yelp Says More Than Half of Restaurants Temporarily Closed Are Now Permanently Shuttered."

4. Steven Hamilton, "From Survival to Revival: How to Help Small Businesses Through the COVID-19 Crisis," Hamilton Project, September 2020, https://www.brookings.edu/wp-content/uploads/2020/09/PP_Hamilton_Final.pdf.

5. Melissa Repko, "Walmart Second-Quarter Results Crush Estimates, as E-commerce Sales Jump 97%," CNBC, August 19, 2020, https://www.cnbc.com/2020/08/18/walmart-wmt-q2–2021-earnings.html.

6. Melissa Repko, "Target Reports a Monster Quarter—Profits Jump 80%, Same-Store Sales Set Record," CNBC, August 19, 2020, https://www.cnbc.com/2020/08/19/target-tgt-q2-2020-earnings.html.

CHAPTER 2: Hindsight Is 2020

1. Jacob Pramuk, "Trump Signs 'Phase One' Trade Deal with China in Push to Stop Economic Conflict," CNBC, January 15, 2020, https://www.cnbc.com/2020/01/15/trump-and-china-sign-phase-one-trade-agreement.html.

2. "Job Market Remains Tight in 2019, as the Unemployment Rate Falls to Its Lowest Level Since 1969," US Bureau of Labor Statistics, April 2020, https://www.bls.gov/opub/mlr/2020/article/job-market-remains-tight-in-2019-as-the-unemployment-rate-falls-to-its-lowest-level-since-1969.htm.

3. "Small Business Optimism Starts New Year as Solid as Ever," NFIB, February 11, 2020, https://www.nfib.com/content/press-release/economy/small-business-optimism-starts-new-year-as-solid-as-ever/.

4. Hannah Knowles and Colby Itkowitz, "Nancy Pelosi Gave Out Souvenir Pens After Sending Impeachment to the Senate—and Republicans Are Fuming," Washington Post, January 16, 2020, https://www.washingtonpost.com/politics/2020/01/16/nancy-pelosi-pens-impeachment/.

5. Rick Scott, "Sen. Rick Scott Urges CDC to Take Swift Action to Combat Threat of the Coronavirus," January 22, 2020, https://www.rickscott.senate.gov/sen-rick-scott-urges-cdc-take-swift-action-combat-threat-coronavirus.

6. J. Edward Moreno, "Government Health Agency Official: Coronavirus 'Isn't Something the American Public Need to Worry About,'" The Hill, January 26, 2020, https://thehill.com/homenews/sunday-talk-shows/479939-government-health-agency-official-corona-virus-isnt-something-the.

7. Ryan W. Miller and Grace Hauck, "15 People Die from Coronavirus in One Day; Death Toll Rises to 41, Chinese Officials Say," *USA Today*, January 24, 2020, updated January 29, 2020, https://www.usatoday.com/story/news/health /2020/01/24/coronavirus-wuhan-china-lockdown-quarantine-us-cases /4562257002/.

8. Chad Terhune et al., "Special Report: How Korea Trounced U.S. in Race to Test People for Coronavirus," Reuters, March 18, 2020, https://www.reuters.com /article/us-health-coronavirus-testing-specialrep/special-report-how-korea -trounced-u-s-in-race-to-test-people-for-coronavirus-idUSKBN2153BW; Soo Rin Kim, Dr. Tiffany Kung, and Dr. Mark Abdelmalek, "Trust, Testing and Tracing: How South Korea Succeeded Where the US Stumbled in Coronavirus Response," ABC News, May 1, 2020, https://abcnews.go.com/Health/trust-testing -tracing-south-korea-succeeded-us-stumbled/story?id=70433504.

9. Saheli Roy Choudhury, "Japan Trades Lower as Many Asian Markets Remain Closed for Lunar New Year," CNBC, January 27, 2020, https://www.cnbc.com /2020/01/27/asia-markets-jan-27-coronavirus-outbreak-affecting-investor -sentiment.html; Zacks Equity Research, "Stock Market News for Jan 27, 2020," Yahoo! Finance, https://finance.yahoo.com/news/stock-market-news -jan-27-150803707.html.

10. Jeff Cox, "Fourth-Quarter GDP Rose Only 2.1% and Full-Year 2019 Posts Slowest Growth in Three Years at 2.3%," CNBC, January 30, 2020, https://www .cnbc.com/2020/01/30/us-gdp-q4–2019-first-reading.html.

11. "Coronavirus Declared Global Health Emergency by WHO," BBC News, January 31, 2020, https://www.bbc.com/news/world-51318246.

12. "Statement on the Second Meeting of the International Health Regulations (2005) Emergency Committee Regarding the Outbreak of Novel Coronavirus (2019-nCoV)," World Health Organization, January 30, 2020, https://www .who.int/news-room/detail/30–01–2020-statement-on-the-second-meeting-of -the-international-health-regulations-(2005)-emergency-committee-regarding -the-outbreak-of-novel-coronavirus-(2019-ncov).

13. Doug Stanglin, Ken Alltucker, and Grace Hauck, "WHO Declares Coronavirus Global Emergency; State Department Raises Travel Warning to Highest Level," *USA Today*, January 30, 2020, https://www.usatoday.com/story/news /world/2020/01/30/coronavirus-death-toll-hits-170-countries-scramble -respond/4618844002/.

14. Fred Imbert, "Dow Plummets 600 Points in Worst Day Since August as Coronavirus Fears Grow," CNBC, January 31, 2020, https://www.cnbc.com

/2020/01/31/stock-market-wall-street-in-focus-after-coronavirus-declares
-global-emergency.html; data analysis with inputs from Macrotrends, https://
www.macrotrends.net.

15. Eustance Huang, "Chinese Stocks Plunge 7% amid Virus Fears on First Trading Day After Lunar New Year Holiday," CNBC, February 3, 2020, https://
www.cnbc.com/2020/02/03/asia-markets-china-markets-coronavirus-caixin
-manufacturing-pmi-in-focus.html.

16. Fred Imbert, "Stock Market Updates Monday: Dow Rebound Loses Steam as
Day Goes On, Tesla Pops 19%," CNBC, February 3, 2020, https://www.cnbc
.com/2020/02/03/stockmarkettodaylive.html.

17. Fred Imbert, "Dow Soars More Than 400 Points, Tesla Surge Leads Nasdaq to
All-Time High," CNBC, February 4, 2020, https://www.cnbc.com/2020/02/04
/us-futures-point-to-wall-street-rally-as-virus-fears-abate.html; "U.S. Factory
Orders Post Largest Increase in Nearly One and a Half Years," Reuters, February 4, 2020, https://www.businessinsider.com/us-factory-orders-post-largest
-increase-in-nearly-one-and-a-half-years-2020-2.

18. John Bacon and Lorenzo Reyes, "Coronavirus Live Updates: Trump Criticizes
Georgia Governor's Reopening Plan; U.S. Deaths Started Sooner Than We
Thought; Market Surges," USA Today, April 22, 2020, https://www.usatoday
.com/story/news/health/2020/04/22/coronavirus-updates-cdc-paycheck
-protection-georgia-states-reopening/2997805001/.

19. Michael R. Pompeo, Secretary of State, "The United States Announces Assistance
to Combat the Novel Coronavirus," statement, US Department of State, February 7, 2020, https://china.usembassy-china.org.cn/the-united-states-announces
-assistance-to-the-novel-coronavirus/.

20. Dian Zhang, Erin Mansfield, and Dinah Voyles Pulver, "U.S. Exported Millions
in Masks and Ventilators Ahead of the Coronavirus Crisis," USA Today, April
3, 2020, https://www.usatoday.com/story/news/investigations/2020/04/02/us
-exports-masks-ppe-china-surged-early-phase-coronavirus/5109747002/.

21. Kim et al., "Trust, Testing and Tracing."

22. Fred Imbert, "Dow Jumps More Than 250 Points to a Record," CNBC, February 12, 2020, https://www.cnbc.com/2020/02/12/us-futures-point-to-higher
-open-after-stocks-hit-fresh-record-highs.html.

23. Fred Imbert, "S&P 500 and Nasdaq Jump to Record Highs, Dow Climbs
More Than 100 Points," CNBC, February 19, 2020, https://www.cnbc.com

/2020/02/19/stock-market-wall-street-in-focus-amid-coronavirus-outbreak
.html.

24. Berkeley Lovelace Jr. and Will Feuer, "CDC Prepares for Possibility Coronavirus Becomes a Pandemic and Businesses, Schools Need to Be Closed,"
CNBC, February 21, 2020, https://www.cnbc.com/2020/02/21/us-health-officials
-prepare-for-coronavirus-outbreak-to-become-pandemic.html; Fred Imbert,
"Dow Drops More Than 200 Points, Posts Losing Week as Coronavirus Fears
Resurface," CNBC, February 21, 2020, https://www.cnbc.com/2020/02/21/us
-futures-point-to-lower-open-on-wall-street.html.

25. Doug Stanglin, "A Dozen Towns in Northern Italy Are Locked Down After
Coronavirus Deaths," *USA Today*, February 24, 2020, https://www.usatoday
.com/story/news/world/2020/02/22/coronavirus-italy-towns-lockdown-deaths
-virus-spreads/4841539002/.

26. Michael Collins and John Fritze, "Trump Puts Vice President Mike Pence in
Charge of Coronavirus Response, Says Nation Is 'Very Ready,'" *USA Today*,
February 26, 2020, https://www.usatoday.com/story/news/politics/2020/02/26
/coronavirus-trump-speak-reporters-he-battles-democrats/4879117002/.

27. Kate Kelly and Mark Mazzetti, "As Virus Spread, Reports of Trump Administration's Private Briefings Fueled Sell-Off," *New York Times*, October 26, 2020,
https://www.nytimes.com/2020/10/14/us/politics/stock-market-coronavirus
-trump.html.

28. John Bacon, "'Seriously People - STOP BUYING MASKS!' Surgeon General
Says They Won't Protect from Coronavirus," *Florida Times-Union*, March 2,
2020, https://www.jacksonville.com/story/news/healthcare/2020/03/02/seriously
-people--stop-buying-masks-surgeon-general-says-they-wont-protect-from
-coronavirus/112244966/.

29. @washingtonpost, Twitter, February 26, 2020, https://twitter.com/washington
post/status/1232659684047441922?s=20.

30. @MSNBC, Twitter, February 28, 2020, https://twitter.com/msnbc/status/1233
478252502638598?lang=en.

31. Scottie Andrew and Jessie Yeung, "Masks Can't Stop the Coronavirus in the
US, but Hysteria Has Led to Bulk-Buying and Price-Gouging," CNN, February
29, 2020, https://edition.cnn.com/asia/live-news/coronavirus-outbreak-02-29
-20-intl-hnk/h_60c0416ca901c2006c1c7c91010b70a4.

32. Neel V. Patel, "Why the CDC Botched Its Coronavirus Testing," *MIT Tech-*

nology Review, March 5, 2020, https://www.technologyreview.com/2020/03
/05/905484/why-the-cdc-botched-its-coronavirus-testing/.

33. Lisa Schnirring, "China Releases Genetic Data on New Coronavirus, Now Deadly," University of Minnesota Center for Infectious Disease Research and Policy, January 11, 2020, https://www.cidrap.umn.edu/news-perspective/2020 /01/china-releases-genetic-data-new-coronavirus-now-deadly; Shawn Boburg et al., "Inside the Coronavirus Testing Failure: Alarm and Dismay Among the Scientists Who Sought to Help," *Washington Post,* April 3, 2020, https://www .washingtonpost.com/investigations/2020/04/03/coronavirus-cdc-test-kits -public-health-labs/?arc404=true.

34. Boburg et al., "Inside the Coronavirus Testing Failure."

35. Ibid.

36. @ScottGottliebMD, Twitter, February 2, 2020, https://twitter.com/scott gottliebmd/status/1224043498816655364.

37. Boburg et al., "Inside the Coronavirus Testing Failure"; Robert P. Baird, "What Went Wrong with Coronavirus Testing in the U.S.," *New Yorker,* March 16, 2020, https://www.newyorker.com/news/news-desk/what-went-wrong-with -coronavirus-testing-in-the-us.

38. "Transcript for CDC Telebriefing: CDC Update on Novel Coronavirus," Centers for Disease Control and Prevention, February 12, 2020, https://www.cdc .gov/media/releases/2020/t0212-cdc-telebriefing-transcript.html.

39. Boburg et al., "Inside the Coronavirus Testing Failure."

40. Jon Cohen, "The United States Badly Bungled Coronavirus Testing—but Things May Soon Improve," *Science,* February 28, 2020, https://www.sciencemag.org /news/2020/02/united-states-badly-bungled-coronavirus-testing-things-may -soon-improve.

41. Ibid.

42. Boburg et al., "Inside the Coronavirus Testing Failure."

43. Robinson Meyer and Alexis C. Madrigal, "The Dangerous Delays in U.S. Coronavirus Testing Haven't Stopped," *The Atlantic,* March 9, 2020, https://www .theatlantic.com/health/archive/2020/03/coronavirus-testing-numbers/607714/; Terhune et al., "Special Report: How Korea Trounced U.S. in Race to Test People for Coronavirus"; "Hospitalization Rates and Characteristics of Pa-

tients Hospitalized with Laboratory-Confirmed Coronavirus Disease 2019—COVID-NET, 14 States, March 1–30, 2020," Centers for Disease Control and Prevention, April 17, 2020, https://www.cdc.gov/mmwr/volumes/69/wr/mm6915e3.htm.

44. Peter Whoriskey and Neena Satija, "How U.S. Coronavirus Testing Stalled: Flawed Tests, Red Tape and Resistance to Using the Millions of Tests Produced by the WHO," *Washington Post*, March 16, 2020, https://www.washingtonpost.com/business/2020/03/16/cdc-who-coronavirus-tests/.

45. "Coronavirus (COVID-19) Update: FDA Issues New Policy to Help Expedite Availability of Diagnostics," US Food and Drug Administration, February 29, 2020, https://www.fda.gov/news-events/press-announcements/coronavirus-covid-19-update-fda-issues-new-policy-help-expedite-availability-diagnostics.

46. Alec Stapp, "Timeline: The Regulations—and Regulators—That Delayed Coronavirus Testing," The Dispatch, March 20, 2020, https://thedispatch.com/p/timeline-the-regulationsand-regulatorsthat.

47. "Proclamation on Declaring a National Emergency Concerning the Novel Coronavirus Disease (COVID-19) Outbreak," The White House, March 13, 2020, https://trumpwhitehouse.archives.gov/presidential-actions/proclamation-declaring-national-emergency-concerning-novel-coronavirus-disease-covid-19-outbreak/; Baird, "What Went Wrong with Coronavirus Testing in the U.S."

48. Larry Buchanan, K. K. Rebecca Lai, and Allison McCann, "U.S. Lags in Coronavirus Testing," *New York Times*, March 17, 2020, https://www.nytimes.com/interactive/2020/03/17/us/coronavirus-testing-data.html.

49. Kyle Lawson, "Coronavirus Risk 'Remains Low' in NYC; Same-Day Testing Now Available, Officials Say," silive.com, March 3, 2020, https://www.silive.com/news/2020/03/coronavirus-risk-remains-low-in-nyc-same-day-testing-now-available-officials-say.html.

50. "Transcript: Mayor de Blasio Updates New Yorkers on City's COVID-19 Preparedness," March 4, 2020, https://www1.nyc.gov/office-of-the-mayor/news/118–20/transcript-mayor-de-blasio-new-yorkers-city-s-covid-19-preparedness.

51. Azi Paybarah and Joseph Goldstein, "2,773 People Are Under Quarantines in New York City," *New York Times*, March 9, 2020, https://www.nytimes.com/2020/03/05/nyregion/coronavirus-new-york-cases.html.

52. Wes Parnell and Shant Shahrigian, "Mayor de Blasio Says Coronavirus Fears

Shouldn't Keep New Yorkers off Subways," *Daily News* (New York), March 5, 2020, https://www.nydailynews.com/coronavirus/ny-coronavirus-bill-de-blasio-coronavirus-subway-20200305-vmjdxjudbndlrjekashqs3hfou-story.html.

53. @senatemajldr, Twitter, March 12, 2020, https://twitter.com/senatemajldr/status/1238152886980395009.

54. John Bresnahan et al., "Senate GOP Crafting New Massive Coronavirus Package at 'Warp Speed,'" Politico, March 17, 2020, https://www.politico.com/news/2020/03/17/white-house-senate-republicans-coronavirus-aid-133732.

55. Clare Foran and Ted Barrett, "Trump Signs Coronavirus Relief Legislation into Law," CNN, March 19, 2020, https://www.cnn.com/2020/03/18/politics/coronavirus-congress-relief-senate-house/index.html.

56. John Fritze, "Trump Declared the Coronavirus Pandemic a National Emergency. What Does That Mean?," *USA Today*, March 13, 2020, https://www.usatoday.com/story/news/politics/2020/03/13/coronavirus-national-emergency-questions-answers-trump/5026463002/.

CHAPTER 3: Fifteen Days to Slow the Spread

1. "Shelley Luther," Vantu News, https://www.vantunews.com/wiki/biography-shelley-luther.

2. LaVendrick Smith, "Dallas Salon Owner Jailed for Reopening in Violation of Court Order," *Dallas Morning News*, May 5, 2020, https://www.dallasnews.com/news/courts/2020/05/05/dallas-salon-owner-ordered-to-spend-a-week-in-jail-for-keeping-salon-open/.

3. "Shelley Luther: Texas Salon Owner Gets 7 Days in Jail for Reopening," Heavy, May 2020, https://heavy.com/news/2020/05/shelley-luther-texas/; "Dallas County Health and Human Services 2019 Novel Coronavirus (COVID-19) Summary," County of Dallas, October 13, 2020, https://www.dallascounty.org/Assets/uploads/docs/hhs/2019-nCoV/COVID-19%20DCHHS%20Summary_101320.pdf.

4. Joanne Rosa, "Salon Owner Defends Decision to Reopen: 'I Could Create a Sterile Environment,'" ABC News, May 11, 2020, https://abcnews.go.com/US/salon-owner-defends-decision-reopen-create-sterile-environment/story?id=70614979.

5. Ibid.

6.   Emma Platoff, "How a Dallas Salon Owner Changed Texas' Reopening Debate," *Texas Tribune*, May 15, 2020, https://www.texastribune.org/2020/05/15/texas-reopening-shelley-luther-dallas-salon-owner/.

7.   Associated Press, "Dallas Salon Owner Who Refused to Close Business Jailed for Defying Order," ABC 7, Dallas, May, 6, 2020, https://abc7.com/dallas-salon-reopens-despite-stay-at-home-order-a-la-mode-shelley-luther-coronavirus/6156173/.

8.   Ibid.

9.   Platoff, "How a Dallas Salon Owner Changed Texas' Reopening Debate."

10. @rwm52, Twitter, July 4, 2020, https://twitter.com/rwm52/status/1279618988281147392.

11. @TedCruz, Twitter, May 5, 2020, https://twitter.com/tedcruz/status/1257840863197179905?s=20.

12. "Governor Abbott Modifies COVID-19 Executive Orders to Eliminate Confinement as a Punishment," State of Texas, May 7, 2020, https://gov.texas.gov/news/post/governor-abbott-modifies-covid-19-executive-orders-to-eliminate-confinement-as-a-punishment.

13. "Texas Lt. Governor Dan Patrick Pays Fine for Salon Owner Who Refused to Close," CBS News, May 8, 2020, https://www.cbsnews.com/news/texas-lt-governor-dan-patrick-paid-fine-shelley-luther-dallas-salon-owner/.

14. Ibid.

15. "DA Will Not Prosecute Case of Two Women Accused of Violating Shutdown Orders," KGNS, May 8, 2020, https://www.kgns.tv/content/news/District-Attorney-will-not-prosecute--570308291.html.

16. Fox News, "Atilis Gym Facing over $1.2M in Fines for Defying NJ's Coronavirus Lockdown Orders, Owner Says," Fox 29, December 11, 2020, https://www.fox29.com/news/atilis-gym-facing-over-1–2m-in-fines-for-defying-njs-coronavirus-lockdown-orders-owner-says.

17. "U.S. Jobless Claims Pass 40 Million: Live Business Updates," *New York Times*, May 28, 2020, https://www.nytimes.com/2020/05/28/business/unemployment-stock-market-coronavirus.html.

18. "15 Days to Slow the Spread," The White House, March 16, 2020, https://trumpwhitehouse.archives.gov/articles/15-days-slow-spread/. Note that this was later changed to "30 days"; see "30 Days to Slow the Spread," The White

House, March 3, 2020, https://trumpwhitehouse.archives.gov/wp-content/up loads/2020/03/03.16.20_coronavirus-guidance_8.5x11_315PM.pdf.

19. John Bacon and Jorge L. Ortiz, "Coronavirus Live Updates: Restrictions Could Last Months; Canada Closes Border; McDonald's Closes Dining Rooms," *USA Today*, March 18, 2020, https://www.usatoday.com/story/news /health/2020/03/16/coronavirus-live-updates-us-death-toll-rises-cases-testing /5053816002/.

20. Sarah Mervosh, Denise Lu, and Vanessa Swales, "See Which States and Cities Have Told Residents to Stay at Home," *New York Times*, April 20, 2020, https:// www.nytimes.com/interactive/2020/us/coronavirus-stay-at-home-order.html.

21. Jackie Borchardt, "Ohio 2020 Recreational Marijuana Legalization Measure Filed: 5 Things to Know," *Columbus Dispatch*, March 2, 2020, https://www .dispatch.com/news/20200302/ohio-2020-recreational-marijuana-legalization -measure-filed-5-things-to-know.

22. Amy L. Knapp, "Coronavirus in Ohio | Local Restaurants React to State Ban," *Canton Repository*, March 16, 2020, https://www.cantonrep.com/news /20200316/coronavirus-in-ohio--local-restaurants-react-to-state-ban.

23. Brad Weisenstein, "Pritzker Forced to Withdraw Criminal Penalties for Small Business Owners Who Defy His Order," Illinois Policy, May 20, 2020, https:// www.illinoispolicy.org/pritzker-forced-to-withdraw-criminal-penalties-for -small-business-owners-who-defy-his-order/.

24. Bryce Hill, "As Many as 21,700 Restaurants Could Close Permanently from COVID-19 Economic Fallout," Illinois Policy, July 2, 2020, https://www.illinois policy.org/as-many-as-21700-restaurants-could-close-permanently-from -covid-19-economic-fallout/; Brad Weisenstein and Ben Szalinski, "Everything You Need to Know About COVID-19 in Illinois," Illinois Policy, daily updates, https://www.illinoispolicy.org/what-you-need-to-know-about-coronavirus-in -illinois/.

25. Ally Marotti, "Restaurants Riled over State's Distribution of COVID-19 Grants," *Crain's Chicago Business*, January 5, 2021, https://www.chicagobusiness .com/restaurants/restaurants-riled-over-states-distribution-covid-19-grants.

26. Nick Sibilla, "Michigan Bans Many Stores from Selling Seeds, Home Garden- ing Supplies, Calls Them 'Not Necessary,'" *Forbes*, April 16, 2020, https:// www.forbes.com/sites/nicksibilla/2020/04/16/michigan-bans-many-stores -from-selling-seeds-home-gardening-supplies-calls-them-not-necessary/#3c3c3 ec75f80.

27. Larry Lee, "Michigan's Stay-at-Home Order 'Decimating' for Garden Centers," Brownfield Ag News for America, April 15, 2020, https://brownfieldagnews .com/news/michigans-stay-at-home-order-decimating-for-garden-centers/.

28. Sabilla, "Michigan Bans Many Stores from Selling Seeds, Home Gardening Supplies, Calls Them 'Not Necessary.'"

29. Larry Lee, "Michigan's Stay-at-Home Order 'Decimating' for Garden Centers."

30. Thomas A. Hemphill and Syagnik Banerjee, "Opinion: Michigan's 'Non-essential' Community Faces Economic Peril," *Detroit News*, June 4, 2020, https:// www.detroitnews.com/story/opinion/2020/06/05/opinion-michigans-non -essential-community-faces-economic-peril/5307920002/.

31. "MEDC COVID-19 Response," Michigan Economic Development Corporation, https://www.michiganbusiness.org/covid19response/.

32. Keisha Lindsay, "Hair Salons/One Client at a Time (Soft Opening April 27th)," petition to NC governor Roy Cooper, MoveOn, https://sign.moveon.org /petitions/hair-salons-one-client-at-a-time-soft-opening-april-27th-2; Melba Newsome, "Spas, Salons Seek a Way Back from COVID Closures," North Carolina Health News, April 21, 2020, https://www.northcarolinahealthnews .org/2020/04/21/spas-salons-seek-a-way-back-from-covid-closures/.

33. "Newsom Gets Failing Grade on Pandemic Response: Letters," *The Sun*, June 3, 2020, https://www.sbsun.com/2020/06/03/newsom-gets-failing-grade-on -pandemic-response-letters/.

34. Eliza Relman, "New York City Mayor Bill de Blasio Violates His Own Government's Recommendations and Hits the Gym in Brooklyn amid the Coronavirus Shutdown," Business Insider, March 16, 2020, https://www.businessinsider .com/nyc-mayor-bill-de-blasio-goes-ymca-announcing-closure-gyms-2020 -3.

35. Andrew M. Cuomo, "Governor Cuomo Signs the 'New York State on PAUSE' Executive Order," March 20, 2020, https://www.governor.ny.gov/news/gov ernor-cuomo-signs-new-york-state-pause-executive-order.

36. Ben Axelson, "Coronavirus Timeline in NY: Here's How Gov. Cuomo Has Responded to COVID-19 Pandemic Since January," Syracuse.com, April 15, 2020, https://www.syracuse.com/coronavirus/2020/04/coronavirus-timeline-in-ny -heres-how-gov-cuomo-has-responded-to-covid-19-pandemic-since-january .html; Julie McMahon, "NY Coronavirus Order for Businesses to Close: What's Considered Essential, Non-Essential?," Syracuse.com, April 9, 2020, https://

www.syracuse.com/coronavirus/2020/03/ny-coronavirus-order-for-businesses
-to-close-whats-considered-essential-nonessential.html.

37. Julie McMahon, "Dog Groomers Divided: Coronavirus Pandemic Shuts Down
    Some, While Others Remain Open," Syracuse.com, April 7, 2020, https://
    www.syracuse.com/coronavirus/2020/04/dog-groomers-divided-coronavirus
    -pandemic-shuts-down-some-while-others-remain-open.html.

38. Andrew M. Cuomo, "Governor Cuomo Signs the 'New York State on PAUSE'
    Executive Order," March 20, 2020, https://www.governor.ny.gov/news/gov
    ernor-cuomo-signs-new-york-state-pause-executive-order.

39. David Harsanyi, "The Left's Coronavirus Narrative Is a Myth," *National Re-
    view*, July 1, 2020, https://www.nationalreview.com/corner/the-lefts-corona
    virus-narrative-is-a-myth/.

40. Andrew Cuomo, "Advisory: Hospital Discharges and Admissions to Nursing
    Homes," New York Department of Health, March 25, 2020, https://skilled
    nursingnews.com/wp-content/uploads/sites/4/2020/03/DOH_COVID19
    __NHAdmissionsReadmissions__032520_1585166684475_0.pdf.

41. Jill Terreri Ramos, "New York's Nursing Home Policy Was Not Fully in
    Line with CDC," Politifact, June 13, 2020, https://www.politifact.com/fact
    checks/2020/jun/13/andrew-cuomo/new-yorks-nursing-home-policy-was-not
    -line-cdc/.

42. Bernard Condon, Matt Sedensky, and Meghan Hoyer, "New York's True Nurs-
    ing Home Death Toll Cloaked in Secrecy," Associated Press, August 10, 2020,
    https://apnews.com/212ccd87924b6906053703a00514647f.

43. Ibid.

44. Bill Hammond, "The Hospital Lobbyists Behind Cuomo's Nursing Home Scan-
    dal," *Wall Street Journal*, September 18, 2020, https://www.wsj.com/articles
    /the-hospital-lobbyists-behind-cuomos-nursing-home-scandal-11600454566.

45. "Andrew Cuomo New York May 20 COVID-19 Press Conference Transcript,"
    Rev, May 20, 2020, https://www.rev.com/blog/transcripts/andrew-cuomo-new
    -york-may-20-covid-19-press-conference-transcript.

46. Fei Zhou et al., "Clinical Course and Risk Factors for Mortality of Adult Inpa-
    tients with COVID-19 in Wuhan, China: A Retrospective Cohort Study," *The
    Lancet*, March 11, 2020, https://www.thelancet.com/journals/lancet/article
    /PIIS0140-6736(20)30566-3/fulltext.

47. "Department of Justice Requesting Data from Governors of States That Issued COVID-19 Orders That May Have Resulted in Deaths of Elderly Nursing Home Residents," US Department of Justice, August 26, 2020, https://www.justice.gov/opa/pr/department-justice-requesting-data-governors-states-issued-covid-19-orders-may-have-resulted; Jonathan Oosting, "Feds Demand Answers from Gov. Whitmer on Michigan Nursing Home Deaths," Bridge Michigan, August 26, 2020, https://www.bridgemi.com/michigan-government/feds-demand-answers-gov-whitmer-michigan-nursing-home-deaths.

48. Jesse McKinley, "Here's Cuomo's Plan for Reopening New York," *New York Times*, May 18, 2020, https://www.nytimes.com/2020/05/04/nyregion/corona virus-reopen-cuomo-ny.html.

49. "Union Members in New York and New Jersey—2019," US Bureau of Labor Statistics, https://www.bls.gov/regions/new-york-new-jersey/news-release/union membership_newyork_newjersey.htm; "Labor Force Trends in New York State," Office of Thomas P. DiNapoli, State Comptroller, September 2017, https://www.osc.state.ny.us/sites/default/files/reports/documents/pdf/2018-12/economic-labor-2017.pdf.

50. Todd Maisel, "Some Businesses Will Not Return Even as City Enters into Phase 2 of Reopening," amNY, June 18, 2020, https://www.amny.com/news/as-city-plods-into-phase-2-reopening-some-businesses-will-not-return/.

51. "Statewide Unemployment Drops to 11 Percent, Payrolls Increase in August," Illinois Department of Employment Security, September 17, 2020, https://www2.illinois.gov/ides/SitePages/NewsArticleDisplay.aspx?NewsID=517; "California Unemployment Lowers to 13.3 Percent in July: Employers Gain 140,400 Non-farm Payroll Jobs," Employment Development Department, State of California, August 21, 2020, https://edd.ca.gov/newsroom/unemployment-august-2020.htm; "NYS Economy Added 244,200 Private Sector Jobs in July 2020," New York State, August 20, 2020, https://www.labor.ny.gov/pressreleases/2020/august-20-2020.shtm.

52. Jorge Fitz-Gibbon, "Nearly One-Third of NY, NJ Small Businesses Reportedly Closed in 2020," *New York Post*, November 29, 2020, https://nypost.com/2020/11/29/nearly-one-third-of-ny-nj-small-businesses-closed-in-2020-report/.

53. "Percent Change in Number of Small Businesses Open," Opportunity Insights, https://tracktherecovery.org/.

54. Wetenkamp, "First Income Tax Was Supposed to Be Temporary," Montgom-

ery & Wetenkamp, July 12, 2011, https://www.mwattorneys.com/blog/first
-income-tax-was-supposed-to-be-temporary/.

55. Mary Papenfuss, "Trump Administration Failed Dry Run 'Crimson Contagion'
Pandemic Exercise," HuffPost, March 20, 2020, https://www.huffpost.com
/entry/crimson-contagion-exercise-trump-administration-failures_n_5e744105
c5b6eab7794560e6; Carol Marin and Don Moseley, "'Crimson Contagion
2019' Simulation Warned of Pandemic Implications in US," NBC 5 Chicago,
March 24, 2020, https://www.nbcchicago.com/news/local/crimson-contagion
-2019-simulation-warned-of-pandemic-implications-in-us/2243832/#.

56. William Cummings, "Trump: Coronavirus Guidelines, Set to Expire Tuesday,
Will Be Extended to April 30," USA Today, March 30, 2020, https://www
.usatoday.com/story/news/politics/2020/03/29/coronavirus-response-updates
-pelosi-fauci/2935369001/.

CHAPTER 4: Breaking America's Backbone

1. @ScottLincicome, Twitter, March 19, 2020, https://twitter.com/scottlincicome
/status/1240814716030771201?s=20.

2. "2018 Small Business Profile," US Small Business Administration Office of Advocacy, https://www.sba.gov/sites/default/files/advocacy/2018-Small-Business
-Profiles-US.pdf.

3. Jennifer Haberkorn, "Congress Begins Work on Third Economic Stimulus
Bill for the Coronavirus Crisis," Los Angeles Times, March 16, 2020, https://
www.latimes.com/politics/story/2020-03-16/economic-stimulus-coronavirus
-congress; Jordain Carney, "McConnell Wants GOP Deal on Third Coronavirus Bill Before Negotiating with Democrats," The Hill, March 17, 2020, https://
thehill.com/homenews/senate/488121-mcconnell-wants-gop-deal-on-third
-coronavirus-bill-before-negotiating-with; John Bresnahan et al., "Senate
GOP Crafting New Massive Coronavirus Package at 'Warp Speed,'" Politico, March 17, 2020, https://www.politico.com/news/2020/03/17/white-house
-senate-republicans-coronavirus-aid-133732; John Bresnahan and Marianne
Levine, "Senate at Impasse on Trillion-Dollar Coronavirus Package," Politico,
March 20, 2020, https://www.politico.com/news/2020/03/20/senate-corona
virus-emergency-stimulus-deal-friday-138788.

4. Sarah D. Wire, "Sidelined in the Final Days of Stimulus Talks, McConnell Again
Learns the Risk of Getting Ahead of Trump," Los Angeles Times, March 27,

2020, https://www.latimes.com/politics/story/2020–03–27/sidelined-stimulus
-talks-mcconnell-risk-getting-ahead-of-trump.

5. Adam Andrzejewski, "Is There Wasteful Spending in the Coronavirus Stimulus Bill?," *Forbes*, March 26, 2020, https://www.forbes.com/sites/adam
andrzejewski/2020/03/26/is-there-wasteful-spending-in-the-coronavirus
-stimulus-bill/#4a70ed8960ae.

6. @RepThomasMassie, Twitter, March 27, 2020, https://twitter.com/RepThomas
Massie/status/1243565641858191361.

7. The Coronavirus Aid, Relief, and Economic Security Act, Public Law 116–
136, 116th Congress, March 27, 2020, https://www.congress.gov/116/plaws
/publ136/PLAW-116publ136.pdf; "A Breakdown of the CARES Act," J.P.Mor-
gan, April 14, 2020, https://www.jpmorgan.com/global/research/cares-act.

8. "The CARES Act Provides Assistance for State, Local, and Tribal Governments," US Department of the Treasury, https://home.treasury.gov/policy
-issues/cares/state-and-local-governments.

9. Naomi Jagoda, "Treasury: 70 Percent of Stimulus Payment Money Sent to Dead
People Has Been Recovered," The Hill, August 31, 2020, https://thehill.com
/policy/finance/514459-treasury-70-percent-of-stimulus-payment-money-sent
-to-dead-people-has-been; Sacha Pfeiffer, "IRS Says Its Own Error Sent $1,200
Stimulus Checks to Non-Americans Overseas," NPR, November 30, 2020,
https://www.npr.org/2020/11/30/938902523/irs-says-its-own-error-sent-1
–200-stimulus-checks-to-non-americans-overseas.

10. Courtesy of Senate Appropriations Committee, "$340 Billion Surge in Emer-
gency Funding to Combat Coronavirus Outbreak," Open the Books, https://
www.openthebooks.com/assets/1/6/US_Senate_Appropriations_Committee
_—_Supplemental_Phase_III.pdf.

11. Adam Andrzejewski and Thomas W. Smith, "Where's the Pork?," Open the
Books, September 2020, https://www.openthebooks.com/assets/1/6/Wheres
_the_Pork_Report_v6.pdf.

12. Peggy McGlone, "Kennedy Center Furloughs 250 in Wake of $25 Million Fed-
eral Grant," *Washington Post*, March 31, 2020, https://www.washingtonpost
.com/entertainment/music/kennedy-center-announces-250-more-layoffs-in
-wake-of-25-million-federal-grant/2020/03/31/461d21ec-72b7–11ea-a9bd-9f8
b593300d0_story.html.

13. Julia Jacobs, "Kennedy Center Drops Furlough of Musicians as They Accept Pay

Cuts," *New York Times*, April 7, 2020, https://www.nytimes.com/2020/04/07
/arts/kennedy-center-national-symphony-orchestra-coronavirus.html.

14. "Allocations for Section 18004(a)(1) of the CARES Act," US Department of
Education, https://www2.ed.gov/about/offices/list/ope/allocationsforsection18
004a1ofcaresact.pdf.

15. @One_Grayman, Twitter, April 17, 2020, https://twitter.com/One_Grayman
/status/1251181013700694018?s=20.

16. "Allocations for Section 18004(a)(1) of the CARES Act," US Department of
Education.

17. Ilana Kowarski, "10 Universities with the Biggest Endowments," *US News
and World Report*, September 22, 2020, https://www.usnews.com/education
/best-colleges/the-short-list-college/articles/10-universities-with-the-biggest
-endowments; James A. Barham, "The 100 Richest Universities: Their Gener-
osity and Commitment to Research," The Best Schools, September 13, 2019,
https://thebestschools.org/features/richest-universities-endowments-generosity
-research/.

18. Wilson Wong, "COVID-19 Turned College Towns into Ghost Towns and Businesses Are Struggling to Survive," NBC News, July 13, 2020, https://www
.nbcnews.com/news/us-news/covid-19-turned-college-towns-ghost-towns
-businesses-are-struggling-n1233521.

19. @Harvard, Twitter, April 21, 2020, https://twitter.com/Harvard/status/12527
37746462007299.

20. @HelenLevinson, Twitter, April 22, 2020, https://twitter.com/HelenLevinson
/status/1253138356453683201?s=20; Luke W. Vrotsos and Cindy H. Zhang,
"Harvard Posts $298 Million Surplus in 2019," *Harvard Crimson*, October
25, 2019, https://www.thecrimson.com/article/2019/10/25/harvard-annual
-financial-report/.

21. @Stanford, Twitter, April 22, 2020, https://twitter.com/Stanford/status/125
2988495787786243.

22. "Harvard Statement on Decision to Not Accept Funds from the CARES Act
Higher Education Emergency Relief Fund," April 22, 2020, Harvard University,
https://www.harvard.edu/media-relations/2020/04/22/harvard-statement-on
-decision-to-not-accept-funds-from-the-cares-act-higher-education-emergency
-relief-fund/; @Harvard, Twitter, April 22, 2020, https://twitter.com/Harvard
/status/1253043752005844993.

23. Thornton Matheson, "Who Benefits from the CARES Act Tax Cuts?," Tax Policy Center, April 17, 2020, https://www.taxpolicycenter.org/taxvox/who -benefits-cares-act-tax-cuts.

24. Andrew Elrod and Mark Engler, "Meet the Bailout's New Slush Fund," Boston Review, March 31, 2020, http://bostonreview.net/class-inequality-politics /andrew-elrod-mark-engler-meet-bailouts-new-slush-fund; Jeanna Smialek, "How the Fed's Magic Money Machine Will Turn $454 Billion into $4 Trillion," *New York Times*, March 27, 2020, https://www.nytimes.com/2020/03/26 /business/economy/fed-coronavirus-stimulus.html.

25. Associated Press, "Watchdogs Question $700M Relief Loan to Struggling Overland Park–Based YRC Worldwide," KSHB, July 21, 2020, https://www.kshb .com/news/coronavirus/watchdogs-question-700m-relief-loan-to-struggling -overland-park-based-yrc-worldwide.

26. Frank Bass, "The Airlines, Due to Get Huge Bailout, Have Spent More Than $300M on Lobbying Since the Last One," Fast Company, March 27, 2020, https://www.fastcompany.com/90483154/the-airlines-due-to-get-huge-bailout -have-spent-a-stunning-amount-on-lobbying-since-the-last-one.

27. Brandon Kochkodin, "U.S. Airlines Spent 96% of Free Cash Flow on Buybacks," Bloomberg, March 16, 2020, https://www.bloomberg.com/news /articles/2020-03-16/u-s-airlines-spent-96-of-free-cash-flow-on-buybacks -chart?sref=hmG4mtJl.

28. Alexander Sammon, "The Airline Bailout Is the CARES Act's Biggest Debacle," *American Prospect*, July 16, 2020, https://prospect.org/economy/airline -bailout-is-the-cares-act-biggest-debacle/.

29. Doug Cameron and Eric Morath, "Covid-19's Blow to Business Travel Is Expected to Last for Years," *Wall Street Journal*, January 17, 2021, https://www .wsj.com/articles/covid-19-pandemics-impact-on-business-travel-hitting-local -economies-11610879401.

30. Robert Freedman, "75% Payroll Rule Makes PPP Loans Useless, Business Owners Say," CFO Dive, May 3, 2020, https://www.cfodive.com/news/payroll -rule-paycheck-protection-program-useless-coronavirus/577213/.

31. Author's interview with Ryan Hoover, April 20, 2020, confirmed via email on September 20, 2020.

32. Ryan Tracy, Chad Day, and Heather Haddon, "Small Business Loans Helped the Well-Heeled and Connected, Too," *Wall Street Journal*, July 6, 2020,

https://www.wsj.com/articles/u-s-releases-names-of-biggest-ppp-borrowers
-11594047600?mod=e2tw.

33. Lisa Desjardins, "It Took 13 Days for the Paycheck Protection Program to Run
Out of Money. What Comes Next?," *PBS NewsHour*, April 16, 2020, https://
www.pbs.org/newshour/politics/it-took-13-days-for-the-paycheck-protection
-program-to-run-out-of-money-what-comes-next.

34. Sarah Hansen, "Ruth's Chris Steak House Returns $20 Million PPP Loan Amid
Public Backlash as Treasury Issues New Guidance," *Forbes*, April 24, 2020,
https://www.forbes.com/sites/sarahhansen/2020/04/23/ruths-chris-steak
-house-returns-20-million-ppp-loan-as-treasury-issues-new-guidance/#a19c8c
06ef7f.

35. Bruce Brumberg, "Alert: SBA Says Paycheck Protection Program Loans Are
Not for Larger 'Small' Businesses with Liquidity Access," *Forbes*, April 23,
2020, https://www.forbes.com/sites/brucebrumberg/2020/04/23/alert-sba-says
-paycheck-protection-program-loans-are-not-for-larger-small-businesses-with
-liquidity-access/?sh=450853f96049.

36. Nathan Vardi, "71 Publicly Traded Companies Got Paycheck Protection Funding Before Money Ran Out," *Forbes*, April 20, 2020, https://www.forbes.com
/sites/nathanvardi/2020/04/20/seventy-one-publicly-traded-companies-got
-paycheck-protection-funding-before-money-ran-out/#56cdde7d5087.

37. Ibid.

38. Ibid.

39. Mary Kate Miller, "US Government Passes Second Round of PPP Funding," Len-
dio, April 24, 2020, https://www.lendio.com/blog/coronavirus/us-government
-passes-second-round-ppp-funding/.

40. Hansen, "Ruth's Chris Steak House Returns $20 Million PPP Loan."

41. Joyce M. Rosenberg, "Billions of Dollars in Aid for Small Businesses Go Un-
claimed," Associated Press, June 29, 2020, https://apnews.com/99928b1013
67ad74358283c82de0fa1a.

42. Ibid.

43. David Benoit and Peter Rudegeair, "Banks Could Get $24 Billion in Fees from
PPP Loans," *Wall Street Journal*, July 7, 2020, https://www.wsj.com/articles
/banks-could-get-24-billion-in-fees-from-ppp-loans-11594134444.

44. Tracy et al., "Small Business Loans Helped the Well-Heeled and Connected,

Too"; Megan Henney, "PPP Ending with $138B Left Over. What Happens to the Money Now?," Fox Business, August 7, 2020, https://www.foxbusiness.com /money/ppp-ending-what-happens-to-leftover-money.

45. @SBAgov, July 6, 2020, Twitter, https://twitter.com/SBAgov/status/128017 8431142092800?s=20.

46. "SBA and Treasury Announce Release of Paycheck Protection Program Loan Data," US Small Business Administration, July 13, 2020, https://www.sba .gov/article/2020/jul/13/sba-treasury-announce-release-paycheck-protection -program-loan-data.

47. "Small Business Majority Responds to the Release of PPP Borrower Information," Small Business Majority, July 6, 2020, https://smallbusinessmajority.org/press -release/small-business-majority-responds-release-ppp-borrower-information.

48. Rick Newman, "The Small Businesses Getting Bailout Loans Aren't What You Think," Yahoo! Finance, July 7, 2020, https://finance.yahoo.com/news/the-small -businesses-getting-bailout-loans-arent-what-you-think-201841546.html.

49. Tracy et al., "Small Business Loans Helped the Well-Heeled and Connected, Too."

50. Allison DeAngelis and Catherine Carlock, Boston Business Journal, "Tom Brady's Lifestyle Brand Collected at Least $350K in PPP Money," NBC 10 Boston, July 6, 2020, https://www.nbcboston.com/news/local/tom-bradys-lifestyle-brand -collected-at-least-350k-in-ppp-money/2154838/; Cassandra Negley, "Companies Owned by Floyd Mayweather, Tom Brady Among Sports Entities Granted PPP Relief Money," Yahoo! Sports, July 7, 2020, https://sports.yahoo.com /floyd-mayweather-tom-brady-companies-sports-organizations-granted-ppp -relief-money-142216529.html.

51. Pablo Maurer and Sam Stejskal, "Some MLS Teams Awarded PPP Loans, Will Soon Decide Whether to Accept Them," The Athletic, May 12, 2020, https:// theathletic.com/1810179/2020/05/12/mls-ppp-loan-decisions/.

52. Ryan Parker, "Kanye West's Yeezy Received $2M-Plus from Federal Pandemic Loan Program," Hollywood Reporter, July 6, 2020, https://www.holly woodreporter.com/news/kanye-wests-yeezy-received-2m-federal-pandemic -loan-1301971.

53. Tatiana Siegel, Alex Weprin, and Ashley Cullins, "Which Hollywood Firms Received Federal Pandemic Loans," Hollywood Reporter, July 6, 2020, https:// www.hollywoodreporter.com/news/hollywood-firms-received-federal-pan demic-loans-1293990.

54. Andrew Kerr, "Paycheck Protection Program Supporting More Than 51 Million Small Business Jobs, Trump Administration Announces," Daily Caller, July 6, 2020, https://dailycaller.com/2020/07/06/paycheck-protection-program-saved -jobs-51-million/; "Forbes: Mapping the Mega Loans Between $1 Million and $10 Million Made to U.S. Small Businesses Through the PPP," Open the Books, July 7, 2020, https://www.openthebooks.com/forbes-mapping-the-mega-loans -between-1-million-and-10-million-made-to-us-small-businesses-through-the -ppp/.

55. Bill Bostock, "The US Catholic Church May Be the Largest Recipient of Federal Coronavirus Aid, with as Much as $3.5 Billion, AP Analysis Says," Business Insider, July 10, 2020, https://www.businessinsider.com/us-catholic-church-3 -billion-coronavirus-loans-not-business-ap-2020-7.

56. Jonathan O'Connell et al., "Treasury, SBA Data Show Small-Business Loans Went to Private-Equity Backed Chains, Members of Congress," *Washington Post*, July 6, 2020, https://www.washingtonpost.com/business/2020/07/06/sba -ppp-loans-data/; Meghan Roos, "McConnell's Wife's Family Business Appears on Trump Admin's List of Companies That Received Most PPP Money," *Newsweek*, July 6, 2020, https://www.newsweek.com/mcconnells-wifes-family -business-appears-trump-admins-list-companies-that-received-most-ppp -1515788.

57. Graham Rapier, "Businesses Connected to Trump Advisor Jared Kushner and His Family Received Millions in Paycheck Protection Loans," Business Insider, July 7, 2020, https://www.businessinsider.com/kushner-family-firms-received -millions-in-paycheck-protection-loans-2020-7.

58. Jeff Cox, "Second-Quarter GDP Plunged by Worst-Ever 32.9% Amid Virus-Induced Shutdown," CNBC, July 30, 2020, https://www.cnbc.com/2020/07/30 /us-gdp-q2-2020-first-reading.html.

59. Rachel Siegel and Andrew Van Dam, "U.S. Economy Contracted at Fastest Quarterly Rate on Record from April to June as Coronavirus Walloped Workers, Businesses," *Washington Post*, July 30, 2020, https://www.washington post.com/business/2020/07/30/gdp-q2-coronavirus/?tidr=a_breakingnews& hpid=hp_no-name_hp-breaking-news%3Apage%2Fbreaking-news-bar.

60. Emily McCormick, "Q2 GDP: US Economy Contracted by Worst-Ever 32.9% in Q2, Crushed by Coronavirus Lockdowns," Yahoo! Finance, July 30, 2020, https://finance.yahoo.com/news/q2-gdp-us-economy-coronavirus-pandemic -consumer-171558880.html.

61. Author's interview with James Rickards, The Roth Effect, October 1, 2020.

62. Maggie Fitzgerald, "U.S. Savings Rate Hits Record 33% as Coronavirus Causes Americans to Stockpile Cash, Curb Spending," CNBC, May 29, 2020, https://www.cnbc.com/2020/05/29/us-savings-rate-hits-record-33percent-as -coronavirus-causes-americans-to-stockpile-cash-curb-spending.html; "Personal Saving Rate," Federal Reserve Bank of St. Louis, https://fred.stlouisfed.org/series /PSAVERT.

63. T. J. McCue, "Amazon Report Cites More Than 1 Million Small Business Sellers on Platform," Forbes, July 24, 2018, https://www.forbes.com/sites/tjmccue /2018/07/24/amazon-report-cites-more-than-1-million-small-business-sellers -on-platform/#161502903e83.

CHAPTER 5: Selling Out Main Street to Wall Street

1. Fred Imbert, "Dow Jumps More Than 800 Points, Nasdaq Hits a Record After Surprise Jobs Surge Boosts Recovery Bets," CNBC, June 5, 2020, https://www .cnbc.com/2020/06/04/stock-market-futures-open-to-close-news.html.

2. "The Employment Situation—May 2020," Bureau of Labor Statistics, https:// www.bls.gov/news.release/archives/empsit_06052020.htm.

3. Board of Governors of the Federal Reserve System, "Who Owns the Federal Reserve?," March 1, 2017, https://www.federalreserve.gov/faqs/about_14986.htm.

4. "Making Sense of the Federal Reserve," Federal Reserve Bank of St. Louis, https://www.stlouisfed.org/in-plain-english/a-closer-look-at-open-market -operations.

5. Murray N. Rothbard, The Case Against the Fed (Auburn, AL: Ludwig von Mises Institute, 2007), https://cdn.mises.org/The%20Case%20Against%20the%20 Fed_3.pdf.

6. Abigail Tucker, "The Financial Panic of 1907: Running from History," Smithsonian, October 9, 2008, https://www.smithsonianmag.com/history/the-financial -panic-of-1907-running-from-history-82176328/; Rothbard, The Case Against the Fed.

7. Rothbard, The Case Against the Fed, 83.

8. Ibid., 117.

9. Ibid., 121.

10. "How Currency Gets into Circulation," Federal Reserve Bank of New York, July 2013, https://www.newyorkfed.org/aboutthefed/fedpoint/fed01.html.

11. Brent Schrotenboer, "US Is 'Printing' Money to Help Save the Economy from the COVID-19 Crisis, but Some Wonder How Far It Can Go," *USA Today*, May 13, 2020, https://www.usatoday.com/in-depth/money/2020/05/12/corona virushow-u-s-printing-dollars-save-economy-during-crisis-fed/3038117001/.

12. Mark Carlson, "A Brief History of the 1987 Stock Market Crash with a Discussion of the Federal Reserve Response," Finance and Economics Discussion Series, Divisions of Research & Statistics and Monetary Affairs, Federal Reserve Board, November 2006, https://www.federalreserve.gov/pubs/feds/2007/200713/200713pap.pdf.

13. Peter Schiff, "My 1987 Correspondence with Alan Greenspan," *The Peter Schiff Show*, April 10, 2016, http://www.schiffradio.com/my-1987-correspondence-with-alan-greenspan/.

14. "United States Fed Funds Rate," Trading Economics, https://tradingeconomics.com/united-states/interest-rate; Kimberly Amadeo, "Fed Funds Rate History: Its Highs, Lows, and Charts," The Balance, Updated February 18, 2021, https://www.thebalance.com/fed-funds-rate-history-highs-lows-3306135; Board of Governors of the Federal Reserve System, "Open Market Operations," March 16, 2020, https://www.federalreserve.gov/monetarypolicy/openmarket.htm.

15. Peter J. Ferrara, "Why the 'Obama Recovery' Took So Long," *Wall Street Journal*, September 10, 2018, https://www.wsj.com/articles/why-the-obama-recovery-took-so-long-1536619545.

16. Board of Governors of the Federal Reserve System, "Federal Reserve Announces It Will Initiate a Program to Purchase the Direct Obligations of Housing-Related Government-Sponsored Enterprises and Mortgage-Backed Securities Backed by Fannie Mae, Freddie Mac, and Ginnie Mae," November 25, 2008, https://www.federalreserve.gov/newsevents/pressreleases/monetary 20081125b.htm; Kimberly Amadeo, "QE1 and How It Stopped the 2008 Recession," The Balance, July 31, 2020, https://www.thebalance.com/what-is-qe1-3305530.

17. Jonathan Allen, "Trump Accuses Fed of Keeping Interest Rates Low to Help Obama," Reuters, November 3, 2015, https://www.reuters.com/article/us-usa-election-trump-fed/trump-accuses-fed-of-keeping-rates-low-to-help-obama-idUSKCN0SS22A20151103.

18. David J. Lynch, "Trump Criticizes Federal Reserve, Breaking Long-Standing Practice," *Washington Post*, July 19, 2018, https://www.washingtonpost.com /business/2018/07/19/trump-criticizes-federal-reserve-breaking-long-standing -practice/.

19. Edward Helmore, "'No Guts, No Vision!' Trump Unhappy After Fed Announces Modest Rate Cut," *The Guardian*, September 18, 2019, https://www.theguardian .com/business/2019/sep/18/federal-reserve-interest-rates-trump-jerome-powell.

20. "Key ECB Interest Rates," European Central Bank, https://www.ecb.europa .eu/stats/policy_and_exchange_rates/key_ecb_interest_rates/html/index.en .html; Jana Randow, Yuko Takeo, and Paul Gordon, "Negative Interest Rates," Bloomberg, August 4, 2020, https://www.bloomberg.com/quicktake/negative -interest-rates?sref=hmG4mtJl.

21. Board of Governors of the Federal Reserve System, "Credit and Liquidity Programs and the Balance Sheet," October 30, 2020, https://www.federalreserve .gov/monetarypolicy/bst_recenttrends.htm; Board of Governors of the Federal Reserve System, "Quarterly Report on Federal Reserve Balance Sheet Developments," August 2019, https://www.federalreserve.gov/monetarypolicy/files /quarterly_balance_sheet_developments_report_201908.pdf.

22. Jeff Cox, "Fed Cuts Rates by Half a Percentage Point to Combat Coronavirus Slowdown," CNBC, March 3, 2020, https://www.cnbc.com/2020/03/03/fed -cuts-rates-by-half-a-percentage-point-to-combat-coronavirus-slowdown.html.

23. Ibid.

24. Jeff Cox, "Fed Boosts Money It's Providing to Banks in Overnight Repo Lending to $175 Billion," CNBC, March 11, 2020, https://www.cnbc.com/2020/03/11 /fed-boosts-money-its-providing-to-banks-in-overnight-repo-lending-to-175 -billion.html.

25. Michael Bloom, Jeff Cox, and Thomas Franck, "'Circuit Breaker' Triggered Again to Keep Stocks from Falling Through Floor. What You Need to Know," CNBC, March 12, 2020, https://www.cnbc.com/2020/03/12/stock-futures-hit -a-limit-down-trading-halt-for-a-second-time-this-week-heres-what-that-means .html/.

26. Jeff Cox, "The Fed to Start Buying Treasurys Friday Across All Durations, Starting with 30-Year Bond," CNBC, March 13, 2020, https://www.cnbc.com /2020/03/13/the-fed-details-moves-to-buy-treasurys-across-all-durations -starting-with-30-year-bond.html; Jeff Cox, "Fed to Pump in More Than $1 Trillion in Dramatic Ramping Up of Market Intervention Amid Coronavirus

Meltdown," CNBC, March 12, 2020, https://www.cnbc.com/2020/03/12/fed
-to-pump-more-than-500-billion-into-short-term-bank-funding-expand-types
-of-security-purchases.html.

27. Steve Liesman, "Federal Reserve Cuts Rates to Zero and Launches Massive
$700 Billion Quantitative Easing Program," CNBC, March 16, 2020, https://
www.cnbc.com/2020/03/15/federal-reserve-cuts-rates-to-zero-and-launches
-massive-700-billion-quantitative-easing-program.html.

28. Loretta Mester, "Statement Regarding My Dissenting Vote at the Meeting
of the Federal Open Market Committee Held on March 15, 2020," Federal
Reserve Bank of Cleveland, March 17, 2020, https://www.clevelandfed.org
/en/newsroom-and-events/speeches/sp-20200317-public-statement-on-dissent
.aspx.

29. Jeff Cox, "Fed's Mester Explains 'No' Vote on Rate Cut, Says She Would Back
Commercial Paper Help," CNBC, March 17, 2020, https://www.cnbc.com
/2020/03/17/feds-mester-explains-no-vote-on-rate-cut-says-she-would-back
-commercial-paper-help.html.

30. Jonathan Garber and Suzanne O'Halloran, "Dow Drops 2,997 Points on Word
Coronavirus Crisis Could Extend Until August," Fox Business, March 16, 2020,
https://www.foxbusiness.com/markets/us-stocks-march-16-2020.

31. Thomas Wade, "Timeline: The Federal Reserve Responds to the Threat of
Coronavirus," American Action Forum, November 2, 2020, https://www
.americanactionforum.org/insight/timeline-the-federal-reserve-responds-to
-the-threat-of-coronavirus/#ixzz6SDPWbLkT; Jeanna Smialek, "Big Banks
Aren't Embracing Fed's Main Street Loan Program," New York Times, July 8,
2020, https://www.nytimes.com/2020/07/08/business/economy/federal-reserves
-lending-coron.html.

32. Dawn Lim, "Federal Reserve Taps BlackRock to Purchase Bonds for the Government," Wall Street Journal, March 24, 2020, https://www.wsj.com/articles
/federal-reserve-taps-blackrock-to-purchase-bonds-for-the-government
-11585085843.

33. Jason Orestes, "Will the Fed Buy Stocks? Here's What It Would Take to Do It,"
TheStreet, April 3, 2020, https://www.thestreet.com/opinion/federal-reserve
-buy-stocks.

34. Brian Croce, "Groups Raise Alarm over Fed, BlackRock Debt-Buying Deal,"
Pensions & Investments, March 30, 2020, https://www.pionline.com/regulation
/groups-raise-alarm-over-fed-blackrock-debt-buying-deal.

35. Paul R. La Monica, "A Key Bank Rule Written in the Wake of the Financial Crisis Just Got Rolled Back," CNN, June 26, 2020, https://www.cnn.com /2020/06/25/investing/fdic-volcker-rule-banks/index.html.

36. Lizzy Gurdus, "Stocks Close Higher as Opposing Forces Pull on the Market—What Investors Should Watch Now," CNBC, June 25, 2020, https://www.cnbc .com/2020/06/25/stocks-rise-as-opposing-forces-pull-on-the-market-what-to -watch.html; Hugh Son and Jessie Pound, "Bank Stocks Surge After Regula- tors Ease Volcker Rule, JPMorgan Chase Climbs 2%," CNBC, June 26, 2020, https://www.cnbc.com/2020/06/25/bank-stocks-reverse-higher-as-regulators -ease-volcker-rule-jpmorgan-chase-rises-2percent.html.

37. Jeff Cox, "Coronavirus Stimulus Just Pushed Fed's Balance Sheet Past $5 Tril- lion for the First Time Ever," CNBC, March 27, 2020, https://www.cnbc.com /2020/03/27/the-feds-balance-sheet-just-passed-5-trillion-for-the-first-time -ever.html.

38. Board of Governors of the Federal Reserve System, "Credit and Liquidity Pro- grams and the Balance Sheet"; "Monthly Statement of the Public Debt of the United States," US Department of the Treasury, January 31, 2004, ftp://ftp .publicdebt.treas.gov/opd/opds012004.pdf.

39. Jeff Cox, "The Fed Is Buying Some of the Biggest Companies' Bonds, Rais- ing Questions over Why," CNBC, June 29, 2020, https://www.cnbc.com/2020 /06/29/the-fed-is-buying-some-of-the-biggest-companies-bonds-raising -questions-over-why.html.

40. Brian Chappatta, "Fed Can't Talk the U.S. Economy into Inflation," Bloomberg, August 28, 2020, https://www.bloombergquint.com/opinion/fed-jackson-hole -meeting-powell-can-t-talk-u-s-economy-into-inflation; Jeff Cox, "Powell An- nounces New Fed Approach to Inflation That Could Keep Rates Lower for Longer," CNBC, August 28, 2020, https://www.cnbc.com/2020/08/27/powell -announces-new-fed-approach-to-inflation-that-could-keep-rates-lower-for -longer.html.

41. Claire Kramer Mills and Jessica Battisto, "Double Jeopardy: Covid-19's Con- centrated Health and Wealth Effects in Black Communities," Federal Re- serve Bank of New York, August 2020, https://www.newyorkfed.org/media library/media/smallbusiness/DoubleJeopardy_COVID19andBlackOwned Businesses.

42. Anjali Sundaram, "Yelp Data Shows 60% of Business Closures Due to the Coro- navirus Pandemic Are Now Permanent," CNBC, September 16, 2020, https://

www.cnbc.com/2020/09/16/yelp-data-shows-60percent-of-business-closures
-due-to-the-coronavirus-pandemic-are-now-permanent.html.

43. Chuck Casto, "Alignable: 34% of Small Businesses Can't Pay October Rent," Alignable, October 8, 2020, https://www.alignable.com/forum/alignable-34 -of-small-businesses-cant-pay-rent-in-october.

44. "USA: Listed Companies," The Global Economy.com, https://www.theglobal economy.com/USA/Listed_companies/.

45. Anneken Tappe, "The Fed Isn't Even Thinking About Raising Rates," CNN, June 10, 2020, https://www.cnn.com/business/live-news/stock-market-news -061020/h_213d00641eab8aacc55ff33db99a1421.

46. Form 10-Q for the quarterly period ended October 1, 2019, The Cheesecake Factory, https://d18rn0p25nwr6d.cloudfront.net/CIK-0000887596/94240e43 –4084–4434-b3c3–9979f45be755.pdf; Form 10-Q for the quarterly period ended September 29, 2015, The Cheesecake Factory, https://d18rn0p25nwr6d .cloudfront.net/CIK-0000887596/9e83e39e-fcd1–4ca2-ad99-a1baba558be5 .pdf; "The Cheesecake Factory Reports Results for Fourth Quarter of Fiscal 2018," The Cheesecake Factory, February 20, 2019, https://investors.thecheese cakefactory.com/news-and-events/news-releases/news-release-details/2019 /The-Cheesecake-Factory-Reports-Results-for-Fourth-Quarter-of-Fiscal-2018 /default.aspx.

47. Paula Seligson, "U.S. Junk Bond Yields Hit Record Low for Second Time This Year," Bloomberg, December 3, 2020, https://www.bloomberg.com/news/articles /2020-12-03/u-s-junk-bond-yields-hit-record-low-for-second-time-this-year.

48. Maggie Fitzgerald, "Many Americans Used Part of Their Coronavirus Stim- ulus Check to Trade Stocks," CNBC, May 21, 2020, https://www.cnbc.com /2020/05/21/many-americans-used-part-of-their-coronavirus-stimulus-check -to-trade-stocks.html.

49. Matthew Fox, "219 'Blank-Check' Companies Raised $73 Billion in 2020, Outpacing Traditional IPOs to Make This the Year of the SPAC, According to Goldman Sachs," Business Insider, December 18, 2020, https://markets.business insider.com/news/stocks/spacs-raised-73-billion-more-than-traditional-ipos -blank-checks-2020-12-1029906693; Christopher M. Barlow et al., "The Year of the SPAC," Skadden, Arps, Slate, Meagher & Flom LLP and Affiliates, January 26, 2021, https://www.skadden.com/insights/publications/2021/01/2021-insights /corporate/the-year-of-the-spac.

50. William Watts, "How Much of the Stock Market's Rise over the Last 11 Years Is Due to QE? Here's an Estimate," MarketWatch, November 15, 2020, https://www.marketwatch.com/story/without-qe-the-s-p-500-would-be-trading-closer-to-1-800-than-3-300-says-societe-generale-11604688442.

51. Whitney Tilson, "Grantham, Kass, and Rocker on a Stock Market Bubble," Whitney Tilson's Daily, January 14, 2021, https://empirefinancialresearch.com/articles/grantham-kass-and-rocker-on-a-stock-market-bubble.

52. Gregory Daco, "Inflation Should Be the Least of Our Worries," The Hill, June 18, 2020, https://thehill.com/opinion/finance/503283-inflation-should-be-the-least-of-our-worries.

53. Ruchir Sharma, "The Rescues Ruining Capitalism," Wall Street Journal, July 24, 2020, https://www.wsj.com/articles/the-rescues-ruining-capitalism-11595603720.

54. Ibid.

55. Jeff Cox, "Highly Indebted 'Zombie' Companies Control More Than 2 Million U.S. Jobs," CNBC, May 21, 2020, https://www.cnbc.com/2020/05/20/highly-indebted-zombie-companies-control-more-than-2-million-us-jobs.html.

56. Hung Tran, "How to Deal with the Coming Pandemic Debt Crisis?," Atlantic Council, May 11, 2020, https://www.atlanticcouncil.org/blogs/new-atlanticist/how-to-deal-with-the-coming-pandemic-debt-crisis/.

57. Reade Pickert, "U.S. Business Debt Soars by Record on Bond Issuance, Loans," Bloomberg, June 11, 2020, https://www.bloomberg.com/news/articles/2020-06-11/u-s-business-debt-soars-by-record-on-bond-issuance-loans?sref=hmG4mtJl; "Financial Accounts of the United States—Z.1; Recent Developments: Debt Outstanding by Sector," Board of Governors of the Federal Reserve System, March, 11, 2021, https://www.federalreserve.gov/releases/z1/20210311/html/recent_developments.htm.

58. Cezary Podkul, "Expected Surge of CLO Downgrades Slow to Arrive," Wall Street Journal, August 28, 2020, https://www.wsj.com/articles/expected-surge-of-clo-downgrades-slow-to-arrive-11598653875.

59. "Our Perspective on the CLO Scare," Fisher Investments, June 23, 2020, https://www.fisherinvestments.com/en-us/marketminder/our-perspective-on-the-clo-scare.

60. Ben Meng, "Calpers Prepares for the Long Haul," Wall Street Journal, June

14, 2020, https://www.wsj.com/articles/calpers-prepares-for-the-long-haul-11
592164054.

CHAPTER 6: Social Justice and Social Costs

1. Ariela Anis, "Black Business Owner Who Invested Life Savings into Minneapolis Restaurant Weeps as Looters Destroy It," Hollywood Unlocked, May 29, 2020, https://hollywoodunlocked.com/black-business-owner-who-invested-life -savings-into-minneapolis-restaurant-weeps-as-looters-destroy-it/; Sam Dorman, "Black Firefighter 'Devastated' After Rioters Destroy Bar He Spent Life Savings to Build," Fox News, May 29, 2020, https://www.foxnews.com/us/black -firefighter-devastated-minneapolis-riots-bar.

2. Dorman, "Black Firefighter 'Devastated' After Rioters Destroy Bar He Spent Life Savings to Build."

3. Josh Penrod, C. J. Sinner, and Mary Jo Webster, "Buildings Damaged in Minneapolis, St. Paul After Riots," *Star Tribune* (Minneapolis), July 13, 2020, https://www.startribune.com/minneapolis-st-paul-buildings-are-damaged -looted-after-george-floyd-protests-riots/569930671/.

4. Molly Hennessy-Fiske, "'We Don't Have Law and Order': Black and Latino Business Owners Face Destruction in Minneapolis," *Los Angeles Times*, May 29, 2020, https://www.latimes.com/world-nation/story/2020-05-29/minneapolis -minority-business-owners-awake-to-destruction.

5. Ibid.

6. Sarah Al-Arshani et al., "How 7 Days of US Protests over the Death of George Floyd Spiraled into Chaos and Deadly Violence," Business Insider, June 1, 2020, https://www.businessinsider.com/protests-death-george-floyd-minneapolis -new-york-denver-2020-5.

7. Nellie Bowles, "Abolish the Police? Those Who Survived the Chaos in Seattle Aren't So Sure," *New York Times*, August 7, 2020, https://www.nytimes .com/2020/08/07/us/defund-police-seattle-protests.html.

8. Bowen Xiao, "Inside Seattle's Lawless, Self-Declared 'Autonomous Zone,'" The Epoch Times, August 25, 2020, https://www.theepochtimes.com/inside -seattles-lawless-self-declared-autonomous-zone_3390380.html.

9. @AP, Twitter, June 22, 2020, https://twitter.com/AP/status/127521796195 1911943; Gene Johnson, "Seattle Will Move to Dismantle Protest Zone, Mayor

Says," Associated Press, June 22, 2020, https://apnews.com/4dcff8f062bae9e 1fe3885c346b44847.

10. Bowles, "Abolish the Police?"

11. "Seattle's Best Resigns," *Wall Street Journal*, August 11, 2020, https://www .wsj.com/articles/seattles-best-resigns-11597188431.

12. Dom Calicchio, "Portland Business Owner on Impact of Riots, Coronavirus: 'It's Terrifying,'" Fox News, July 29, 2020, https://www.foxnews.com/media /portland-business-owner-on-impact-of-riots-coronavirus-its-terrifying.

13. @TaraLaRosa, Twitter, September 9, 2020, https://twitter.com/TaraLaRosa /status/1303909615512453126?s=20; "Man Charged with Arson in Connection to Oregon Wildfire," ABC 7, September 12, 2020, https://abc7.com/wildfire -oregon-fire-in-arson/6420067/.

14. Jamie Goldberg, "Insurers Balk at Covering Portland Businesses; Brokers Say Downtown Upheaval Has Made Carriers Wary," *The Oregonian*, December 12, 2020, https://www.oregonlive.com/business/2020/12/insurers-balk-at-covering -portland-businesses-brokers-say-downtown-upheaval-has-made-carriers -wary.html.

15. Bowles, "Abolish the Police?"

16. Sabri Ben-Achour, "Economically, Riots Endure," Marketplace, June 1, 2020, https://www.marketplace.org/2020/06/01/riots-lasting-economic-impact/.

17. William J. Collins and Robert A. Margo, "The Labor Market Effects of the 1960s Riots," working paper 10243, National Bureau of Economic Research, January 2004, https://www.nber.org/papers/w10243; Rav Avora, "Violence Hurts the Communities Protesters Want to Protect," *Foreign Policy*, August 14, 2020, https://foreignpolicy.com/2020/08/14/violence-hurts-the-communities- protesters-want-to-protect/.

18. William J. Collins and Robert A. Margo, "The Economic Aftermath of the 1960s Riots: Evidence from Property Values," working paper 10493, National Bureau of Economic Research, May 2004, https://www.nber.org/papers/w104 93; Avora, "Violence Hurts the Communities Protesters Want to Protect."

19. Joe Cahill, "What's at Stake—for All of Us—if Looting Flares Up Again," *Crain's Chicago Business*, August 11, 2020, https://www.chicagobusiness.com /joe-cahill-business/whats-stake-all-us-if-looting-flares-again.

20. Ibid.

21. Amanda Vinicky, "Illinois Exodus: Census Data Finds People Continue to Leave State," WTTW, December 23, 2020, https://news.wttw.com/2020/12/23 /illinois-exodus-census-data-finds-people-continue-leave-state; Bryce Hill, "Illinois Sees Worst Population Decline Since World War II," Illinois Policy, December 22, 2020, https://www.illinoispolicy.org/illinois-sees-worst-population -decline-since-world-war-ii/.

22. Rob Garver, "Economic Damage from Civil Unrest May Persist for Decades," Voice of America, June 2, 2020, https://www.voanews.com/usa/nation-turmoil -george-floyd-protests/economic-damage-civil-unrest-may-persist-decades.

CHAPTER 7: A Couple Hundred Days' Worth of "Fifteen Days to Slow the Spread"

1. "The Employment Situation—October 2020," US Bureau of Labor Statistics, https://www.bls.gov/news.release/pdf/empsit.pdf.

2. "March 2020: Dr. Anthony Fauci Talks with Dr Jon LaPook About COVID-19," *60 Minutes*, March 8, 2020, https://www.cbsnews.com/video/march-2020-dr -anthony-fauci-talks-with-dr-jon-lapook-about-covid-19/.

3. "Small Business Optimism Is Falling, July 2020 Index Reports," NFIB, August 19, 2020, https://www.nfib.com/content/analysis/economy/july-2020-sbet -small-business-optimism-is-falling/.

4. Alex Tavlian, "Sour Grapes Emerge as Most Calif. Wineries Close While Newsom's Winery Remains Open," *The Sun*, July 2, 2020, http://sjvsun.com /california/sour-grapes-emerge-as-most-calif-wineries-close-while-newsoms -winery-remains-open/; "Ask 17: Why Is the Winery Founded by Gov. Newsom Still Open?," KGET, July 3, 2020, https://www.kget.com/health/coronavirus /ask-17-why-is-the-winery-founded-by-gov-newsom-still-open/.

5. @NYGovCuomo, Twitter, July 21, 2020, https://twitter.com/NYGovCuomo /status/1285602348446945281?s=20.

6. handshakesbarandgrill, Instagram, July 17, 2020, https://www.instagram.com /p/CCwHxMUAjzc/?utm_source=ig_embed; @Maxtropolitan, Twitter, July 17, 2020, https://twitter.com/Maxtropolitan/status/1284312486745866241/photo /1.

7. "Bars Get Creative to Avoid NY's Food with Alcohol Rule but 'Cuomo Chips' Aren't Enough, Gov. Says," NBC 4 New York, July 24, 2020, https://www.nbc

newyork.com/news/local/bars-get-creative-to-avoid-nys-food-with-alcohol
-rule-but-cuomo-chips-arent-enough-gov-says/2529749/.

8. Don Cazentre, "Chips? Chips and Salsa? Cuomo's Rules on Food Sales at Bars
Still Causing Confusion," Syracuse.com, July 21, 2020, https://www.syracuse
.com/restaurants/2020/07/chips-chips-and-salsa-cuomos-rules-on-food-sales
-at-bars-still-causing-confusion.html.

9. "Unemployment Rate 16.1 Percent in Massachusetts, 4.5 Percent in Utah, in
July 2020," U.S. Bureau of Labor Statistics, August 27, 2020, https://www.bls
.gov/opub/ted/2020/unemployment-rate-16-point-1-percent-in-massachusetts
-4-point-5-percent-in-utah-in-july-2020.htm.

10. Jon Blistein, "MTV Video Music Awards to Take Place in Brooklyn with Governor Cuomo's OK," *Rolling Stone*, June 29, 2020, https://www.rollingstone.com
/music/music-news/mtv-video-music-awards-2020-brooklyn-andrew-cuomo
-1022116/.

11. "Employment and Unemployment Among Youth Summary," US Bureau of
Labor Statistics, August 18, 2020, https://www.bls.gov/news.release/youth
.nr0.htm; @LizAnnSonders, Twitter, July 6, 2020, https://twitter.com/LizAnn
Sonders/status/1280085129113763840/photo/1.

12. Carmen Reinicke, "US Shocks Economists by Adding 2.5 Million Jobs in
May as Unemployment Declines to 13.3%," Business Insider, June 5, 2020,
https://www.businessinsider.com/may-jobs-report-unemployment-rate-declines
-nonfarm-payrolls-surprise-increase-2020-6.

13. @nytimes, Twitter, July 31, 2020, https://twitter.com/nytimes/status/12892766
41181437955?s=20.

14. Beth LeBlanc, Craig Mauger, and Melissa Nann Burke, "High Court Strikes
Down Whitmer's Emergency Powers; Gov Vows to Use Other Means," *Detroit News*, October 2, 2020, https://www.detroitnews.com/story/news/local
/michigan/2020/10/02/michigan-supreme-court-strikes-down-gretchen
-whitmers-emergency-powers/5863340002/.

15. Jeff Cox, "Job Growth Stronger Than Expected in October, Unemployment
Rate Slides to 6.9%," November 6, 2020, CNBC, https://www.cnbc.com
/2020/11/06/jobs-report-october-2020.html.

16. Beth McKenna, "Amazon's Earnings Breeze Past Expectations: 5 Metrics
You Should See," The Motley Fool, October 30, 2020, https://www.fool.com
/investing/2020/10/30/amazons-earnings-breeze-past-expectations-5-metric/;

Hugh Langley, "Alphabet's Q3 Revenue Jumps 14% as the Company Bounces Back from a Historic Slump," Business Insider, October 29, 2020, https://www.businessinsider.com/google-alphabet-earnings-q3-2020-advertising-cloud-youtube-other-bets-2020-10.

17. Data from Yahoo! Finance, November 6, 2020, https://finance.yahoo.com.

18. Gina Francolla, "Monday's Session by the Numbers," CNBC, November 2, 2020, https://www.cnbc.com/2020/11/02/stock-market-today-live.html.

19. Paula Gardner, "Whitmer Administration Leaves Restaurants in Dark on New COVID Rule," Bridge Michigan, November 2, 2020, https://www.bridgemi.com/business-watch/whitmer-administration-leaves-restaurants-dark-new-covid-rule.

20. "NFIB: Argues Gov. Evers' Action Is Illegal, Irresponsible," WisBusiness.com, October 16, 2020, https://www.wisbusiness.com/2020/nfib-argues-gov-evers-action-is-illegal-irresponsible/.

21. "Military Suicides Have Increased by as Much as 20% During the Coronavirus Pandemic," CBS News, September 28, 2020, https://www.cbsnews.com/news/military-suicides-increase-coronavirus-pandemic/; Ann Pietrangelo, "Suicide Ideation Is Increasing During COVID-19: How Best to Cope," Healthline, August 23, 2020, https://www.healthline.com/health-news/suicidal-ideation-is-increasing-during-covid-19-how-best-to-cope; Cory Stieg, "Could You Get PTSD from Your Pandemic Experience? The Long-Term Mental Health Effects of Coronavirus," CNBC, September 16, 2020, https://www.cnbc.com/2020/04/17/long-term-mental-health-ptsd-effects-of-covid-19-pandemic-explained.html.

22. Stephen Sawchuk, "COVID-19's Harm to Learning Is Inevitable. How Schools Can Start to Address It," EducationWeek, August 19, 2020, https://www.edweek.org/ew/articles/2020/08/20/covid-19s-harm-to-learning-is-inevitable-how.html.

23. Emma Dorn et al., "COVID-19 and Student Learning in the United States: The Hurt Could Last a Lifetime," McKinsey & Company, June 2020, https://www.mckinsey.com/industries/public-and-social-sector/our-insights/covid-19-and-student-learning-in-the-united-states-the-hurt-could-last-a-lifetime.

24. Ibid.

25. Olivia Rockeman, "Summers Says COVID-19 Will End Up Costing U.S. $16 Trillion," Bloomberg, October 12, 2020, https://www.bloomberg.com/news

/articles/2020–10-12/summers-says-covid-19-will-end-up-costing-u-s-16-trillion ?sref=hmG4mtJl.

26. Lauren Thomas, "Turning a Dead Mall into a Warehouse Will Slash Its Value as Much as 90%, Barclays Predicts," CNBC, October 15, 2020, https://www .cnbc.com/2020/10/15/mall-values-could-b.html.

27. "2020 IPOs," Stock Analysis, https://stockanalysis.com/ipos/2020-list/.

28. Ibid.

29. Erika Adams and Tanay Warerkar, "Restaurants and Bars Account for 1.4 Percent of COVID-19 Spread in New York," Eater New York, December 11, 2020, https://ny.eater.com/2020/12/11/22169841/restaurants-and-bars -coronavirus-spread-data-new-york; "'SNL' Gets to Game Lockdown Rules While Small Biz Gets Hammered," New York Post, October 8, 2020, https:// nypost.com/2020/10/08/snl-gets-to-game-lockdown-rules-while-small-biz -gets-hammered/.

30. Eric Groves, "Special Report: COVID Crisis Relief Needed to Keep Small Business Economy Afloat," Alignable, December 10, 2020, https://www.align able.com/forum/special-report-covid-crisis-needed-to-keep-small-business -economy.

31. Eric Rosenbaum, "Small Business Confidence Drops to All-Time Low After Biden Election," CNBC, November 30, 2020, https://www.cnbc.com/2020 /11/30/small-business-confidence-hits-all-time-low-after-biden-election.html ?__source=twitter%7Cmain.

32. Damian J. Troise, "S&P 500 Closes Out 2020 at Record High After a Quiet Trading Day but a Year of Wild Swings," USA Today, December 31, 2020, https://www.usatoday.com/story/money/2020/12/31/dow-jones-stocks-were -flat-early-trading-after-year-sharp-swings/4099199001/.

33. Daniel Sparks, "Apple Stock: Buy, Sell, or Hold After Soaring 81% in 2020?," The Motley Fool, December 31, 2020, https://www.fool.com/investing/2021 /01/01/apple-stock-buy-sell-or-hold-after-soaring-81-in-2/; "Amazon.com, Inc. (AMZN)," Yahoo! Finance, https://finance.yahoo.com/quote/AMZN/history ?period1=1577750400&period2=1610064000&interval=1d&filter =history&frequency=1d&includeAdjustedClose=true; Travis Hoium, "Tesla Stock Surged 695% in 2020. Is It a Buy for 2021?," The Motley Fool, December 30, 2020, https://www.fool.com/investing/2020/12/30/tesla-stock-surged-695 -in-2020-is-it-a-buy-for-202/.

CHAPTER 8: Protecting the Smallest Minority

1. Jonathan Hoenig, *A New Textbook of Americanism: The Politics of Ayn Rand* (Capitalistpig Publications, 2018).

2. Patrice Onwuka, "L.A. Restaurant Owner Fights Back Against Government's COVID-19 Double Standards," Independent Women's Forum, December 7, 2020, https://www.iwf.org/2020/12/07/l-a-restaurant-owner-fights-back-against-governments-covid-19-double-standards/; "$185K Raised to Help Sherman Oaks Restaurant Owner Who Voiced Frustration over LA County Dining Ban in Viral Video," ABC 7, December 10, 2020, https://abc7.com/sherman-oaks-angela-marsden-viral-video-pineapple-hill-saloon-and-grill/8653073/.

3. Onwuka, "L.A. Restaurant Owner Fights Back Against Government's COVID-19 Double Standards."

4. Lee Fang, "Hollywood Deployed Lobbyists to Win Exemptions to Strict California Lockdown," The Intercept, December 11, 2020, https://theintercept.com/2020/12/11/hollywood-covid-filming-california-lockdown/.

5. "COVID-19: States Should Not Abuse Emergency Measures to Suppress Human Rights—UN Experts," United Nations Human Rights, Office of the High Commissioner, March 16, 2020, https://www.ohchr.org/EN/NewsEvents/Pages/DisplayNews.aspx?NewsID=25722.

6. Stephon Bagne, "The Use of Eminent Domain Powers to Combat COVID-19," JD Supra, April 22, 2020, https://www.jdsupra.com/legalnews/the-use-of-eminent-domain-powers-to-36832/.

7. "State Authority, Individual Rights Clash Amid Pandemic," American Bar Association, April 27, 2020, https://www.americanbar.org/news/abanews/aba-news-archives/2020/04/state-authority-individual-rights-clash/.

CHAPTER 9: America's Worst Trade Deal

1. John Dickerson, "The Hardest Job in the World," *The Atlantic*, May 2018, https://www.theatlantic.com/magazine/archive/2018/05/a-broken-office/556883/.

2. "The True Size of Government," Volcker Alliance, September 29, 2017, https://www.volckeralliance.org/true-size-government.

3. Dickerson, "The Hardest Job in the World."

4. "Dow Jones Industrial Average," Wikipedia, https://en.wikipedia.org/wiki/Dow
    _Jones_Industrial_Average.

5. Dave Kowal, "How Many Federal Laws Are There? No One Knows," Kowal
    Communications, Inc., February 7, 2013, http://www.kowal.com/?q=How
    -Many-Federal-Laws-Are-There%3F.

6. Clark Neily and Dick M. Carpenter II, "Government Unchecked," Center for
    Judicial Engagement, September 2011, http://www.ij.org/images/pdf_folder
    /other_pubs/grvnmtunchkd.pdf.

7. John Baker, "Revisiting the Explosive Growth of Federal Crimes," Heritage
    Foundation, June 16, 2008, https://www.heritage.org/report/revisiting-the
    -explosive-growth-federal-crimes#_ftnref6.

8. Rebecca M. Blank, "Trends in the Welfare System," in *Welfare, the Family,
    and Reproductive Behavior: Research Perspectives* (Washington, DC: National
    Academy Press, 1998), https://www.ncbi.nlm.nih.gov/books/NBK230340/pdf
    /Bookshelf_NBK230340.pdf, 33–49, at 33.

9. Ibid.

10. Council of Economic Advisers, "Government Employment and Training Pro-
    grams: Assessing the Evidence on Their Performance," Executive Office of the
    President of the United States, June 2019, https://trumpwhitehouse.archives
    .gov/wp-content/uploads/2019/06/Government-Employment-and-Training
    -Programs.pdf.

11. Damon Dunn, *Punting Poverty: Breaking the Chains of Welfare* (San Francisco:
    Pacific Research Institute, 2020), 19.

12. "21.3 Percent of U.S. Population Participates in Government Assistance Pro-
    grams Each Month," United States Census Bureau, May 28, 2015, https://www
    .census.gov/newsroom/press-releases/2015/cb15–97.html.

13. Neily and Carpenter, "Government Unchecked."

14. "Federal Grants to State and Local Governments: A Historical Perspective on
    Contemporary Issues," Congressional Research Service, May 22, 2019, https://
    fas.org/sgp/crs/misc/R40638.pdf.

15. Samual Stebbins, "How Much Money Does Your State Receive from the Fed-
    eral Government? Check Out This List," *USA Today*, March 20, 2019, https://

www.usatoday.com/story/money/economy/2019/03/20/how-much-federal
-funding-each-state-receives-government/39202299/; Rockefeller Institute, "Giving or Getting? New York's Balance of Payments with the Federal Government,"
Rockefeller Institute of Government, September 2017, https://rockinst.org/issue
-area/giving-getting-new-yorks-balance-payments-federal-government-2/;
Laura Schultz and Michelle Cummings, "Giving or Getting? New York's Balance
of Payments with the Federal Government," Rockefeller Institute of Government, January 8, 2019, https://rockinst.org/wp-content/uploads/2019/01/1-7
-19b-Balance-of-Payments.pdf.

16. Ruchir Sharma, "The Rescues Ruining Capitalism," *Wall Street Journal*, July
    24, 2020, https://www.wsj.com/articles/the-rescues-ruining-capitalism-11595
    603720.

17. Gloria Guzman, "New Data Show Income Increased in 14 States and 10 of the
    Largest Metros," United States Census Bureau, September 26, 2019, https://
    www.census.gov/library/stories/2019/09/us-median-household-income-up-in
    -2018-from-2017.html; "Monthly Federal Spending/Revenue/Deficit Charts,"
    usgovernmentspending.com, November 5, 2020, https://www.usgovernment
    spending.com; Bureau of Economic Analysis, October 29, 2020, https://apps
    .bea.gov/national/pdf/SNTables.pdf.

18. "John Adams to Abigail Adams, 7 July 1775," National Archives, https://
    founders.archives.gov/documents/Adams/04-01-02-0160.

19. Author's interview with Britt Raybould, October 7, 2020.

20. Sharma, "The Rescues Ruining Capitalism."

21. David Wessel, "How Worried Should You Be About the Federal Deficit and
    Debt?," Brookings Institution, July 8, 2020, https://www.brookings.edu/policy
    2020/votervital/how-worried-should-you-be-about-the-federal-deficit-and
    -debt/.

CHAPTER 10: Losing the Branding on Capitalism

1. Eugene Kiely, "'You Didn't Build That,' Uncut and Unedited," FactCheck.org,
   July 24, 2012, https://www.factcheck.org/2012/07/you-didnt-build-that-uncut
   -and-unedited/.

2. Rob Wildeboer and Chip Mitchell, "'Winning Has Come Through Revolts':
   A Black Lives Matter Activist on Why She Supports Looting," WBEZ, August

12, 2020, https://www.wbez.org/stories/winning-has-come-through-revolts-a
-black-lives-matter-activist-on-why-she-supports-looting/398d0f3f-73d0-4f2e-
ae32-04cceba0d322.

3.   Tom Bemis, "Karl Marx Is the Most Assigned Economist in U.S. College
Classes," MarketWatch, January 31, 2016, https://www.marketwatch.com
/story/communist-manifesto-among-top-three-books-assigned-in-college
-2016-01-27; "2019 Annual Poll," Victims of Communism Memorial Foundation, 2019, https://victimsofcommunism.org/annual-poll/2019-annual-poll/;
"'Meet Today's Typical Millennial,'" Jon Sutz Multimedia Consulting for Law
and Advocacy, http://www.jonsutz.com/mttm/.

4.   "2019 Annual Poll," Victims of Communism Memorial Foundation; Jon Tal-
ton, "This Era's Capitalism Is Driving Many Among the Young to Socialism,"
Seattle Times, November 27, 2020, https://www.seattletimes.com/business
/this-eras-capitalism-is-driving-many-among-the-young-to-socialism/.

5.   @TeenVogue, Twitter, October 17, 2018, https://twitter.com/TeenVogue/status
/1052641654367313921.

6.   Michelle Li, "How to Have the Perfect Night In with These 7 Outfits," Teen
Vogue, February 4, 2020, https://www.teenvogue.com/story/best-lingerie-lounge
wear-this-season; Gianluca Russo, "Ariana Grande Is Releasing a 'R.E.M.'
Perfume. It'll Be Her Sixth," Teen Vogue, August 6, 2020, https://www.teen
vogue.com/story/ariana-grande-rem-fragrance.

7.   Christina Maxouris, "Cardi B Gave Her Husband (a Whole Lot of) Cash
in a Fridge for His Birthday," CNN, December 17, 2019, https://www.cnn
.com/2019/12/17/entertainment/cardi-b-offset-cash-fridge-trnd/index.html;
Philip Bump, "Cardi B: Here's Where Your Tax Money Is Going," Washington
Post, March 23, 2018, https://www.washingtonpost.com/news/politics/wp
/2018/03/23/cardi-b-heres-where-your-tax-money-is-going/.

8.   Kandist Mallett, "The Coronavirus Pandemic Demonstrates the Failures of
Capitalism," Teen Vogue, March 24, 2020, https://www.teenvogue.com/story
/coronavirus-pandemic-failures-capitalism.

9.   Ian Hathaway, "Almost Half of Fortune 500 Companies Were Founded by
American Immigrants or Their Children," Brookings, December 4, 2017, https://
www.brookings.edu/blog/the-avenue/2017/12/04/almost-half-of-fortune-500
-companies-were-founded-by-american-immigrants-or-their-children/.

10.   Mark J. Perry, "Why Socialism Failed," Foundation for Economic Education,
May 31, 1995, https://fee.org/articles/why-socialism-failed/.

11. Harry Enten, "Congress' Approval Rating Hasn't Hit 30% in 10 Years. That's a Record," CNN, June 1, 2019, https://www.cnn.com/2019/06/01/politics/poll-of-the-week-congress-approval-rating/index.html.

12. "Average Income Around the World," WorldData.info, 2019, https://www.worlddata.info/average-income.php; "Global Wealth Databook 2019," Credit Suisse Research Institute, https://www.credit-suisse.com/media/assets/corporate/docs/about-us/research/publications/global-wealth-databook-2019.pdf.

13. Ben Carlson, "Many Top-Earners Lose Their Wealth Within a Decade of Getting It," Business Insider, July 1, 2018, https://www.businessinsider.com/many-top-earners-lose-their-wealth-within-a-decade-of-getting-it-2018-7.

14. Patrick Winters and Marion Halftermeyer, "U.S. Mints More Than Half of World's New Millionaires," Bloomberg, October 21, 2019, https://www.bloombergquint.com/global-economics/u-s-mints-more-than-half-of-new-millionaires-on-booming-stocks.

15. "8 Small Business Revenue Statistics," Fundera, https://www.fundera.com/resources/small-business-revenue-statistics.

16. Jerry Hirsch, "Elon Musk's Growing Empire Is Fueled by $4.9 Billion in Government Subsidies," *Los Angeles Times*, May 30, 2015, https://www.latimes.com/business/la-fi-hy-musk-subsidies-20150531-story.html.

17. "Illinois Report Card, 2019–2020," Illinois State Board of Education, https://www.illinoisreportcard.com/district.aspx?source=environment&source2=perstudentspending&Districtid=15016299025.

18. "Data: Breaking Down the Where and Why of K–12 Spending," EducationWeek, September 24, 2019, https://www.edweek.org/ew/section/multimedia/the-where-and-why-of-k-12-spending.html.

19. Dominic Rushe, "The US Spends More on Education Than Other Countries. Why Is It Falling Behind?," *The Guardian*, September 7, 2018, https://www.theguardian.com/us-news/2018/sep/07/us-education-spending-finland-south-korea.

20. Ibid.

21. Mark J. Perry, "Chart of the Day: Administrative Bloat in US Public Schools," American Enterprise Institute, March 9, 2013, https://www.aei.org/carpe-diem/chart-of-the-day-administrative-bloat-in-us-public-schools/.

22. "Operating Schools During COVID-19: CDC's Considerations," Centers for

Disease Control and Prevention, July 23, 2020, https://www.cdc.gov/corona
virus/2019-ncov/community/schools-childcare/reopening-schools.html.

23. Damian Kavanagh and Benjamin Scafidi, "One Sector Is Flourishing During
the Pandemic: K-12 Private Schools," The Hill, November 29, 2020, https://
thehill.com/opinion/education/527623-one-sector-is-flourishing-during-the
-pandemic-k-12-private-schools/.

24. Damon Dunn, *Punting Poverty: Breaking the Chains of Welfare* (San Francisco:
Pacific Research Institute, 2020), 14.

25. Adam Smith, *An Inquiry into the Nature and Causes of the Wealth of Nations*
(New York: Oxford University Press, 1993), 22.

26. "Charitable Giving Statistics," National Philanthropic Trust, https://www
.nptrust.org/philanthropic-resources/charitable-giving-statistics/; Leslie Al-
brecht, "The U.S. Is the No. 1 Most Generous Country in the World for the Last
Decade," MarketWatch, December 7, 2019, https://www.marketwatch.com
/story/the-us-is-the-most-generous-country-but-americans-say-debt-is-keeping
-them-from-giving-more-to-charity-2019-10-18.

CHAPTER 11: Trading Capitalism for Cronyism

1. Tim Evans, Emily Hopkins, and Tony Cook, "'Reeks of Cronyism': Indiana
Still Hiding Nursing Home Coronavirus Info, Advocates Say," *Indianapolis Star*, May 1, 2020, https://www.indystar.com/story/news/investigations
/2020/05/01/coronavirus-reporting-indiana-nursing-homes-lags-many-other
-states/3048806001/.

2. "Total Lobbying Spending in the United States from 1998 to 2019," Statista,
March 4, 2020, https://www.statista.com/statistics/257337/total-lobbying
-spending-in-the-us/.

3. Lee Drutman, "How Corporate Lobbyists Conquered American Democracy,"
The Atlantic, April 20, 2015, https://www.theatlantic.com/business/archive/2015
/04/how-corporate-lobbyists-conquered-american-democracy/390822/.

4. "History of Lobbying in the United States," Wikipedia, https://en.wikipedia
.org/wiki/History_of_lobbying_in_the_United_States.

5. Clive S. Thomas, Ronald J. Hrebenar, and Anthony J. Nownes, "Interest Group
Politics in the States: Four Decades of Developments—the 1960s to the Present," The Council of State Governments, 2008, https://knowledgecenter.csg

.org/kc/system/files/thomas.pdf; Drutman, "How Corporate Lobbyists Conquered American Democracy."

6. Murray N. Rothbard, *The Case Against the Fed* (Auburn, AL: Ludwig von Mises Institute, 2007), https://cdn.mises.org/The%20Case%20Against%20the%20Fed_3.pdf.

7. Ibid., 85.

8. Robert Higgs, "Government Growth," The Library of Economics and Liberty, https://www.econlib.org/library/Enc/GovernmentGrowth.html; Robert Higgs, "The Growth of Government in the United States," Independent Institute, August 1, 1990, https://www.independent.org/news/article.asp?id=1390; "Total Government Spending in the United States, Fiscal Year 2021," us governmentspending.com, November 5, 2020, https://www.usgovernment spending.com/total.

9. Bethany Blankley, "Report: State Spending Accelerated in Fiscal 2019, Led by Increases in Transportation," The Center Square, November 28, 2019, https://www.thecentersquare.com/national/report-state-spending-accelerated-in-fiscal-2019-led-by-increases-in-transportation/article_e94e2db6-1047-11ea-8136-4fe940915fea.html.

10. Michael Katz, "State Pension Unfunded Liabilities Nearly $6 Trillion," Chief Investment Officer, March 29, 2019, https://www.ai-cio.com/news/state-pension-unfunded-liabilities-nearly-6-trillion/.

11. Thomas et al., "Interest Group Politics in the States."

12. Aaron Renn, "Cities That Lost Amazon's HQ2 Contest Can Still End Up Ahead," *The Atlantic*, November 15, 2018, https://www.theatlantic.com/ideas/archive/2018/11/silver-lining-losing-amazons-hq2-contest/575893/; "Amazon HQ2," Wikipedia, https://en.wikipedia.org/wiki/Amazon_HQ2.

13. Lydia DePillis, "How Trump's Trade War Is Making Lobbyists Rich and Slamming Small Businesses," ProPublica, January 6, 2020, https://www.propublica.org/article/how-trump-trade-war-is-making-lobbyists-rich-and-slamming-small-businesses.

14. Craig Eyermann, "Why Does the Federal Government Have 1.4 Billion Pounds of American Cheese Stockpiled?," Foundation for Economic Education, March 5, 2019, https://fee.org/articles/why-does-the-federal-government-have-14-billion-pounds-of-american-cheese-stockpiled/; Emily Moon, "What Will the U.S. Government Do with 1.4 Billion Pounds of Cheese?," *Pacific Standard*, January

10, 2019, https://psmag.com/economics/what-will-the-us-government-do-with
-1-4-billion-pounds-of-cheese.

15. Todd Zywicki and James Sherk, "Auto Bailout or UAW Bailout? Taxpayer
Losses Came from Subsidizing Union Compensation," The Heritage Foundation, June 13, 2012, https://www.heritage.org/taxes/report/auto-bailout-or-uaw
-bailout-taxpayer-losses-came-subsidizing-union-compensation.

16. Rothbard, *The Case Against the Fed*, 86.

17. John Taylor, "The Danger of Regulatory Capture," PolicyEd, October 11, 2018,
https://www.policyed.org/intellections/danger-regulatory-capture/video.

18. Roisin McCord, Edward S. Prescott, and Tim Sablik, "Explaining the Decline in
the Number of Banks Since the Great Recession," Federal Reserve Bank of Richmond, March 2015, no. 15–03, https://www.richmondfed.org/publications
/research/economic_brief/2015/eb_15-03.

19. Steve Maas, "Small Business Lending Declined After Dodd-Frank Passed,"
NBER Digest, June 2018, https://www.nber.org/digest/jun18/jun18.pdf, 2.

20. "How Dodd-Frank Stole the Recovery by Killing Small-Business Growth,"
Investor's Business Daily, June 15, 2018, https://www.investors.com/politics
/editorials/dodd-frank-killed-small-business-growth/.

21. Thomas C. Leonard, "Op-Ed: Minimum Wages Were First Designed to Keep
Women and Minorities Out of Jobs," *Los Angeles Times*, April 5, 2016, https://
www.latimes.com/opinion/op-ed/la-oe-0405-leonard-minimum-wage-2016
0405-story.html; Carrie Sheffield, "On the Historically Racist Motivations
Behind Minimum Wage," *Forbes*, April 29, 2014, https://www.forbes.com
/sites/carriesheffield/2014/04/29/on-the-historically-racist-motivations-behind
-minimum-wage/#24cb1c2211bb.

22. "Agencies Lobbied by Lockheed Martin, 2017," The Center for Responsive
Politics, https://www.opensecrets.org/federal-lobbying/clients/agencies?cycle=
2017&id=d000000104; "Ex–Energy Secretary Rick Perry Rejoins Energy
Transfer's Board," *Dallas Morning News*, January 3, 2020, https://www.dallas
news.com/business/energy/2020/01/04/ex-energy-secretary-rick-perry-rejoins
-energy-transfers-board/; "New Report: Gas Pipeline Giant, Kelcy Warren,
Inflated Politicians with $2.7 Million," Sierra Club, January 31, 2017, https://
www.sierraclub.org/texas/blog/2017/01/new-report-gas-pipeline-giant-kelcy
-warren-inflated-politicians-27-million.

23. Walter Donway, "Crony Capitalism Versus 'Making' Money," Atlas Society,

May 7, 2012, https://www.atlassociety.org/post/crony-capitalism-versus-making
-money.

24. "About Us: American Federation of Teachers," AFT, https://www.aft.org
/about; "About NEA," National Education Association, https://www.nea.org
/about-nea; "National Education Association (NEA)," InfluenceWatch, https://
www.influencewatch.org/labor-union/national-education-association-nea/;
Douglas N. Harris, "Teacher Unions May Be More Important Than Ever in
2020," Brookings, June 5, 2019, https://www.brookings.edu/blog/brown-center
-chalkboard/2019/06/05/teacher-unions-may-be-more-important-than-ever
-in-2020/; "Teachers Unions," Center for Responsive Politics, 2020, https://www
.opensecrets.org/industries/contrib.php?ind=L1300&Bkdn=Source&cycle
=2020.

25. Greg LeRoy et al., "Shortchanging Small Business," Good Jobs First, October
2015, http://www.goodjobsfirst.org/sites/default/files/docs/pdf/shortchanging
.pdf.

26. Philip Mattera, "Subsidizing the Corporate One Percent," Good Jobs First,
February 2014, https://www.goodjobsfirst.org/sites/default/files/docs/pdf/sub
sidizingthecorporateonepercent.pdf; Philip Mattera and Kasia Tarczynska,
"Uncle Sam's Favorite Corporations," Good Jobs First, March 2015, http://www
.goodjobsfirst.org/sites/default/files/docs/pdf/UncleSamsFavoriteCorporations
.pdf.

27. Isaac Stanley-Becker, Desmond Butler, and Nick Miroff, "In Coronavirus
Scramble for N95 Masks, Trump Administration Pays Premium to Third-Party
Vendors," Washington Post, April 15, 2020, https://www.washingtonpost.com
/national/coronavirus-trump-masks-contracts-prices/2020/04/15/9c186276-
7f20-11ea-8de7-9fdff6d5d83e_story.html; Jen Wilson, "CBJ Morning Buzz:
Honeywell, Lowe's and Nucor CEOs Among Those Tapped for Trump's Advisory Groups; Banks Grapple with Tech Problems," Charlotte Business Journal,
April 16, 2020, https://www.bizjournals.com/charlotte/news/2020/04/16/cbj
-morning-buzz-local-notables-among-execs-tapped.html.

28. Stanley-Becker, Butler, and Miroff, "In Coronavirus Scramble for N95 Masks,
Trump Administration Pays Premium to Third-Party Vendors."

29. Rachael Levy, "Kodak Shifts into Drug Production with Help of $765 Million
U.S. Loan," Wall Street Journal, July 28, 2020, https://www.wsj.com/articles
/kodak-lands-765-million-u-s-loan-in-start-of-medical-supply-chain-fix
-11595930400.

30. Scott Lincicome, "The Government's Plan to Turn Kodak into a Pharmaceutical Company Sure Seems Underdeveloped," Cato Institute, July 29, 2020, https://www.cato.org/blog/governments-plan-turn-kodak-pharmaceutical -company-sure-seems-underdeveloped.

31. Dave Michaels and Theo Francis, "Kodak Loan Disclosure and Stock Surge Under SEC Investigation," *Wall Street Journal*, August 4, 2020, https:// www.wsj.com/articles/kodak-loan-disclosure-and-stock-surge-under-sec -investigation-11596559126; "Eastman Kodak's Top Executive Reportedly Got Trump Deal Windfall on an 'Understanding,'" CNBC, August 3, 2020, https:// www.cnbc.com/2020/08/01/eastman-kodaks-top-executive-reportedly-got -trump-deal-windfall-on-an-understanding.html; Rob Lenihan, "Kodak Trading Choppy as Loan Controversy Awaits Vote Result," TheStreet, November 4, 2020, https://www.thestreet.com/investing/kodak-share-trading-choppy-as -loan-controversy-awaits-election-result.

32. Rebecca Hughes and Patch Staff, "Officials Phase Out Hospital Site Beds at McCormick Place," Patch, May 8, 2020, https://patch.com/illinois/chicago /officials-phase-out-hospital-site-beds-mccormick-place; Heather Cherone, "Field Hospital at McCormick Place Will Close After Treating Few Patients as Curve Bends," WTTW, May 1, 2020, https://news.wttw.com/2020/05/01 /field-hospital-mccormick-place-will-close-after-treating-few-patients-curve -bends; "Temporary COVID-19 Field Hospital at Javits Center Closing," Spectrum News NY1, May 1, 2020, https://www.ny1.com/nyc/all-boroughs/news /2020/05/01/javits-center-temporary-covid-19-field-hospital-closing.

33. @RentsTweets, Twitter, July 28, 2020, https://twitter.com/RentsTweets/status /1288150110011035648?s=20.

CHAPTER 12: Trading Places

1. "Major Foreign Holders of Treasury Securities," as of end of December 2020, Department of the Treasury/Federal Reserve Board, February 16, 2021, https:// ticdata.treasury.gov/Publish/mfh.txt.

2. "Deng Xiaoping," Wikipedia, https://en.wikipedia.org/wiki/Deng_Xiaoping; Catherine H. Keyser, "Three Chinese Leaders: Mao Zedong, Zhou Enlai, and Deng Xiaoping," Asia for Educators, Columbia University, 2020, http://afe .easia.columbia.edu/special/china_1950_leaders.htm.

3. Don Oberdorfer, "Trade Benefits for China Are Approved by Carter,"

Washington Post, October 24, 1979, https://www.washingtonpost.com
/archive/politics/1979/10/24/trade-benefits-for-china-are-approved-by-carter
/febc46f2-2d39-430b-975f-6c121bf4fb42/.

4. "Poverty Headcount Ratio at $1.90 a Day (2011 PPP) (% of Population)—
China," World Bank Development Research Group, https://data.world
bank.org/indicator/SI.POV.DDAY?locations=CN; "The World Bank in China,"
World Bank, https://www.worldbank.org/en/country/china/overview.

5. Bernard Gwertzman, "U.S. Decides to Sell Weapons to China in Policy Reversal," *New York Times*, June 17, 1981, https://www.nytimes.com/1981/06/17
/world/us-decides-to-sell-weapons-to-china-in-policy-reversal.html.

6. "China Retail Sales," Photius Coutsoukis, July 1987, https://photius.com
/countries/china/economy/china_economy_retail_sales.html; "History of Trade
of the People's Republic of China," Wikipedia, https://en.wikipedia.org/wiki
/History_of_trade_of_the_People%27s_Republic_of_China.

7. Ben Baden, "40 Years of US-China Commercial Relations," *China Business
Review*, January 1, 2013, https://www.chinabusinessreview.com/40-years-of
-us-china-commercial-relations/.

8. Thomas W. Lippman, "Bush Makes Clinton's China Policy an Issue," *Washington Post*, August 20, 1999, https://www.washingtonpost.com/wp-srv/politics
/campaigns/wh2000/stories/chiwan082099.htm.

9. Don Ake, "Ake's Take: We're Addicted to Cheap Chinese Goods," FTR, June 19,
2019, https://www.ftrintel.com/blog/akes-take-were-addicted-to-cheap-chinese
-goods/.

10. Robert E. Scott, "We Can Reshore Manufacturing Jobs, but Trump Hasn't
Done It," Economic Policy Institute, August 10, 2020, https://www.epi.org
/publication/reshoring-manufacturing-jobs/.

11. Baden, "40 Years of US-China Commercial Relations."

12. "US Relations with China 1949–2020," Council on Foreign Relations, https://
www.cfr.org/timeline/us-relations-china.

13. "Poverty Headcount Ratio at $1.90 a Day (2011 PPP) (% of Population)—
China," World Bank Development Research Group.

14. Lujie Chen, Tao Yue, and Xiande Zhao, "8 Ways Brands Can Fight Counterfeits
in China," *Harvard Business Review*, May 10, 2018, https://hbr.org/2018/05
/8-ways-brands-can-fight-counterfeits-in-china.

15. "Trade in Fake Goods Is Now 3.3% of World Trade and Rising," OECD, March 18, 2019, https://www.oecd.org/newsroom/trade-in-fake-goods-is-now-33-of-world-trade-and-rising.htm; Mark Litke, "China Big in Counterfeit Goods," ABC News, January 7, 2006, https://abcnews.go.com/WNT/story?id=130381&page=1.

16. Elizabeth Schulze, "Counterfeit Goods from China Are Crushing American Small Businesses—and They're Calling on Trump to Fight Back," CNBC, March 1, 2020, https://www.cnbc.com/2020/02/28/small-businesses-are-pushing-trump-to-fight-chinese-counterfeits.html; Leticia Miranda and Megha Rajagopalan, "Small American Businesses Are Struggling Against a Flood of Chinese Fakes," BuzzFeed News, April 4, 2017, https://www.buzzfeednews.com/article/leticiamiranda/small-businesses-struggle-flood-of-chinese-fakes.

17. Byung-Chul Han, *Shanzhai: Deconstruction in Chinese*, translated by Philippa Hurd (Cambridge, MA: MIT Press, 2017); summary, https://mitpress.mit.edu/books/shanzhai.

18. Scott Cendrowski, "Disney Characters Spark Controversy at China's New Anti-Disneyland," *Fortune*, May 31, 2016, http://fortune.com/2016/05/31/disney-characters-china-disneyland/.

19. Julie Weed, "Welcome to the Haiyatt. In China, It's Not the Hotel It Sounds Like," *New York Times*, April 28, 2014, https://www.nytimes.com/2014/04/29/business/international/sound-alike-hotels-in-china-borrow-western-brands-prestige.html?_r=0.

20. "Starbucks Wins Chinese Logo Case," BBC News, January 2, 2006, http://news.bbc.co.uk/2/hi/business/4574400.stm; "Schultz' Starbucks Wins China Copyright Case," *Forbes*, January 2, 2006, https://www.forbes.com/2006/01/02/schultz-starbucks-china-cx_cn_0102autofacescan01.html#77e980775351.

21. Tribune News Service, "China 'Has Taken the Gloves Off' in Its Theft of US Technology Secrets," *South China Morning Post*, November 19, 2018, https://www.scmp.com/news/world/united-states-canada/article/2173843/china-has-taken-gloves-its-thefts-us-technology.

22. Grant Clark, "What's Intellectual Property and Does China Steal It?: Quick Take," Bloomberg, December 4, 2018, https://www.bloomberg.com/news/articles/2018-12-05/what-s-intellectual-property-and-does-china-steal-it-quicktake.

23. Chad P. Bown and Melina Kolb, "Trump's Trade War Timeline: An Up-to-Date Guide," Peterson Institute for International Economics, April 19, 2018,

Updated January 24, 2020, https://www.wita.org/wp-content/uploads/2020/02
/trump-trade-war-timeline.pdf.

24. Josh Horwitz, "A Startup Challenging Starbucks in China Is Now Worth
$1 Billion," July 11, 2018, Quartz, https://qz.com/1325403/luckin-coffee
-startup-challenging-starbucks-in-china-worth-1-billion/.

25. Julie Zhu, "Timeline—Luckin Coffee's Journey from Hot Startup to $5bln
Share Wipeout," Reuters, April 3, 2020, https://www.reuters.com/article/luckin
-investigation-timeline/timeline-luckin-coffees-journey-from-hot-startup-to
-5bln-share-wipeout-idUSL8N2BR2K5.

26. "Anonymous," "Luckin Coffee: Fraud + Fundamentally Broken Business,"
Muddy Waters Research, January 31, 2020, https://drive.google.com/file/d
/1LKOYMpXVo1ssbWQx8j4G3-strg6mpQ7F/view.

27. Tonya Garcia, "Luckin Coffee to Be Delisted from the Nasdaq," Market-
Watch, June 26, 2020, https://www.marketwatch.com/story/luckin-coffee-to
-be-delisted-from-the-nasdaq-2020-06-26; Amelia Lucas, "Luckin Coffee
Fires CEO, COO After Sales Fraud Investigation," CNBC, May 12, 2020,
https://www.cnbc.com/2020/05/12/luckin-coffee-fires-ceo-coo-after-sales
-fraud-investigation.html; Zhu, "Timeline—Luckin Coffee's Journey from Hot
Startup to $5bln Share Wipeout."

28. Mark R. Hake, "3 Key Takeaways from the Luckin Coffee Stock Fraud,"
InvestorPlace, May 19, 2020, https://investorplace.com/2020/05/lk-stock-fraud
-lessons-muddy-waters-research/.

29. Scott Eden, "SEC Probes China Stock Fraud Network," TheStreet, December 21,
2010, https://www.thestreet.com/markets/emerging-markets/sec-probes-china
-stock-fraud-network-10952277.

30. Katanga Johnson, "Top U.S. Market's Audit Watchdog Gives Gloomy Forecast for Quality Bookkeeping at U.S.-Listed Chinese Firms," Reuters, July 9,
2020, https://www.reuters.com/article/us-usa-sec-china/top-u-s-markets-audit
-watchdog-gives-gloomy-forecast-for-quality-bookkeeping-at-u-s-listed-chines
e-firms-idUSKBN24A331.

31. "Chinese Companies Listed on Major U.S. Stock Exchanges," U.S.-China Economic and Security Review Commission, October 2, 2020, https://www.uscc
.gov/chinese-companies-listed-major-us-stock-exchanges.

32. Dave Michaels, "White House Seeks Crackdown on U.S.-Listed Chinese
Firms," Wall Street Journal, August 6, 2020, https://www.wsj.com/articles

/trump-administration-seeks-crackdown-on-chinese-companies-with-shares
-traded-in-u-s-11596748284.

33. Daniel Flatley and Ben Bain, "Senate Approves Bill to Require Chinese Cos.
to Give PCAOB Access to Audits," *Accounting Today*, May 21, 2020, https://
www.accountingtoday.com/articles/senate-approves-bill-to-require-chinese
-companies-to-give-pcaob-access-to-audits; Reshma Kapadia, "Why De-
listing Chinese Companies Won't Be Easy," *Barron's*, July 11, 2020, https://
www.barrons.com/articles/why-delisting-chinese-companies-wont-be-easy
-51594486137; Office of Congressman Brad Sherman, "Congress Passes Legislation to De-List Chinese Companies Unless U.S. Has Access to Audit Workpa-
pers," December 2, 2020, https://sherman.house.gov/media-center/press-releases
/congress-passes-legislation-to-de-list-chinese-companies-unless-us-has.

34. Adi Robertson, "The Big Legal Questions Behind Trump's TikTok and
WeChat Bans," The Verge, August 10, 2020, https://www.theverge.com/2020
/8/10/21358505/trump-tiktok-wechat-tencent-bytedance-china-ban-executive
-order-legal-sanctions-rules.

35. Arjun Kharpal, "Here's Where Things Stand with the Messy TikTok Deal,"
CNBC, September 25, 2020, https://www.cnbc.com/2020/09/25/tiktok-deal
-timeline-the-latest-in-the-messy-saga-as-ban-looms.html; John D. McKinnon,
Georgia Wells, and Kate Davidson, "TikTok Deal Makers Await Court Ruling on U.S. Ban," *Wall Street Journal*, October 22, 2020, https://www.wsj
.com/articles/tiktok-deal-makers-await-court-ruling-on-u-s-ban-11603359016.

36. Byron Tau, "U.S. Government Contractor Embedded Software in Apps to Track
Phones," *Wall Street Journal*, August 7, 2020, https://www.wsj.com/articles
/u-s-government-contractor-embedded-software-in-apps-to-track-phones-11
596808801?mod=e2tw.

37. William Gallagher, "Six Apple Production Lines Capable of $5 Billion in
Exports Allegedly Moving to India," AppleInsider, August 3, 2020, https://
appleinsider.com/articles/20/08/03/six-apple-production-lines-capable-of-5
-billion-in-exports-allegedly-moving-to-india; Koya Jibiki, "Southeast Asia Vies
for Foreign Manufacturers Leaving China," Nikkei Asia, July 4, 2020, https://
asia.nikkei.com/Economy/Southeast-Asia-vies-for-foreign-manufacturers
-leaving-China.

38. Marco Rubio, "We Need a More Resilient American Economy," *New York
Times*, April 20, 2020, https://www.nytimes.com/2020/04/20/opinion/marco
-rubio-coronavirus-economy.html.

39. Jen Wieczner, "The Case of the Missing Toilet Paper: How the Coronavirus Exposed U.S. Supply Chain Flaws," *Fortune*, May 18, 2020, https://fortune .com/2020/05/18/toilet-paper-sales-surge-shortage-coronavirus-pandemic -supply-chain-cpg-panic-buying/; Chris Gilmore, "Increase in Bidet Sales Due to Coronavirus Pandemic," WFLX Fox 29, April 27, 2020, https://www.wflx .com/2020/04/27/bidet-sales-rise-due-coronavirus-pandemic/.

40. Katherine Ellen Foley and Tim McDonnell, "The Cheaper, Greener Alternatives to Clorox Wipes," Quartz, August 11, 2020, https://qz.com/1890296/clorox -wipes-shortage-the-best-disinfecting-wipe-alternatives/amp/.

41. Adrienne Vogt, "These Unknown Store Brands Took Over Store Shelves While Purell and Clorox Disappeared," CNN, August 5, 2020, https://www.cnn .com/2020/08/05/business/hand-sanitizer-purell-clorox/index.html.

42. "New Chinese Billionaires Outpace U.S. by 3:1: Hurun," Reuters, February 26, 2020, https://www.reuters.com/article/us-china-economy-wealth/new-chinese -billionaires-outpace-u-s-by-3-to-1-hurun-idUSKCN20K0YB.

43. Steven Lee Myers, Jin Wu, and Claire Fu, "China's Looming Crisis: A Shrinking Population," *New York Times*, January 17, 2020, https://www.nytimes.com /interactive/2019/01/17/world/asia/china-population-crisis.html; Charlie Campbell, "China's Aging Population Is a Major Threat to Its Future," *Time*, February 7, 2019, https://time.com/5523805/china-aging-population-working-age/.

44. Martin Crutsinger, "U.S. Trade Deficit Surged in July to Highest in 12 Years," PBS, September 3, 2020, https://www.pbs.org/newshour/economy/u-s-trade -deficit-surged-in-july-to-highest-in-12-years.

CHAPTER 13: Decentralization Versus Centralization

1. Thomas Sowell, *Basic Economics*, 5th ed. (New York: Basic Books, 2015), 220–21.

2. Mark Perry, "Thomas Sowell on the Cruelty of Minimum Wage Laws," American Enterprise Institute, June 29, 2017, https://www.aei.org/economics/thomas -sowell-on-the-cruelty-of-minimum-wage-laws/.

3. Sam Dean, "The New Burger Chef Makes $3 an Hour and Never Goes Home. (It's a Robot)," *Los Angeles Times*, February 27, 2020, https://www.latimes .com/business/technology/story/2020-02-27/flippy-fast-food-restaurant-robot -arm.

4. Peter Romeo, "Wage Hikes Force Large-Scale Restaurant Closings, Study Finds," *Restaurant Business*, April 16, 2019, https://www.restaurantbusiness online.com/workforce/wage-hikes-force-large-scale-restaurant-closings-study -finds.

5. "New Upwork Study Finds 36% of the U.S. Workforce Freelance amid the COVID-19 Pandemic," Upwork, September 15, 2020, https://www.upwork .com/releases/new-upwork-study-finds-36-of-the-us-workforce-freelance-amid -the-covid-19-pandemic.

6. Carol Roth, "California and Federal Politicians Want to Destroy Millions of Freelance Jobs—We Can't Let Them Win," Fox Business, March 1, 2020, https://www.foxbusiness.com/markets/california-federal-politician-freelance -jobs-carol-roth.

7. Ibid.

8. Kevin McCarthy, "Democrats' Failed AB5 Continues to Hurt Californians," press release, US House of Representatives, August 21, 2020, https://kevin mccarthy.house.gov/media-center/press-releases/democrats-failed-ab5-continues -to-hurt-californian.

9. Sara Ashley O'Brien, "Prop 22 Passes in California, Exempting Uber and Lyft from Classifying Drivers as Employees," CNN, November 4, 2020, https:// www.cnn.com/2020/11/04/tech/california-proposition-22/index.html.

10. "Should the U.S. Adopt a Value-Added Tax? David R. Henderson: No: It Makes It Too Easy for the Government to Raise Money," *Wall Street Journal*, February 28, 2016, https://www.wsj.com/articles/should-the-u-s-adopt-a-value-added -tax-1456715703/.

11. Kent Hoover, "10 Regulations That Give Small Business Owners the Worst Headaches," The Business Journals, April 28, 2016, https://www.bizjournals .com/bizjournals/washingtonbureau/2016/04/10-regulations-that-give-small -business-owners-the.html.

12. Leora Klapper, Anat Lewin, and Juan Manuel Quesada Delgado, "The Impact of the Business Environment on the Business Creation Process," Policy Research Working Paper no. WPS 4937, World Bank, 2009, https://openknowledge .worldbank.org/handle/10986/4131 License: CC BY 3.0 IGO"; Ryan Hahn, "Entrepreneurship—The Key to Prosperity?," World Bank, November 19, 2008, https://blogs.worldbank.org/psd/entrepreneurship-the-key-to-prosperity.

13. Scott Shane, "Small Business's Problem with Government Regulation," Small

Business Trends, July 26, 2013, https://smallbiztrends.com/2011/01/small
-business%E2%80%99s-problem-with-government-regulation.html.

14. Ibid.

15. "37 Ways Donald Trump Has Remade the Rules for Business," *Wall Street Journal*, January 17, 2018, https://www.wsj.com/articles/how-donald-trump
-has-remade-the-rules-for-business-1516190400.

16. Emily H. Wein, Rachel B. Goodman, and Thomas B. Ferrante, "COVID-19: States Waive In-State Licensing Requirements for Health Care Providers," *National Law Review*, March 17, 2020, https://www.natlawreview.com
/article/covid-19-states-waive-state-licensing-requirements-health-care
-providers; "COVID-19 State Emergency Response: Temporarily Suspended and Waived Practice Agreement Requirements," American Association of Nurse Practitioners, October 7, 2020, https://www.aanp.org/advocacy/state/covid
-19-state-emergency-response-temporarily-suspended-and-waived-practice
-agreement-requirements.

17. Jeffrey A. Singer, "Transitioning from Medical Licensure to Certification: Architects Show a Way," *Orange County Register*, August 7, 2020, https://
www.ocregister.com/2020/08/07/transitioning-from-medical-licensure-to
-certification-architects-show-a-way/.

18. Jarrett Dieterle and Shoshana Weissmann, "Congress Moves on Occupational Licensing Reform, but There's More to Do," The Hill, July 29, 2018, https://
thehill.com/opinion/civil-rights/399291-congress-moves-on-occupational
-licensing-reform-but-theres-more-to-do.

19. "Hair Braiding Schools in Illinois," Beauty Schools Directory, 2020, https://
www.beautyschoolsdirectory.com/programs/hair-braiding-school/il.

20. Shirley Svorny and Michael F. Cannon, "Health Care Workforce Reform: COVID-19 Spotlights Need for Changes to Clinician Licensing," Policy Analysis no. 899, Cato Institute, August 4, 2020, https://www.cato.org/publications
/policy-analysis/health-care-workforce-reform-covid-19-spotlights-need
-changes#right-skilling-vs-wrong-skilling.

21. "At What Cost? State and National Estimates of the Economic Costs of Occupational Licensing," Institute for Justice, January 1, 2020, https://ij.org/report
/at-what-cost; "Standing Up for Natural Hair Braiders' Right to Earn an Honest Living," Braiding Freedom: A Project of the Institute for Justice, http://braiding
freedom.com/braiding-initiative/standing-up-for-natural-hair-braiders-right
-to-earn-an-honest-living/.

22. "Standing Up for Natural Hair Braiders' Right to Earn an Honest Living."

23. Andrew Wimer, "Florida House and Senate Advance Occupational Licensing Reform Bills," Institute for Justice, February 20, 2020, https://ij.org/press-release/florida-house-and-senate-advance-occupational-licensing-reform-bills/; Governor Ron DeSantis, "Governor Ron DeSantis Signs 'The Occupational Freedom and Opportunity Act' to Remove Unnecessary Barriers to Employment," news release, June 30, 2020, https://www.flgov.com/2020/06/30/governor-ron-desantis-signs-the-occupational-freedom-and-opportunity-act-to-remove-unnecessary-barriers-to-employment/.

24. Chris Carter, "Illinois House Bill Would Eliminate Licensing for Barbers, Cosmetologists," WAND 17, March 5, 2020, https://www.wandtv.com/news/illinois-house-bill-would-eliminate-licensing-for-barbers-cosmetologists/article_0ad27670-5f32-11ea-b4bd-27f88206c8fb.html.

25. Dieterle and Weissmann, "Congress Moves on Occupational Licensing Reform, but There's More to Do."

26. Joe Setyon, "N.Y. Food Police Shut Down a 7-Year-Old's Lemonade Stand. This Bill Makes Sure They Can't Do It Again," Reason, May 1, 2019, https://reason.com/2019/05/01/n-y-food-police-shut-down-a-7-year-olds-lemonade-stand-this-bill-makes-sure-they-cant-do-it-again/.

27. Adrienne Vogt, "These Unknown Store Brands Took Over Store Shelves While Purell and Clorox Disappeared," CNN, August 5, 2020, https://www.cnn.com/2020/08/05/business/hand-sanitizer-purell-clorox/index.html.

28. "Apply for Licenses and Permits," US Small Business Administration, https://www.sba.gov/business-guide/launch-your-business/apply-licenses-permits.

29. "Workers' Compensation Insurance: It's the LAW," Illinois Workers' Compensation Commission, 2020, https://www2.illinois.gov/sites/iwcc/about/Pages/insurance.aspx.

Index

About the Author

CAROL ROTH is a "recovering" investment banker, entrepreneur, TV pundit and host, speaker, prolific content creator, and *New York Times* bestselling author of *The Entrepreneur Equation*. She has worked in a variety of capacities across industries, including currently as an outsourced chief customer officer (CCO), as a director on public and private company boards, and as a strategic business advisor.

Carol advocates for small business, small government, and big hair. Prior to the pandemic lockdowns, Carol was often on an airplane, but currently spends her time in Chicago with her husband, Kurt.

You can connect with Carol via her website at CarolRoth.com.